KEY GEOGRAPHY

New
Places

DAVID WAUGH & TONY BUSHELL

First published in 1995 by:
Stanley Thornes (Publishers) Ltd
New edition 2001

This edition published in 2005 by:
Nelson Thornes Ltd
Delta Place
27 Bath Road
CHELTENHAM
GL53 7TH
United Kingdom

09 / 10 9 8 7 6

A catalogue record for this book is available from the British Library

New edition ISBN 978 0 7487 5439 7
This edition ISBN 978 0 7487 9396 9

Page make-up by eMC Design, www.emcdesign.org.uk
Illustrations by Jane Cope, Hardlines, Lovell Johns Limited/Maps
International, Angela Lumley, Richard Morris, Oxford Design and
Illustrators, Tim Smith and Shaun Williams
Edited by Katherine James
Picture research by Penni Bickle and Sue Sharp

Printed in China

The previous page shows favelas and skyscrapers
in Rio de Janeiro

Acknowledgements

The authors and the publishers are grateful to the following for
permission to reproduce photographs and other copyright material
in this book.

AA Photo Library: 71 (bottom right); Alamy/ Jon Arnold Images:
163 (left), 171 (right); Alamy/ Julio Etchart: 15 (top); Alamy/ LMR
Group: 165 (right); Alamy/ Panorama Stock: 150 (bottom left) ;
Alec Gillespie Photography: 116 (top); Andes Press Agency: 19
(middle bottom), 36 (middle left), 65, 164 (left); Art Directors &
Trip Photo Library: 112 (left), 116 (bottom), 123 (right), 127 (left),
128, 137, 151 (bottom), 170; Associated Press: 84 (both), 173
(middle); The Automobile Association: 82; Benetton UK: 78 (logo);
Penni Bickle: 126; Cephas: 71 (top right), 74, 92, 97 (bottom right),
101, 102 (middle & bottom left); Corbis: 30 (middle), 68 (bottom),
93 (both), 94 (right); Corbis/ Alan Schein Photography: 172; Corbis/
Alison Wright: 171 (middle); Corbis/ David Ball: 169 (right), 173
(right); Corbis/ Photowood Inc: 171 (left); Corbis/ Richard Klune:
169 (left); Corbis RF (NT): cover; Corel 290 (NT): cover; Corel 696
(NT): cover; vcEye Ubiquitous/ Hutchison Library: 30 (top), 36
(middle right), 71 (bottom left), 98 (bottom left), 103 (bottom),
105 (left), 123 (left), 144 (right); Fiat UK Limited: 78 (logo); Frank
Lane Picture Agency: 48 (top) ; Geopix Ltd/ Chris Rowley: 142,
144 (left both), 145 (all), 146 (all), 148 (both), 149 (top both), 150
(top and bottom right), 151 (middle), 152 (top), 153 (left), 154
(top both and bottom left), 156 (all), 157 (left), 161 (bottom);
Geoscience: 68 (top); Getty Images: 5 (left both), 24 (top), 25
(bottom), 42 (bottom right), 71 (top left), 80 (top left), 81 (top);
Heritage Image Partnership/ Spectrum Colour Library: 56 (top), 72
(left), 76 (bottom), 96 (left), 97 (bottom middle), 98 (bottom right),
100 (left), 105 (right); Images of Africa: 42 (bottom left), 43 (left),
54 (top), 56 (bottom), 58 (top), 62; ImageState/ Images Colour
Library: 5 (right), 97 (top), 100 (right), 102 (top); Intermediate
Technology: 17, 53 (bottom left), 58 (bottom left), 61 (top and
middle) ; Japan Information and Cultural Centre: 102 (bottom

right); Japan National Tourist Organisation: 97 (bottom left),
103 (top); John Birdsall Photography: 164 (right); John Cleare/
Mountain Camera Picture Library: 45 (left), 71 (middle left);
Katz: 19 (middle top), 80 (bottom), 81 (bottom); London Aerial
Photography: 124, 130; Magnum Photos: 165 (left); Neil Setchfield
Photography: 173 (left); Network Photographers: 121; Newham
Borough Council: 120; Newslink Africa: 5 (middle); Northumbria
Tourist Office: 117 (top); Offside Sports Photography: 18 (bottom
left); Olivetti UK Limited: 78 (logo); Maps reproduced from
Ordnance Survey Mapping with the permission of Her Majesty's
Stationary Office © Crown Copyright; Licence no: 07000U: 125,
131; Panos Pictures: 4 (bottom right), 29 (top), 36 (bottom right),
53 (top); Pirelli SpA of Milan: 78 (logo); Port of Tokyo/ Tokyo
Metropolitan Government: 99; Rex Features: 4 (top), 15 (bottom),
57 (top), 96 (right); Robert Harding Picture Library: 18 (bottom
right), 94 (left), 163 (right); Sally & Richard Greenhill: 127 (right);
Science Photo Library: 20, 42 (top), 98 (top), 112 (right), 140;
John Seely: 61 (bottom); Skishoot-Offshoot: 76 (top); Skyscan:
167 (right); Skyscan/ B Evans: 167 (left); South American Pictures:
4 (bottom left), 19 (top), 24 (bottom both), 25 (top), 28 (left), 31,
32 (top left), 33; Still Pictures: 18 (top left), 28 (right), 29 (bottom
both), 32 (top right & bottom both), 36 (top both), 43 (right), 48
(bottom left), 54 (bottom), 159 ; Sue Cunningham Photographic:
cover, 19 (bottom), 32 (bottom left), 36 (bottom left); Simon
Warner: 122; David Waugh: 5 (top), 44 (both), 45 (right), 53
(bottom right), 56 (middle), 57 (bottom), 58 (bottom right), 147
(both), 149 (bottom left), 152 (bottom both); David Waugh/ Chris
Rowley: 143 (both), 149 (bottom right), 153 (right), 157 (right);
Jonathan Waugh: 151 (top), 154 (bottom right); Judith Waugh: 52
(top); Woodfall Wild Images: 117 (bottom); World Pictures: 48
(bottom right), 49 (top), 72 (right), 161 (top); Zanussi Ltd: 78 (logo)

Every effort has been made to contact copyright holders.
The publishers apologise to anyone whose rights have been
inadvertently overlooked, and will be happy to rectify and errors or
omissions.

Contents

1 Development

Differences in world development

All countries are different. Some, for example, are rich and have high standards of living. Others are poor and have lower standards of living. Countries that differ in this way are said to be at different stages of development.

Map **A** shows the distribution of these countries. Notice that the richer countries are mainly in the 'North' and the poorer countries are in the 'South'.

Activities

1 Complete a larger copy of table **B**.

B

	Continent	Developed or developing?
Brazil		
Italy		
Japan		
Kenya		
UK		
China		

2 Complete a copy of the crossword by solving the following clues. All of these answers can be found on these two pages.

Across
1 Country with a population density of 21 per km².
2 London is its capital city.
3 Continent between the Atlantic and Indian Oceans.
4 Ocean between South America and Africa.
5 Tropic to the south of the Equator.
6 Country in North America.
7 Developed country in southern Europe.
8 The capital city of Italy.
9 Developed country in North America.

Down
5 Tropic to the north of the Equator.
10 Developing country in Asia.
11 African country on the Equator.
12 Country with a population density of 336 per km².
13 Ocean between Asia and North America.
14 Developed country south of the Equator.
15 Capital city of Kenya.
16 Captial city of Brazil.

UK

- Area (size)   244 880 km²
- Population   60 million
- Population density   245 per km²
- Capital city   London

A

Canada

PACIFIC OCEAN

NORTH AMERICA

USA

R. Mississippi

ATLANTI

Mexico

R. Amazon

Brazil

SOUTH AMERICA

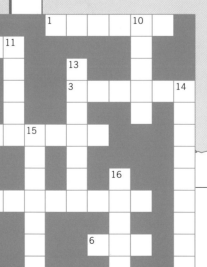

Brazil

- Area (size)   8 511 965 km²
- Population   182 million
- Population density   21 per km²
- Capital city   Brasilia

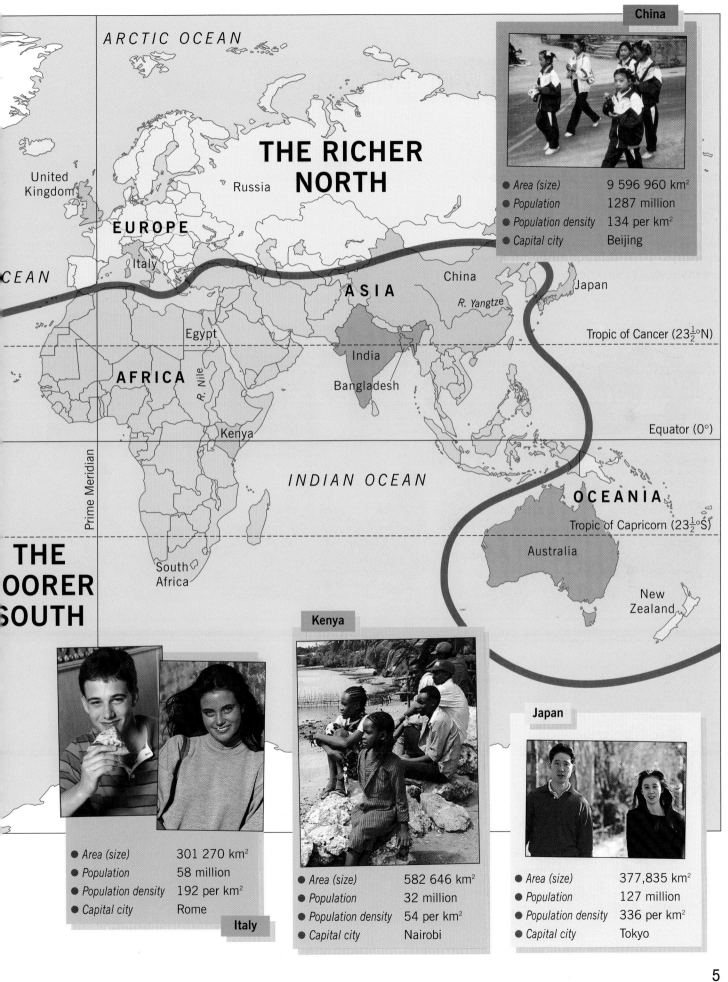

ARCTIC OCEAN

THE RICHER NORTH

United Kingdom

Russia

EUROPE

Italy

OCEAN

ASIA

China

Japan

R. Yangtze

Egypt

AFRICA

R. Nile

India

Bangladesh

Kenya

Tropic of Cancer (23½°N)

Equator (0°)

Prime Meridian

INDIAN OCEAN

OCEANIA

Tropic of Capricorn (23½°S)

Australia

New Zealand

South Africa

THE POORER SOUTH

China

- *Area (size)*   9 596 960 km²
- *Population*   1287 million
- *Population density*   134 per km²
- *Capital city*   Beijing

- *Area (size)*   301 270 km²
- *Population*   58 million
- *Population density*   192 per km²
- *Capital city*   Rome

Italy

Kenya

- *Area (size)*   582 646 km²
- *Population*   32 million
- *Population density*   54 per km²
- *Capital city*   Nairobi

Japan

- *Area (size)*   377,835 km²
- *Population*   127 million
- *Population density*   336 per km²
- *Capital city*   Tokyo

What is development?

As we grow up in life we change and slowly progress through several stages. First we are babies, then children, then teenagers and eventually adults. Each stage can be seen as a step forward in our growth and mental ability. Progress like this is called **development**.

In geography, development follows the same pattern. People and places change as they develop. Geographers are interested in the effects of these changes and the

differences that each stage of development produces. They are also concerned about how development can best be achieved.

Look at the drawings **A** and **B** below. Drawing **A** shows some features that are typical of countries at an early stage of development. Drawing **B** shows similar features, but this time in a more developed country.

A

B

Development is about growth and change. It can help countries progress and become better places in which to live. Many countries in the world are very poor. Development is not just about making them rich, it is also about improving living conditions and ensuring a better **quality of life** and **standard of living** for everyone.

Read what the people in drawing **C** are saying. Notice that there are many different aspects to development. Which ones do you think are the most important?

C

Development is when people have freedom and equal rights and are allowed to vote.

Development is when people have enough food to eat and clean water to drink.

Development should provide equal opportunities for everyone.

Development should make a country rich and improve standards of living.

Development reduces poverty and improves living conditions.

Development is when everyone can go to school and is able to read and write.

Development should help people live a longer and healthier life.

Development should enable people to earn a good living.

What is development?

Development means that people are happier and enjoy life more.

Activities

1 Make a larger copy of diagram **D**.
   a) Complete the diagram by putting the following statements into the correct boxes.
   b) Add one more statement to each box.

- Modern shopping centres
- Slum living conditions
- Few facilities in schools
- High-paid jobs available
- Few goods for sale
- Unreliable transport
- Good health care
- Efficient transport
- Good-quality education
- Many jobs done by hand

D

Developing

○
○
○

Developed

○
○
○

2 Look at the statements about development in drawing **C**.
   a) Write out the three statements that are most important to you.
   b) For each of the people in **E** below, write out three statements that you think are most important to them.

E

The leader of a country

An old person

A homeless person

Summary

Development is a process of growth and change. It can help countries and regions progress and make them better places in which to live.

How can we measure development?

Measuring development is not easy. The most commonly used method is to look at wealth. The best way to measure wealth is to work out a country's **gross national product per capita**.

Gross national product per capita is the total amount of money earned by a country divided by the total number of people living in that country. To make comparisons between countries easier, this is always given in United States dollars (US$).

Based upon wealth, people try to fit countries into one of two groups:

1 The richest ones are said to be **more economically developed countries (MEDCs)**. This is usually shortened to **developed countries**. Their inhabitants have high standards of living.

2 The poorest ones are said to be **less economically developed countries (LEDCs)**. This is usually shortened to **developing countries**. Their inhabitants have much lower standards of living.

A

To most people, development means how rich or poor a country is. People who live in rich countries usually have a high **standard of living**.

B

In 2003 the UK earned $1 530 000 million. If you divide this by the UK's total population of 60 million this gives a GNP per capita of $25 500.

C

Countries in the richer 'North' have high GNPs, e.g.
USA $36 300
Japan $28 700
UK $25 500
Italy $25 100

Countries in the poorer 'South' have much lower GNPs, e.g.
Brazil $7600
China $4700
India $2600
Kenya $1100

D

The **gross national product (GNP)** is the total value of all the goods and services produced by a country in a year.

GNP per capita is what each person in the country would earn if the amount were shared out equally.

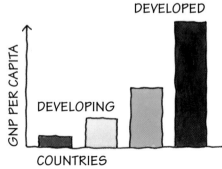

Usually, the more developed a country is, the higher its **GNP per capita** is.

Whilst GNP is easy to use and gives a good indication of how developed a country is, it does not tell the full story. For example, a country may produce lots of oil but very little food. Or it may have a very large army but not many schools.

To find out what a country is really like we need to look at a variety of other indicators as well as GNP. The three main types of indicator are shown in drawing **E**.

Development can be measured in many different ways.

Economic indicators give information about the general wealth of a country. They measure such things as energy use, trade, income and industrial output.

Social indicators are about people and how they live, what they do and what quality of life they have. They look at services such as education, health care and housing.

Cultural indicators look at the effect of traditions, religion and the way of life.

Look at map **F**. It shows the pattern of economic development using GNP as an indicator. Notice how the world is divided very clearly into the rich and the poor.

Most of the 'richer', developed countries are found in the North whilst the 'poorer', developing countries are in the South.

Activities

1 Write out the meaning of each of the following terms. The Glossary at the back of the book will help you.
   • Development
   • Developed country
   • Developing country
   • Standard of living
   • Quality of life
   • GNP per capita

2 a) Name the countries numbered 1 to 10 on map **F**. Map **A** on pages 4 and 5 will help you.
   b) List the countries under these headings:
      • 'Richer' developed countries
      • 'Poorer' developing countries
   Drawing **C** and the statistics at the back of the book will help you.

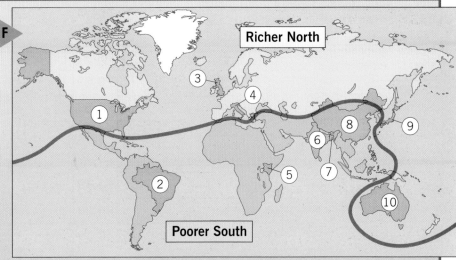

F

Richer North

Poorer South

Summary

There are many different ways of measuring development. The most commonly used method is to look at wealth using GNP.

How can population be used to measure development?

A good way of measuring development is to use population statistics. Countries at different stages of development have different population features. Some of these features are explained in drawing **A**.

Look carefully at the statistics for Kenya and the UK. Notice the differences between the countries. Kenya is a developing country whilst the UK is a developed country.

Now look at the **population pyramids** shown in drawings **B** and **C**. They show the proportion of males and females and the percentage of people in different age groups.

They are useful because they show the present **population structure** and so help measure development. They also enable comparisons to be made between countries and help forecast future trends. This can help a country identify problems and plan for the future.

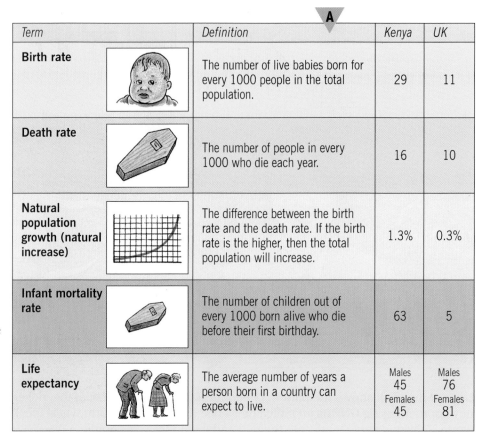

A

Term		Definition	Kenya	UK
Birth rate		The number of live babies born for every 1000 people in the total population.	29	11
Death rate		The number of people in every 1000 who die each year.	16	10
Natural population growth (natural increase)		The difference between the birth rate and the death rate. If the birth rate is the higher, then the total population will increase.	1.3%	0.3%
Infant mortality rate		The number of children out of every 1000 born alive who die before their first birthday.	63	5
Life expectancy		The average number of years a person born in a country can expect to live.	Males 45 Females 45	Males 76 Females 81

B

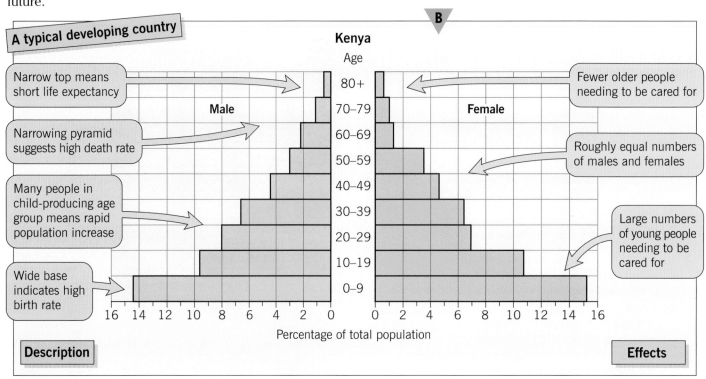

A typical developing country

Kenya

Age

Narrow top means short life expectancy

Narrowing pyramid suggests high death rate

Many people in child-producing age group means rapid population increase

Wide base indicates high birth rate

Male

Female

Fewer older people needing to be cared for

Roughly equal numbers of males and females

Large numbers of young people needing to be cared for

Percentage of total population

Description

Effects

Activities

Activities

1 Write out the meaning of the following terms:
 a) Birth rate
 b) Death rate
 c) Natural increase
 d) Infant mortality
 e) Life expectancy.

2 Make a larger copy of table **D**.
 a) Put the following terms into the correct columns.

Low birth rate   High death rate   Low death rate

High birth rate   High infant mortality

Low infant mortality

Long life expectancy

Short life expectancy

Low natural increase   High natural increase

 b) Put the shape of the population pyramid into the correct columns.
 c) Put these countries into the correct columns:

● Brazil ● Italy ● Japan ● Kenya ● UK ● China

The statistics at the back of the book will help you.

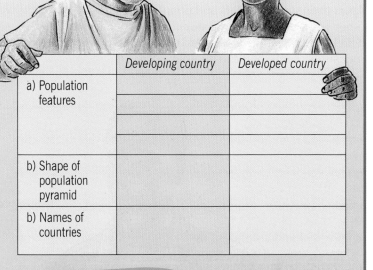

	Developing country	Developed country
a) Population features		
b) Shape of population pyramid		
b) Names of countries		

Summary

Population features such as birth rates, death rates, natural population growth, infant mortality rates and life expectancy can be used to measure development. These are examples of **social indicators**.

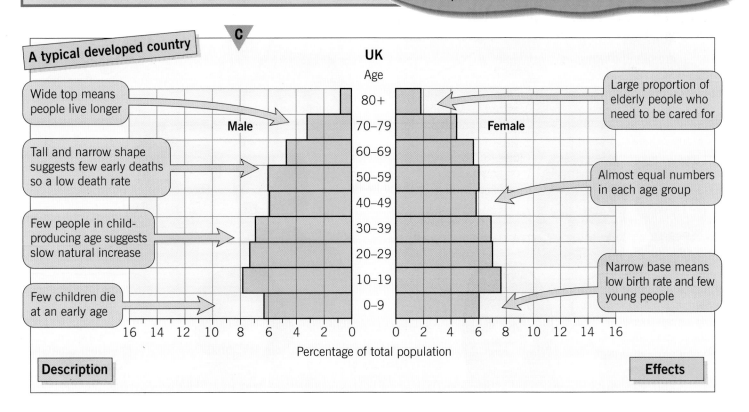

A typical developed country

C

UK

Wide top means people live longer

Tall and narrow shape suggests few early deaths so a low death rate

Few people in child-producing age suggests slow natural increase

Few children die at an early age

Large proportion of elderly people who need to be cared for

Almost equal numbers in each age group

Narrow base means low birth rate and few young people

Male   Female

Age: 80+, 70–79, 60–69, 50–59, 40–49, 30–39, 20–29, 10–19, 0–9

16 14 12 10 8 6 4 2 0   0 2 4 6 8 10 12 14 16

Percentage of total population

Description   **Effects**

How else may development be measured?

Apart from wealth (GNP) and population there are many other ways of trying to measure the level of a country's development. Most of these are either **social** or **economic** measures. Some of these alternatives are described in drawing **A** and are listed in table **E**. Table **E** also gives some actual figures for these measures. Further statistics for measuring development for a selection of countries can be found at the back of the book.

A

Developing countries

Developed countries

Jobs (employment)

Most people are farmers or are employed in other primary activities such as forestry or mining. Many jobs are done by hand.

Most people are employed in manufacturing or in providing services. Many jobs are done by machines and computers.

Many houses do not have electricity, a water supply or sewerage. People cannot afford TVs and videos.

Most houses have electricity, a water supply and sewerage. People can afford TVs and videos.

Many people still live in rural areas.

Most people live in towns and cities.

Living in towns (urban dwellers) and housing amenities

Not everyone goes to school. Schools and the training of teachers are expensive. There are also many children of school age.

We often cannot afford to build enough hospitals, to train nurses and doctors, or to provide vaccines and health care. Many people have a poor diet.

Every child has the opportunity to go to school and often goes on to higher education.

Education and health

We have hospitals, trained nurses and doctors and vaccines. Most people have plenty to eat and have a good diet.

Rural areas have poor transport links. Transport in urban areas is congested and old.

We use lots of energy – to many of us all we need to do is to press a switch.

Transport and use of energy

We cannot afford to use much energy. This can prevent us from developing more rapidly.

Most places have fast, efficient transport links with cars, buses, trains and planes.

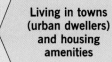

Measuring development is not easy. The main problem is that development is rarely spread evenly.

B

This problem is greatest in developing countries where there is a huge gap between the rich and poor. The rich are very rich and have very high standards of living whilst the poor are very poor and live a very difficult life.

Human Development Index (HDI)

C

In 1990 the United Nations created its own measure of development, called the **Human Development Index**. It combines information on health, education and wealth. It therefore measures **social** as well as **economic** progress and gives a good guide to a country's overall well-being.

The HDI 'League table' lists 175 countries. Those in this book are ranked as follows:

9	Japan
13	UK
21	Italy
65	Brazil
104	China
146	Kenya

The HDI has the advantage of being able to show differences in levels of development **within** a country as well as **between** countries.

Activities

1 a) Make a larger copy of table **D**.
  b) Using information from table **E**, complete your table to show the rank order of the four countries for each measure of development. The most developed will score 1 and the least developed will score 4.
  c) Add the scores together for each country and complete the Total row.

2 Write out the countries from your completed table as a 'League table of development'.
The country with the lowest score will be most developed and should be at the top of the league.

3 Write a paragraph to describe some of the features of:
  a) a developed country and
  b) a developing country.

D

	UK	Brazil	Kenya	China
GNP per capita (highest first)				
Life expectancy (highest first)				
Primary jobs (lowest first)				
Living in towns (highest first)				
Going to school (highest first)				
People per doctor (lowest first)				
Owning a car (highest first)				
Total				

E

	UK	Brazil	Kenya	China
GNP per capita	$25 500	$7600	$1100	$4700
Life expectancy	78	71	45	72
Primary jobs (%)	2	53	70	50
Living in towns (%)	92	78	25	29
Going to school (%)	100	50	24	71
People per doctor	300	1000	10 130	1000
Owning a car (per 1000)	476	80	15	10

Summary

A wide range of measures can be used to show differences in the level of development between various places in the world.

What is meant by interdependence?

Most countries want to be **independent**. They would prefer to make their own decisions as to how they develop and how their people live. However, no country has everything that it needs. This means that each country has to work with other countries if it is to develop and improve its standard of living.

When countries work together and rely on each other for help they are said to be **interdependent**.

One of the main ways that countries become interdependent is by selling goods to each other. They buy things that they need or would like to have. They then sell things to make money to pay for what they have bought. The exchanging of goods and materials like this is called **trade**.

Unfortunately, as drawing **A** shows, it is the richer, developed countries that make the most money from trade. The poorer, developing countries earn little and gradually grow poorer as they struggle to pay for the expensive goods that they need.

In time the developing country may have to ask the developed country for **aid**. Aid is a form of help and is another way in which countries become interdependent. If it is planned carefully, aid can help a country progress. However, it can also make it more reliant on other countries and therefore less independent.

Drawing **B** shows some different types of aid.

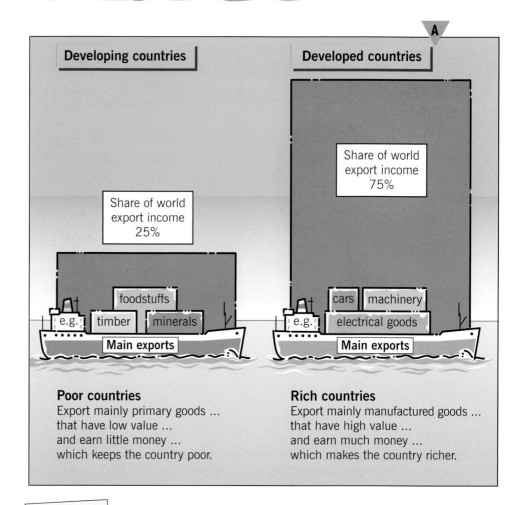

A

Developing countries

Share of world export income 25%

foodstuffs

e.g. timber minerals

Main exports

Developed countries

Share of world export income 75%

cars machinery

e.g. electrical goods

Main exports

Poor countries
Export mainly primary goods ...
that have low value ...
and earn little money ...
which keeps the country poor.

Rich countries
Export mainly manufactured goods ...
that have high value ...
and earn much money ...
which makes the country richer.

AID

B

Can be given by countries or organisations such as the United Nations or Oxfam.

Short-term aid

Brings help quickly to people in emergencies such as earthquakes, floods, famine and civil wars.
This aid may be food, clothing, shelter or medical supplies.

Long-term aid

Tries to improve the standard of living and quality of life. It can include:
• **money** to pay for new schemes
• **skilled people** such as doctors, teachers and engineers
• **equipment** for hospitals and factories
• **big projects** such as new roads or power stations.

Most countries are now more interdependent than in the past. Because of improvements in transport and communications, companies and large organisations are able to have offices and factories almost anywhere in the world. Many locate in the poorer countries where costs are low. Ideas and lifestyles are also spreading more easily as television and the internet become more accessible.

This process is called **globalisation**. Globalisation means the way companies, ideas and lifestyles are spreading around the world with increasing ease.

Globalisation is an important reason for countries becoming more interdependent.

C A McDonald's takeaway in China

Activities

1 a) What is meant when a country is said to be interdependent?
  b) Why does a country have to trade?

2 a) Make a larger copy of diagram **D** and complete it using the following statements:
   • which cost little money
   • that earn much money
   • mainly primary goods.
  b) Draw a similar diagram to show how trade affects poor countries.

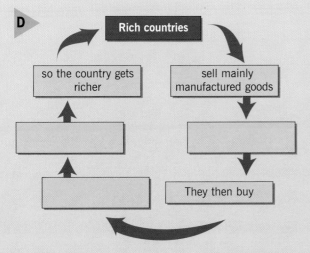
D

Rich countries → sell mainly manufactured goods

so the country gets richer

They then buy

3 Look at photo **E**. Make a list of the short-term and long-term aid that you think the country needs most. Give reasons for your answers.

E Food aid in Somalia

Summary

Countries need to be interdependent if they are to develop and share in the earth's resources.

What is sustainable development?

Development is about change for the better. It is about progress and improvement both for the country itself and the people who live in it. Unfortunately it is very easy for countries that want to develop and to make progress, to waste resources and damage the environment.

The richer countries are the worst offenders. With only 25 per cent of the world's population, they use 75 per cent of the earth's natural resources. Many of the resources are non-renewable and can only be used once. They often cause pollution of air, land and water.

The poorer countries add to the problem. They have rapidly rising populations who want to improve their standards of living. They rarely have enough money or the technology to provide or use additional resources without damaging the environment.

Most people agree that the solution to the problem is **sustainable development**. Sustainable development is a way of improving people's quality of life without wasting resources or harming the environment.

A

Sustainable development ...
- is progress that can continue year after year
- uses, but does not waste, natural resources
- improves, but does not threaten, ways of life
- neither harms the present, nor destroys the future environment
- is sensible development which can bring benefits now and in the future.

B

Low-energy lights with automatic timers

Glass-fibre insulation in the ceiling

Electrical equipment switched off when not in use

Door closed during lessons

SUSTAINABLE DEVELOPMENT

Draught-proofing on door

Double-glazed windows

Waste materials like paper, cans and plastics re-used or recycled

Wall cavities filled with foam

CLOTHES

Thermostats on radiators to control temperature

Paper used sparingly

Carpet on floor

Books, equipment and furniture handled with care

Clothing recycled

Drawing **B** shows how sustainable methods can help conserve resources and save energy in the classroom. Which of these methods apply to your classroom?

Sustainable development in poorer, developing countries can be difficult to achieve. The best schemes tend to be small and use **appropriate technology**. These schemes meet the needs of the local people and the environment in which they live. They are more likely to be sustainable and can help improve the quality of life for people today without damaging the future.

C

Appropriate technology …
• is usually small-scale
• uses local skills and knowledge
• uses local raw materials and technology
• uses renewable resources
• does not damage the environment
• uses limited amounts of money
• develops local skills and trains local people
• develops products needed by local people at a price they can afford
• encourages local people to work together.

D Processing locally grown cashew nuts in Kenya

Activities

1 Write out the meaning of the following terms. The Glossary at the back of the book will help you.
   a) Sustainable development
   b) Renewable resources
   c) Non-renewable resources
   d) Appropriate technology

2 Make a larger copy of diagram **E**. Complete it by adding five advantages of sustainable development.

3 Look at drawing **B**.
   a) Give two methods that help conserve resources.
   b) Give two methods that help save energy.
   c) How many of the methods apply to your classroom?
   d) How could you improve your classroom as an example of sustainable development?

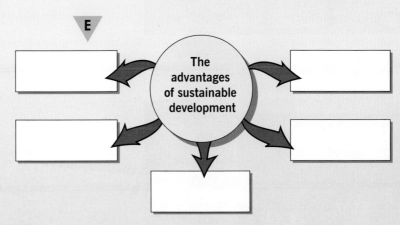

E

The advantages of sustainable development

Summary

Sustainable development should lead to an improvement in people's quality of life and standard of living without wasting natural resources or spoiling the environment.

What is Brazil like?

Almost everybody has heard of Brazil but few people have much idea of what Brazil is really like. What do you know about Brazil? What images come to mind when you think about the country?

Most people, when asked that question, would probably come up with football, coffee, the River Amazon, Rio de Janeiro and perhaps Indians and the rainforest. Which of these would you have thought about? Would you have added any others?

Brazil in fact, is very difficult to describe. It is a huge country. It is bigger than all of Europe put together and almost 30 times larger than Great Britain. Because of its size it has a great variety of physical features, climate and types of vegetation. There are also great variations in how people live, their wealth and overall quality of life. Indeed Brazil can best be described as a land of contrasts. Look at the photos on these pages. They show some of the contrasts.

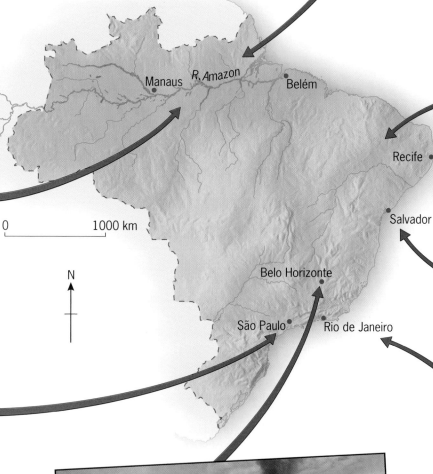

Amerindians live a traditional way of life in the hot, wet rainforest.

A mixture of people from all over the world now live in Brazil. The team that played in the 2002 World Cup final is typical of that mix.

Brazil is one of the fastest growing industrial nations in the world. Industry has brought wealth but it has also caused pollution.

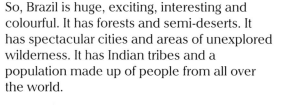
Living conditions can be very difficult. These stilt houses are on the banks of the Amazon.

So, Brazil is huge, exciting, interesting and colourful. It has forests and semi-deserts. It has spectacular cities and areas of unexplored wilderness. It has Indian tribes and a population made up of people from all over the world.

But it is the contrast between the rich and the poor that people notice more than anything else. On the one hand there is the appalling poverty of the slums. On the other there is the high-class life-style of the wealthy. That is Brazil's great problem and the one that is causing the most concern.

Peasant farmers try to make a living in the hot, dry semi-desert of the north-east.

Poverty and unhealthy living conditions are common in Brazil. These slum houses are in Salvador.

For rich and poor alike the beach is the place to be for social life, sport and leisure. This is Copacabana beach.

Activities

1 Work with a partner and make a list of things that come to mind when you think of Brazil.

2 From the photos and their captions find:
   a) one place that is hot and wet and one place that is hot and dry
   b) one place that is jungle and one place that is semi-desert
   c) two examples of wealth and two examples of poverty
   d) one example of traditional lifestyles and one example of mixed nationalities
   e) one example of difficult working conditions and one example of economic wealth.

Write your answers in a table like the one below.

Contrasts in Brazil		
a) Climate		
b) Vegetation		
c) Standard of living		
d) Population		
e) Economic		

3 a) Describe at least four things that you think are good about Brazil. Write a paragraph of about 50 words.
   b) Make a list of at least six things that you think are problems in Brazil.

Summary Brazil is a land of contrast. There are great differences between how the rich and the poor live.

What are Brazil's main physical features?

River Amazon

- Second longest river in the world
- 6280 km (3925 miles) in length
- Over 300 km wide at its mouth
- More than 1100 tributaries flow into it
- Has source in Peru at height of 5200 m (17000 ft)
- Ocean going ships can sail 3200 km up river
- Contains 20% ($\frac{1}{5}$th) of world's total river water

Amazon rainforest

- Largest rainforest on earth
- Mainly flat and low-lying
- A few hills and low mountain ranges
- Over 40000 species of plants and animals
- Home to over a third of all species on earth
- Mostly uninhabited
- Home of Amerindians
- Still large areas unexplored
- Always hot and wet
- Rains on most days

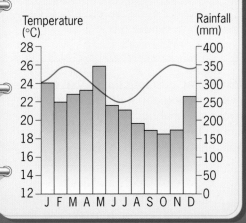

Temperature (°C) — Rainfall (mm)
J F M A M J J A S O N D

Coastal lowlands

- Highlands fall steeply into the sea
- Some narrow, flat stretches of land
- Area once rainforest
- Forest now cleared for farming and settlement
- Warm temperatures, ample rainfall, good soils – excellent for growing crops
- Inland areas cooler than coast
- East coast is the most populated area of Brazil

The photos that make up this picture of South America were taken from 830 km (520 miles) above the earth's surface by an orbiting satellite. The colours have been changed slightly (**enhanced**) to show the relief features and drainage patterns more clearly. The red dashed line has been added to show Brazil's border.

Dense forest and areas of lush vegetation show up as bright green. Drier regions are brown or yellow. Notice the river Amazon and its tributaries. Can you also see the snow-capped mountains of the Andes in the west of South America?

North-east Brazil

- Mostly flat-topped highland
- Some areas of flat coastal lowland
- Very dry. No rain at all in some years
- Mainly rough scrub and thorn bushes
- Too dry for much else to grow
- Vegetation called caatinga
- Difficult living conditions

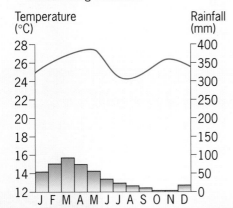

Brazilian Highlands

- Mainly flat-topped hills and plateaux
- Height between 1000 and 2000 metres
- Include highest parts of Brazil
- Hot, wet summers
- Warm, dry winters
- Grassland and open forest

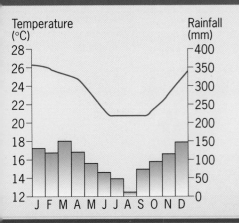

Activities

1 Make a larger copy of the map below. Complete the descriptions of each region using information from these two pages.

Brazil – main physical regions

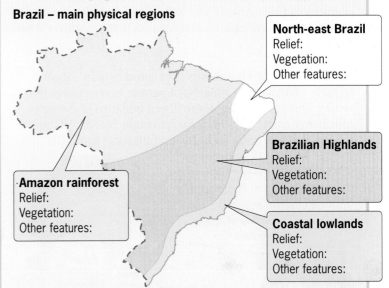

North-east Brazil
Relief:
Vegetation:
Other features:

Brazilian Highlands
Relief:
Vegetation:
Other features:

Amazon rainforest
Relief:
Vegetation:
Other features:

Coastal lowlands
Relief:
Vegetation:
Other features:

2 Match the following regions with the correct climate descriptions. Use the climate graphs to complete the temperature and rainfall figures for November.

North-east Brazil ⟩ ⟨ Hot (26°C) and very wet (180 mm)

Amazon rainforest ⟩ ⟨ Warm (___°C) and medium rainfall (____ mm)

Coastal lowlands ⟩ ⟨ Hot (___°C) and very dry (__ mm)

3 Write out the following paragraph and fill in the missing spaces.

The River Amazon
The Amazon is the _____ longest river in the world (the Nile is the longest river). It flows ___ km from its source in ____ to its mouth in the _____ . Ocean-going ships can sail ___ km upriver. At its _____ the Amazon is over 300 km wide. The river has over ____ tributaries. It drains 6.5 million km² of rainforest and is important for transport and trade.

Summary

Brazil is a huge country with a great variety of physical features. Much of the land is flat and there are few mountains. The Amazon is Brazil's greatest river.

People in Brazil

Look at diagram **A** which shows some people who live in Brazil. Notice how different each of them looks and what varied backgrounds they have. If you stand on a street corner in a Brazilian city you will see even more variety. Nearly every race, culture and religion in the world will be represented.

Just 500 years ago Brazil was populated only by tribal Indians. Today it is a mixture of people from all over the world. This change has come about because of the large number of migrants who have arrived in Brazil and the mixing that has gone on between different races. The

Portuguese first came to what we now know as Brazil in 1500. They ruled the country as a colony for over 300 years. They brought slaves from Africa to work on plantations and helped develop tolerant attitudes towards new citizens from foreign countries. The slaves were quickly followed by immigrants from other parts of Europe, Asia and North America.

Most modern Brazilians are proud of their mixed origins. There is much inter-marriage and this is one reason why there are very few racial problems and practically no colour prejudice in Brazil.

A

We are the original Amerindians. Most of us live in the Amazon forest but there aren't many of us left now

We come from Japan. Most of us live in and around São Paulo. We like to keep our traditions and tend to live together and keep to ourselves.

We Portuguese were the first Europeans to settle here. We set up modern Brazil and gave the country our language.

We Germans have been coming here since the 1880s. We have brought industry and business skills to Brazil.

Our people first came here as slaves over 400 years ago. Our background and African culture are an important part of Brazilian life.

We are Italians. Some of our people went straight to the cattle ranches in the south but most took work on the coffee plantations near São Paulo.

Brazil has a population of 182 million – more than three times that of the UK. So where do they live and why are some parts of Brazil very crowded whilst others are almost uninhabited?

Map **C** shows **population distribution** in Brazil. You will notice that most people live near the coast in the south-east of the country. Towards the north and west the **population density** is very **sparse**. The reasons for this uneven distribution are due to **positive** and **negative factors**.

B

Negative factors discourage people from living in an area
- Difficult living conditions
- Poor farming
- Few resources available

Positive factors attract people to an area
- Pleasant living conditions
- Good farming
- Resources available for industry

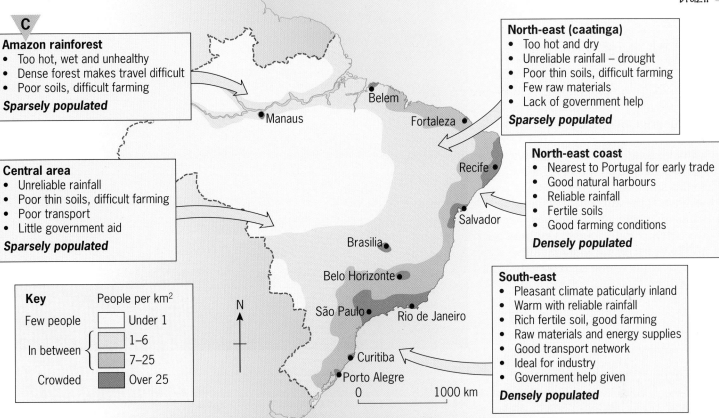

C

Amazon rainforest
- Too hot, wet and unhealthy
- Dense forest makes travel difficult
- Poor soils, difficult farming

Sparsely populated

North-east (caatinga)
- Too hot and dry
- Unreliable rainfall – drought
- Poor thin soils, difficult farming
- Few raw materials
- Lack of government help

Sparsely populated

North-east coast
- Nearest to Portugal for early trade
- Good natural harbours
- Reliable rainfall
- Fertile soils
- Good farming conditions

Densely populated

Central area
- Unreliable rainfall
- Poor thin soils, difficult farming
- Poor transport
- Little government aid

Sparsely populated

South-east
- Pleasant climate paticularly inland
- Warm with reliable rainfall
- Rich fertile soil, good farming
- Raw materials and energy supplies
- Good transport network
- Ideal for industry
- Government help given

Densely populated

Key	People per km²
Few people	Under 1
In between	1–6
	7–25
Crowded	Over 25

Cities: Manaus, Belem, Fortaleza, Recife, Salvador, Brasilia, Belo Horizonte, São Paulo, Rio de Janeiro, Curitiba, Porto Alegre

N

0 1000 km

Activities

1 a) Who were the original inhabitants of Brazil?
   b) Name five countries or regions from which immigrants came to Brazil.
   c) Which people gave their language to Brazil?
   d) Which people arrived as slaves?
   e) Which people prefer to keep together?

2 Which three of the following are reasons for there being little racial discrimination or colour prejudice in Brazil?
- All the people are of the same race
- The Portuguese encouraged tolerance
- Everyone is the same colour
- There is much inter-marriage
- Brazilians are proud of their mixed origin.

3 Draw table **D** and put the following in the correct columns:

• densely populated • sparsely populated • very few people • crowded • too hot and wet • pleasant climate • good water supply • raw materials nearby • dense forest• good energy supplies • difficult travel• unhealthy conditions • much industry • rich fertile soil • poor soils • difficult farming • good farming • mainly negative factors • mainly positive factors.

D

South-east	Amazon rainforest

4 a) List the cities from sketch **E** in order of size. Give the biggest first.
   b) In which part of Brazil are the four largest cities?

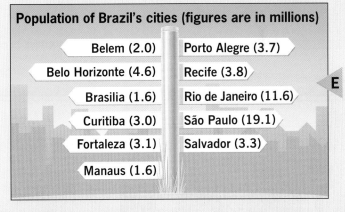

Population of Brazil's cities (figures are in millions)

Belem (2.0)	Porto Alegre (3.7)
Belo Horizonte (4.6)	Recife (3.8)
Brasilia (1.6)	Rio de Janeiro (11.6)
Curitiba (3.0)	São Paulo (19.1)
Fortaleza (3.1)	Salvador (3.3)
Manaus (1.6)	

E

5 Draw a bar graph to show the number of people in each of the cities in sketch **E**.
- Arrange the bars in order of size with the biggest on the left.
- Use different colours for the cities that are inland to those that are within 200 km of the coast.
- Give your graph a title.

Summary

Brazil is a mixture of people from all over the world. The south-east is the most densely populated. Population decreases towards the north and west.

23

The best of Brazil

For many people, Brazil is a dream holiday destination. A pleasant climate, a varied landscape, and friendly people are just a start. Add to this sun-clad beaches, historic sights and the adventure of the Amazon jungle, and Brazil has everything for the tourist. One way to see Brazil is by a multi-centre holiday. Here is one such holiday advertised by a tour company as 'The best of Brazil'.

A

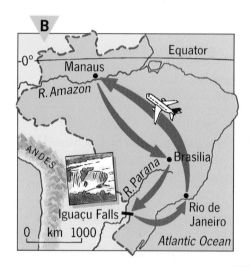

B

C

The Rio Carnival Four magical days of noise, excitement, music and non-stop dancing. A festival of street parties, parades, fancy dress and firecrackers. Endless wine, food and fun with very, very friendly people. This is Brazil at its best, a never to be forgotten experience.

Day 1 Rio
Excursion to the summit of Corcovado mountain and the statue of Christ the Redeemer. Spectacular views of the bays and beaches. Afternoon free to visit Copacabana and Ipanema beaches or stroll along elegant avenues of shops and boutiques.

Day 2 Rio
Morning tour of the city including ascent of Sugar Loaf Mountain by cable car. Optional cruise to one of the nearby tropical islands. Evening at a top nightclub and dancing to the 'Samba beat'.

Day 3 Rio/Manaus
Early flight to Manaus. Travel downriver by canoe to experience the thrill of the Amazon (**E**). A chance to see thousands of colourful birds leave their roosts and fish jump from the waters of the river. An evening expedition by boat searching for alligators by torchlight (**D**).

Day 4 Amazon
In the morning explore the rainforest with a local guide. There are more plants and animal species here than anywhere else in the world. Over 42,000 different species of insects have been recorded so be well prepared with insect repellent! In the afternoon visit an Indian village to experience the local way of life and perhaps buy traditionally made crafts.

Day 5 Amazon
Canoe trip to Lake Acajituba to see rubber trees, Brazil nuts and variety of palms. In the afternoon a fishing trip. There are 1500 species of edible fish here. You may even catch piranha.

Day 6 Manuas/Brasilia
Morning flight to Brasilia. Afternoon city tour to view the exciting modern architecture of this ultra modern capital.

Day 7 Brasilia/Iguaçu
Fly via São Paulo to Iguaçu (**F**). Guided tour of one of the world's most spectacular waterfalls. Don't miss the thrilling helicopter flight which takes you right over the Falls.

Day 8 Iguaçu
A full day of relaxation at Iguaçu Falls set in a sub-tropical forest full of exotic birds and butterflies. Opportunity to cross the border to visit Paraguay and Argentina.

Day 9 Iguaçu/Rio
Morning flight to Rio. Day at leisure in city.

D

E

F

Postcard from
Das Cataratas Hotel, Iguaçu Falls

Dear Paul and Christine,

We're at Iguaçu Falls now. They are absolutely breathtaking. We have just walked along a narrow pathway carved out of the rocks and we're right beside the falls. There are over 275 separate waterfalls here. They empty a million gallons of water every second into the foaming Parana River. The sound is deafening. We are going on a boat trip later to Garganta do Diablo (Devil's Throat). That's below the falls so we might get a bit wet! Some of our friends have booked the helicopter trip.

   With best wishes
      Joanne

G

Activities

1 List four features that make Brazil an interesting holiday destination.

2 Draw a star diagram like the one below to show at least six attractions of Rio de Janeiro.

H

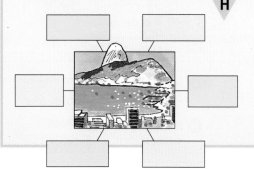

3 Imagine that you are on Day 5 of the Best of Brazil holiday. Write a postcard to a friend describing the most enjoyable parts of your holiday so far.

4 Imagine that you are flying from Iguaçu to Rio on Day 9. Write in your diary how you spent your time at Iguaçu and what impressed you about the falls.

5 Working in pairs, design a poster advertising Brazil as a holiday destination.
- Try to include a map, labelled photos or sketches, and short descriptions.
- Make the poster as colourful and interesting as possible.
- Your teacher may have some travel brochures which could help you.

Summary   Brazil is a land of contrasts. It has varied and often spectacular scenery and a way of life that is both interesting and exciting.

Brazil's 'Golden Triangle'

The south-east is where most people in Brazil live. It is the richest area of the country and has always been the most important industrial region. Because of this, the three main cities of São Paulo, Rio de Janeiro and Belo Horizonte have become known as the '**Golden Triangle**'.

The south-east region is made up mainly of highland that slopes steeply into the sea. On the narrow, coastal plain there is little space for development and the climate is uncomfortably hot and wet. Inland on the high plateau the climate is much cooler and healthier. It is here where most industry and **commercial farming** is located.

Coffee provided early wealth for the region. The climate and rich 'terra rossa' soil proved perfect for growing this crop and São Paulo quickly developed as the 'coffee capital of the world'. Santos became important as the port for São Paulo. Immigrants flocked to the area to work on the coffee plantations called **fazendas**. Over half a million were Italian. Others came from different parts of Europe and other parts of Brazil, mainly in the 1890s.

The profit from coffee was put to good use. Much of it was invested in other industries and on good roads and railways. At first the new industries were small in scale and linked to local resources. Factories processing food and producing leather goods, textiles, clothes and paper were the most common.

More recently, the mining of nearby mineral resources, the building of new power stations and an increase in government aid has helped the Golden Triangle develop **heavy industries**. Brazil now has steel, chemical, shipbuilding, aircraft and car industries all located in the area. These industrial developments have attracted even more migrants to the area in search of work.

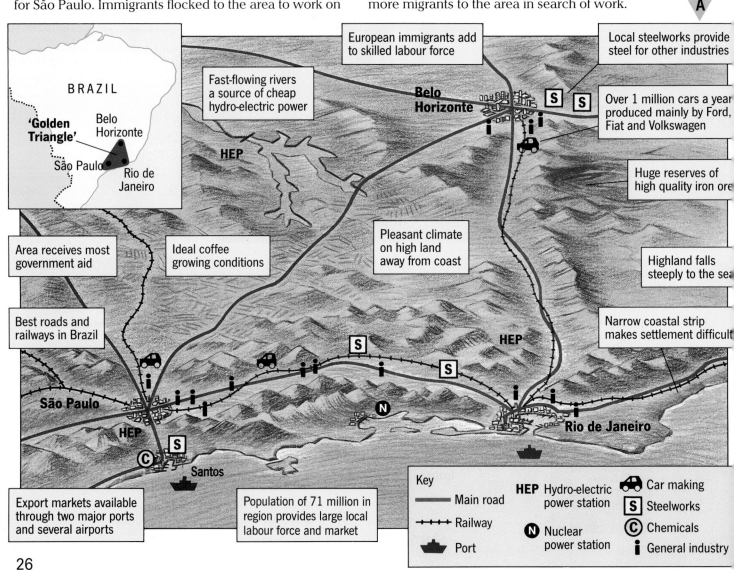

European immigrants add to skilled labour force

Local steelworks provide steel for other industries

Fast-flowing rivers a source of cheap hydro-electric power

Over 1 million cars a year produced mainly by Ford, Fiat and Volkswagen

Huge reserves of high quality iron ore

Area receives most government aid

Ideal coffee growing conditions

Pleasant climate on high land away from coast

Highland falls steeply to the sea

Best roads and railways in Brazil

Narrow coastal strip makes settlement difficult

Export markets available through two major ports and several airports

Population of 71 million in region provides large local labour force and market

BRAZIL

'Golden Triangle'

Belo Horizonte

São Paulo

Rio de Janeiro

Belo Horizonte

São Paulo

HEP

Santos

Rio de Janeiro

Key

— Main road

+ Railway

Port

HEP Hydro-electric power station

N Nuclear power station

Car making

S Steelworks

C Chemicals

General industry

The success of the south-east has brought many benefits but it has also caused some problems . . .

Only the rich people have made money from the factories. Most of the workers are paid very low wages.

Wildlife has been lost as forests have been cleared to make way for factories and more coffee plantations

Cars and factories pollute the air in our cities

Millions of people live in poor quality housing with no water, electricity or proper sanitation

Our rivers, lakes and even the sea are polluted by waste from towns and factories

As more people come to the area in search of work, there are not enough jobs to go round and unemployment increases

Traffic congestion is a problem here. There are just too many cars.

Many of the largest industries are multi-nationals owned by foreigners. This means that most of the profits leave Brazil.

Activities

1 Draw a simple sketch map of the region shown in map **A** as follows:
a) Draw in the coastline and name the Atlantic Ocean.
b) Mark and name São Paulo, Belo Horizonte, Rio de Janeiro and Santos.
c) Draw in and name the 'Golden Triangle'.
d) Shade the narrow coastal strip green and shade the highland brown.

2 a) Make a larger copy of diagram **C** below.
b) Write the following labels in the correct places: Santos, narrow coastal plain, highland, mineral resources, much industry, hot and wet, pleasant climate, coffee growing.
c) With help from your diagram suggest why fewer people live on the coast than inland.

D

Raw materials
Nearby, there are huge supplies of…

Labour
Large labour force from local population of… and skilled workers from…

Energy
This is mainly cheap…

Reasons for growth in the Golden Triangle

Transport
Roads and railways are…

Investment
Profit from coffee and aid from…

Market
Large local market and exports by sea from…

3 Make a larger copy of diagram **D**, above, and complete it using information from map **A**.

4 Study diagram **B** and list the problems of Brazil's south-east. Write no more than ten words for each one. Underline those that are damaging to the environment.

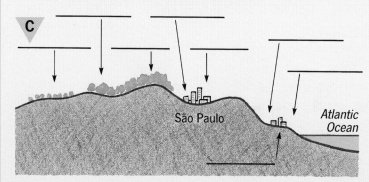

C

São Paulo

Atlantic Ocean

Summary

The south-east is Brazil's wealthiest and most populated region. The Golden Triangle has many industries and attracts large numbers of migrants in search of work.

São Paulo: the rich...

A

Hello,

my name is Maria and I live in São Paulo with my parents and brother. My father is a manager at the Ford car factory on the outskirts of town. My mother works in an office. We have a nice house in the suburbs with a large garden. A maid comes in on most days to cook the meals and keep the house clean.

My brother Carlos is two years older than me and we go to school together. I like geography and languages and hope to go to University eventually. During the week I work hard at school and I have a lot of homework.

At weekends we often go to our small beach house at Ubatura, a beach resort on the Atlantic coast. If we don't go there I like to go downtown.

São Paulo city centre is like any modern city. It has huge skyscrapers, lovely shops, lots of restaurants and plenty of nightlife. Rua Augusta is the best for fashion shops. My brother sometimes takes me to a disco near there. I like to dance the Samba.

São Paulo is the biggest and wealthiest city in Brazil. It is very crowded and always seems to be busy. The area around the city is the most important in Brazil for agriculture and industry. Over 90% of Brazilian-made cars are manufactured here. New factories and offices seem to open up nearly every day.

Like many families in São Paulo we are well off and have a good standard of living. Not everyone in our city is so lucky though. Some people here are very poor indeed and live a very difficult life.

Activities

1 Unscramble the following to give five features of São Paulo's city centre.

> prakysrecss • sphso • trustearna eflingthi • sdoisc

2 Why is the area around São Paulo important?

3 a) What jobs do Maria's mother and father have?
   b) Maria's family is wealthy. Give five features of her way of life that show this.

4 Make a larger copy of sketch **C** showing Roberto's house. Complete it by answering the questions.

C Life in a favela

a) How many people are in Roberto's family?

b) Where does the family live?

c) How many rooms does the house have?

h) How have conditions been improved?

d) What is the house made from?

g) What problems do the sewers cause?

f) How does Roberto earn money?

e) How does Roberto's father earn money?

...and the poor

B

Hello,

I'm Roberto and am 12 years old. I live with my parents and four sisters on the outskirts of São Paulo. Our home is in a slum district known in Brazil as a favela. Our house is very basic. We built it ourselves with any materials that we could find. There are only two small rooms. In one we work, eat and relax. In the other we sleep. It is very crowded but we are making improvements all the time.

My father makes sandals from old car tyres. He sells them at a small market on the edge of our favela. On a good day he can make over one cruzado (about 80p). I only go to school in the mornings. There are very few books and there never seems to be any pens or paper to work with. In the afternoons and weekends I go to the city centre to work as a shoe-shiner. I will have to give up school soon and work full-time. My family needs the money.

The smell of our favela is very unpleasant. Open sewers run down the streets and even under houses. The place is dirty and disease is a problem. My two youngest sisters nearly died from diarrhoea when they were just babies. The council tries to improve conditions here. They recently provided us with piped water and electricity which is a great help. Nearly half of São Paulo's people live in slum conditions like us.

5 Copy and complete the paragraph on the right using the words from drawing **D**.

D

unhealthy · education · electricity · sewage · favela · poor

A slum district in Brazil is called a _____. It is an area of _____ quality housing which often lacks _____, a water supply and _____ disposal. People in these areas earn little money, have poor _____ and live in crowded, _____ conditions. *Favelas* are mainly the result of large numbers of newcomers moving to cities from the countryside.

Summary

Standards of living vary considerably in the São Paulo area. Some people are wealthy and have a good quality of life. Other people are extremely poor and live in slum conditions.

29

People in the Amazon rainforest

In the north and west of Brazil is the Amazon rainforest. This is the least populated region of the country and is the home of many different Amerindian tribes. The Kayapo are one of these tribes. They live on the Xingu river, a tributary of the Amazon.

Photo **A** shows a traditional Kayapo village. The circle of wooden buildings with palm-leafed thatched roofs are where the families live. The central house is used only by men. They meet socially here and make the decisions that affect the whole village.

Like most Amerindian people, the Kayapo use face and body paint. Red and black are the most common colours. Both of these are made from the juice of plants. On special occasions feathered head-dresses, nose pieces and ear plugs are worn. The men wear a round wooden disc between the chin and a stretched lower lip (photo **B**). All of the ornaments are made from materials found in the forest.

The Kayapo live by hunting, fishing and collecting food from the forest (photo **D**). A few crops are grown but only just enough for the villagers themselves. People who live like this are called **hunter-gatherers** and **subsistence farmers**. The forest provides the Indians with an excellent diet. They have a choice of over 250 fruits and hundreds of different vegetables, nuts and leaves.

Shifting cultivation

A clearance is made by cutting down trees and burning the vegetation. This is called slash and burn.

Crops are planted and grow well in the warm, humid conditions.

Within four or five years the soil becomes exhausted and the harvest gets poorer and poorer.

The clearing is abandoned and the farmers move on.

The clearing gradually grows over and the natural forest returns.

As well as hunting and gathering food, the Kayapo make their own 'gardens' in small forest clearings. In these they grow fruit trees and crops including manioc, maize, sweet potatoes, pineapples, peppers and beans. The Indian women, especially, are expert forest gardeners. They work in a careful and organised way, improving the soil at the same time. After a while, however, the heavy rains wash away the nutrients in the soil and crops no longer grow so well. The Kayapo then move away and make a new **forest garden**. This type of farming is called **shifting cultivation** (photo **C**).

Forest uses

- Plants and trees are used as building materials.
- The Indians have a use for 90 per cent of the forest plants.
- Face and body paints are made from plants.
- Body ornaments are made from animal bones and teeth, birds' feathers and tree bark.
- Nine species of stingless bee are used to produce honey.
- Musical instruments are made from animal bones and skins, bamboo and nutshells.
- Medicines are made from over 650 different forest plants.

D

Kayapo Indians in the forest

Forest care

- Small-scale farming allows soil to be used again later.
- Limits are put on numbers of wild animals and birds hunted to ensure species survival.
- Clean and orderly villages help reduce waste and pollution.
- Useful new trees and shrubs have been added to the forest.
- Soil quality is improved in the clearings by adding fertiliser made from plant leaves, ashes and termite nests.
- Spare food and forest products are traded to reduce waste.

Activities

1 Answer the questions below. The first letters are given in drawing **E**. Write out your completed answers.
   a) Least populated region of Brazil
   b) An Amerindian tribe
   c) Where the Kayapo live
   d) Worn by Kayapo men
   e) A forest clearing used for growing crops
   f) A type of farming, where people move from one place to another
   g) Where just enough food is grown for the village
   h) Someone who collects and hunts food
   i) A method of forest clearance

E (drawing with labels: HG, SF, SC, SB, AR, XR, FG, WD, KI)

2 a) Make a larger copy of diagram **F**.
   b) Put these labels into the correct boxes.

Plant crops

Soil loses goodness

Burn the vegetation

Cut down the forest

Harvest crops

Abandon clearing and move on

   c) Why is clearing the forest called slash and burn?
   d) Why is this method of farming called shifting cultivation?

3 Draw a star diagram to show how useful the forest is to the Kayapo Indian. Write no more than four words for each use.

4 a) How do the Indians reduce waste in the forest?
   b) How do the Indians care for the forest?

F

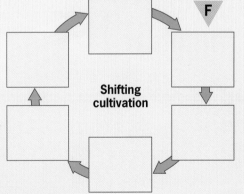

Shifting cultivation

Summary

The Indians depend on the forest for their life. They have a great respect for all plants and animals and are careful not to damage the environment.

31

What is happening to the Amazon rainforest?

The Amerindians are not the only people with an interest in the rainforest. Since the 1970s the Brazilian government has encouraged the development of the Amazon region. The aim has been to bring wealth to the area by using its natural resources. Some of the developments are shown below.

B

New roads Many new roads have been built deep into the rainforest. The Trans-Amazonian Highway is the longest. It stretches 5300 km (3300 miles) across Brazil from east to west. The roads help move timber, cattle and crops to markets. People from other parts of Brazil have settled along these roads.

A

Mining Huge deposits of iron ore, gold, copper, bauxite and other minerals have been discovered in the rainforest. Mining companies have felled trees and built roads through the forest to reach these deposits.

C

Power stations An unlimited water supply and ideal river conditions have led to the development of many hydro-electric power (HEP) stations. HEP stations provide cheap and plentiful energy for industry, transport and domestic use. More than 125 new HEP dams are to be built in the next 15 years. The reservoirs behind the dams flood large areas of forest.

D

Ranching Large areas of the forest have been bought by multi-national companies for cattle ranching. These companies have burnt down the forest and replaced the trees with grass. The beef from the cattle ranches has largely gone to fast-food chains in the United States and Europe to make into burgers.

Developments in the rainforest have brought many benefits. They have provided jobs for people, brought money into the region and helped Brazil's industry and agriculture. However, there have been problems. Large parts of the rainforest have been destroyed and the Amerindian way of life has been put under serious threat.

6000 people lost their homes because of the Tucurui HEP scheme

New roads have brought in settlers. Some of our people have been murdered by them.

Cattle ranchers burn the forest, ruin the soil and leave the mess for us

New roads cut through the forest and damage our land

Some of the plants we use to make medicines have disappeared

We don't want development, we just want to live as we are

Mining waste and chemicals have poisoned our rivers

Huge areas of forest have been cleared for mining

There is not as much wildlife now that the trees have been felled

We were forced off our land by violent cattle ranchers

Many Indians have died from diseases brought in by settlers

HEP schemes have put large areas of forest under water

E

Chief Raoni of the Kayapo
We want nothing from the white man. He has brought us only death, illness and murder. He has stolen and destroyed our forest. We want to be left alone to live with our ancestors. We want to stay here. It is our right.

Activities

1 a) What minerals may be found in the forest?
 b) What is the cattle ranching meat mainly used for?
 c) What advantages have new roads brought to the area?
 d) Why is the Amazon region good for HEP?

2 Give three benefits that developments in the rainforest have brought.

3 Look at photo A of mining in the rainforest. For each of the following people say what their feelings might be about the new development. Give reasons for your answers.
 ● A Kayapo Indian
 ● A Brazilian mine owner
 ● A European tourist

4 Make a copy of the table below. Complete it using information from diagram E above.

Problems of development

Mining	New roads	HEP	Ranching	Others

5 Work with a partner for this task.
 a) Imagine you are Chief Raoni. Make a list of reasons why you are against rainforest development.
 b) Imagine you are a government minister. Make a list of reasons why development of the rainforest should go ahead.
 c) Display your arguments as an attractive and interesting poster.

Summary

There have been many changes to the Amazon rainforest. These have brought benefits to some people but caused problems for others.

Two regions compared

A

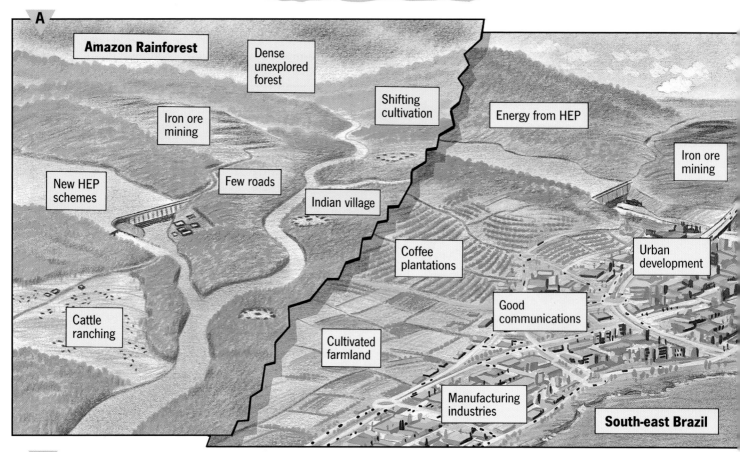

Amazon Rainforest

Dense unexplored forest

Shifting cultivation

Energy from HEP

Iron ore mining

Iron ore mining

New HEP schemes

Few roads

Indian village

Urban development

Coffee plantations

Cattle ranching

Good communications

Cultivated farmland

Manufacturing industries

South-east Brazil

B

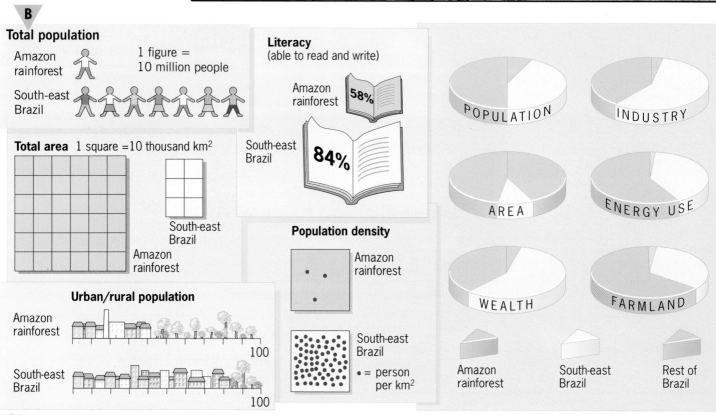

Total population

Amazon rainforest

1 figure = 10 million people

South-east Brazil

Literacy
(able to read and write)

Amazon rainforest **58%**

South-east Brazil **84%**

Total area   1 square = 10 thousand km²

South-east Brazil

Amazon rainforest

Population density

Amazon rainforest

South-east Brazil

• = person per km²

Urban/rural population

Amazon rainforest

100

South-east Brazil

100

POPULATION   INDUSTRY

AREA   ENERGY USE

WEALTH   FARMLAND

Amazon rainforest

South-east Brazil

Rest of Brazil

As we have seen, South-east Brazil is very different to the Amazon rainforest (diagrams **A** and **B**). The South-east is a small region but it has nearly half of Brazil's population and most of its wealth. The area's original wealth came from enormous coffee plantations. Nowadays, modern industry powered by cheap hydro-electricity is the biggest source of income. South-east Brazil is densely populated. It has the country's largest cities, densest network of roads and railways, and highest standards of living.

The Amazon rainforest is in complete contrast. The area is huge yet very few people live there. Most of the population is concentrated in river towns like Manaus. The Amerindians live mainly in isolated villages deep in the jungle. The region is poor and provides only a tiny proportion of Brazil's wealth.

Although this area is rich in resources, development is proving difficult because of unhealthy living conditions, poor communications and vast distances. There is also concern that developments can damage the rainforest and destroy the Indian way of life.

Activities

1 Draw table **C** and complete it by putting the features from drawing **A** in the correct columns.

C

Amazon rainforest	South-east Brazil	Amazon rainforest and South-east Brazil

2 a) Make two copies of star diagram **E** below.
  b) In the centre of the first one write 'Amazon rainforest'. In the centre of the second one write 'South-east Brazil'.
  c) Unscramble the words below and use them to complete your diagrams. Some words can be used more than once.

D

PooaSula
rooeinr
ewt
wol
toh
ehahlty
slepaatn
ertopuseug
aprsysle
eHolzoBritnoe
eedsnyl
oreiRdjieoan
gihh
toh

E

1 The main language is _____

2 The climate is _____ and _____

3 The area is _____ populated

4 The main town or towns _____

5 Most people have a _____ standard of living

6 A mineral mined here is _____

F

Fact File

	Amazon rainforest	South-east Brazil
Population (most or least)		
Area (largest or smallest)		
How crowded (most or least)		
Urban population (most or least)		
Able to read or write (most or least)		
% of Brazil's industry (57 or 3)		
% of Brazils wealth (4 or 57)		
% of Brazil's cultivated farmland (33 or 2)		

3 a) Make a larger copy of Fact File **F** above.
  b) Choose from the brackets the correct word or number for each column.
  c) Add more information to your Fact File to help you compare the two regions.

4 Imagine that you are a writer for a geographical magazine. Write two short articles of about 100 words each to describe the main features of:
  a) the Amazon rainforest
  b) South-east Brazil.

Summary

The South-east and the Amazon rainforest are two important but very different regions of Brazil.

How developed is Brazil?

A

The good life – Copacabana beach, Rio de Janeiro

A poor family in a Rio de Janeiro favela

Carajas iron ore mine doubles production

New HEP station opens at Tucurui

HIGH-TECH SPACE PROGRAMME READY FOR SATELLITE LAUNCH

Modern office blocks, São Paulo

An old forge in the poor part of town

Health-carers helpless as killer disease strikes Indians

CAR INDUSTRY ACCLAIMED AS SUCCESS OF THE DECADE

FOOD SHORTAGES A PROBLEM FOR CITY HOMELESS

Niteroi bridge, Rio de Janeiro

Horse drawn water cart near Manaus

Rio – over two million slum dwellers

Young Brazilians top unemployment league

As we have seen, countries are at different levels of **development** or progress. **Developed countries** are generally wealthy. They have high levels of industrial development and most of the people have a good standard of living. **Developing countries** are usually poor. They are in the process of building up their industry and farming. For many of their people the benefits of good health care, education and housing may not be available. Some people in these countries do not even have enough food to eat.

So how developed is Brazil? Look at the information above and try to decide.

As you will see from the previous page it is really quite difficult to label Brazil as either developed or developing. There are many people in the country who are wealthy and who have a very good standard of living. There are many others, however, who live in poverty and do not have adequate food, housing or health care. This is the problem in Brazil. The rich are very rich but the poor are very poor.

In fact Brazil is a rapidly developing country. Since the 1960s it has made tremendous industrial progress and is now one of the wealthier countries of the world. As yet, however, the wealth has not reached many of Brazil's people and for them, hardship continues to be a way of life.

Like many less developed countries, Brazil has had to make choices about the way to develop. It has chosen rapid industrialisation as its way forward. This has brought wealth and economic success to the country. Unfortunately for many of its people, it has not yet brought an improvement in standards of living.

Look at the table B. It compares Brazil with some of her South American neighbours and the UK using **development indicators**.

GNP and energy use are examples of **economic indicators**. They tell us about the general wealth of the country.

Social indicators like infant mortality and school attendance help us measure the standard of living that people have.

B

Indicator of development	Argentina	Brazil	Bolivia	Colombia	Ecuador	Paraguay	Peru	UK
GNP per capita (US$) (earnings per person per year)	10 500	7600	2500	6100	3200	4300	5000	25 500
Energy use (tonnes of coal equivalent per 1000 people)	183	77	36	77	73	23	49	499
Adult literacy (%)	97	86	87	92	93	94	91	99
Infant mortality (deaths per 1000 births)	16	32	56	22	32	28	37	5

Activities

1 Give the meaning of the terms:
- Development
- Developed country
- Developing country.

2 Look at the information on the opposite page. Make a list of all the features you would expect to find in:
a) a developed country;
b) a developing country.
c) Why is it difficult to describe Brazil as either developed or developing?

3 List the South American countries from table **B** in order of:
a) GNP per capita (highest first)
b) Energy use (highest first)
c) Adult literacy (highest first)
d) Infant mortality (lowest first)

4 Copy out and complete the following sentences.

- Using economic indicators, Brazil is _____ developed than most South American countries.
- Using social indicators, Brazil is _____ developed than most South American countries.
- Using both economic and social indicators, Brazil is _____ developed than the UK.

5 Brazil has been described as 'a rich country full of poor people'. Suggest reasons for this description.

Summary

Brazil has developed quickly since the 1960s. It is now one of the world's leading industrial countries. Many Brazilians have gained little from this development.

How interdependent is Brazil?

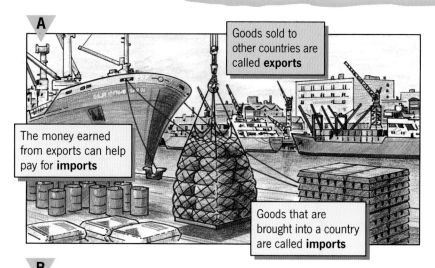

A

Goods sold to other countries are called **exports**

The money earned from exports can help pay for **imports**

Goods that are brought into a country are called **imports**

All countries need help from other countries if they are to make progress. Help for Brazil has come in many ways. For example:

- Foreign banks have given loans;
- Large **multi-national companies** have invested money in developing resources and industry;
- Rich countries and voluntary organisations have provided **aid**;
- **Trade** has been developed with countries around the world.

When countries work together like this, and rely on each other for help, they are said to be **interdependent**.

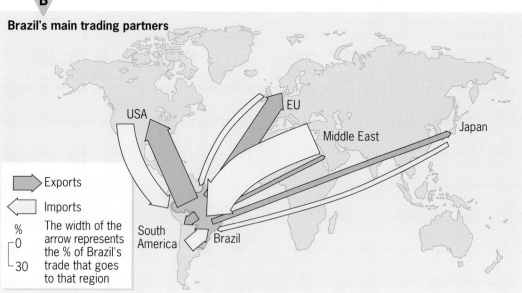

B

Brazil's main trading partners

USA

EU

Middle East

Japan

South America

Brazil

Exports

Imports

%
0
30

The width of the arrow represents the % of Brazil's trade that goes to that region

The development of trade has been particularly important to Brazil. In the past, **primary goods** such as coffee and soya beans have been the main **exports**. Recently, with the rapid growth of industry, more money has been made from exporting **manufactured products** such as cars, clothes and shoes. Brazil also needs to **import** goods and resources from other countries (diagram **A**). These include oil, chemicals and heavy machinery for industry. A large variety of foodstuffs that are not available in Brazil are also imported.

Map **B** shows Brazil's main trading partners. Notice that the **European Union (EU)** and the USA receive over half of Brazil's exports. Most oil supplies are imported from the Middle East.

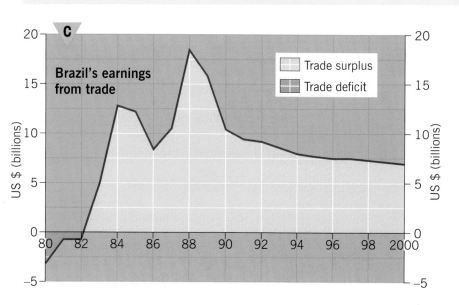

C

Brazil's earnings from trade

Trade surplus

Trade deficit

US $ (billions)

20 15 10 5 0 -5

80 82 84 86 88 90 92 94 96 98 2000

Look carefully at graph **C**. It shows that Brazil now has a **trading surplus**. This means that it has earned more money from exports than it has spent on imports. The extra money can easily be spent. It can be used to improve living standards or be invested in further industrial development. It can also help pay off loans and so reduce Brazil's huge **national debt**.

In the past, political problems have restricted Brazil's interdependence with other South American countries. Now however, these problems have largely been overcome. In the last ten years, the biggest increase in Brazil's foreign trade has been with other countries on the South American continent.

Many countries around the world have joined together to form trading organisations. These organisations encourage trade between countries and also work together and help each other in many other ways. In doing this they become interdependent.

Brazil is a member of several groups. One of these is LAFTA, the Latin American Free Trade Association of which Brazil has been a member for many years. LAFTA's membership includes Mexico as well as most of the South American countries. Another is MERCOSUL, a small group of four countries which have recently joined together as the South American Common Market. The aims of MERCOSUL are shown in diagram **D**.

D MERCOSUL - aims of the South American Common Market

Improve communications between the four countries

Encourage more trade between the four countries

Reduce taxes to make goods from other MERCOSUL countries cheaper

Develop closer social and political links

Activities

1 Make a copy of crossword **E** and complete it using these clues.
1 Export products like cars, clothes and shoes
2 Money owed by a country
3 The exchange of goods and materials between countries.
4 A large business or company
5 A trade organisation
6 This is a form of help
7 Goods or resources brought into a country
8 A trading organisation
9 When countries work together and rely on each other.
10 Goods or resources sold to another country
11 A major primary export for Brazil

2 a) Make a copy of table **F** and complete it with help from map **B**.
b) List Brazil's export markets in order of importance. Give the largest first.
c) List Brazil's import markets in order of size. Give the largest first.

E

3 a) Why is there a high percentage of imports from the Middle East?
b) Why might you expect the percentage of exports to other South American countries to be higher? (Think of Brazil's location.)

4 a) What is a trading surplus?
b) In which year was Brazil's first trading surplus?
c) In which year was Brazils highest trading surplus and how much was it worth?
d) What can Brazil do with a trading surplus?

5 a) What is meant when a country is said to be interdependent?
b) Give four ways in which a country may be interdependent.

Name of region	Imports (%)	Exports (%)
	20	24
	5	30
	15	10
	44	4
	6	7

F

Summary

The development of links with countries in South America and the rest of the world have helped Brazil to become interdependent.

Can development be sustainable?

Sustain: to keep in existence; to keep up; to maintain, prolong

Brazil has made spectacular progress in recent years. During the 1960s and 1970s industrial growth was so rapid and successful that it was called an **'economic miracle'**. The miracle brought great riches to some people and made Brazil very wealthy.

Unfortunately industrial growth has also brought problems. As we have seen, large areas of the Amazon rainforest have been cleared, wildlife has been lost and the Indian way of life has been threatened. Some people worry that this so-called development and progress is actually damaging Brazil . They say that development should bring about an improvement in living conditions for people. At the same time, however, it should not harm or destroy the environment nor prevent people in the future from achieving similar standards of living. Development like this is called **sustainable development**.

Sustainable development is sensible development. It uses but does not waste resources. It improves but does not threaten ways of life. It looks after the needs of today but does not damage the future.

Sustainable development needs good planning. It also needs the co-operation of people and nations and it requires a commitment to conservation. Brazil and other countries in the world are now showing a greater concern for the damaging effects of industrial growth. Steps to improve the quality of development are already being made. We just hope that it's not too late!

Commercial logging is one example of an industry that if managed correctly may be sustainable.

Commercial logging – the problems

Commercial logging is the second largest cause of rainforest destruction. Most of the timber taken from the forest is exported to the richer countries. It is used in the construction industry and for making furniture, plywood, veneers, wood pulp and paper. Trees are a renewable resource, but only if they are used and managed carefully. At present this is not happening and logging has become a wasteful and damaging forest activity.

- After forest clearance the soil quickly loses its fertility and is unable to support new vegetation

- The areas of land that have been cleared are so large that it is difficult for vegetation to return

- Because of costs, logging companies rarely replace felled trees with new ones

- Amazon Indians have been moved off their land and wildlife has been destroyed

- Government regulations are rarely heeded

- Heavy machinery compacts the soil and damages drainage. This makes recultivation difficult.

- Only about 5% of the forest trees are actually wanted by the loggers. Unfortunately to obtain those, they damage or destroy 65% of the remaining ones.

- Soil left without tree cover is quickly washed away by heavy rains. Insufficient soil is left for new plant growth.

Commercial logging – a sustainable industry?

We are considering whether to put a tax on hardwood products. The money collected would be spent on reafforestation schemes.

The International Trade and Timber Organisation

We have created areas where logging activities are either banned completely or strictly controlled

National Park Service of Brazil

The United Nations

Our intention is to reduce international trade in logging. We think that this can be done by taxing endangered hardwoods such as mahogany and so reduce logging profits.

The International Tropical Timber Organisation

Our main advice to logging companies is to:
- limit the number of trees felled in an area
- leave enough trees for the forest to recover
- protect the trees that are left
- plant two trees for every one tree felled
- have a working plan that is agreed by conservationists and is enforced.

Manager of Habitat shop

Like many other high street furniture shops, we have banned the sale of all rainforest products that are not produced in a sustainable way.

Activities

1 a) Write out the meaning of 'sustain'.
   b) Give four facts about sustainable development.
   c) Give three needs of sustainable development.

2 a) Make a list of at least ten uses of timber.
   b) Give three ways in which commercial logging can damage the soil.
   c) Why is logging a wasteful and damaging activity?

3 One way of making the logging industry more sustainable is to reduce the amount of timber taken from the forest.
   a) Which organisations support this method?
   b) How do they plan to bring this about?

4 Imagine that you work for the International Tropical Timber Organisation. Design a poster to show how you think logging can be made a sustainable industry. Try to add drawings for each of your suggestions.

Plantation owner

We only want certain trees from the forest so we have cleared some areas and planted only the types that we need. This makes it much easier to look after the trees and means that we don't have to keep destroying more and more forest.

Worldwide Fund for Nature

We recognise the need for timber products. Our researchers are trying to find out how many trees may be felled in an area without causing permanent damage to the wildlife.

Summary

Sustainable development is progress that can go on year after year. If practised properly, logging in the rainforest could be a sustainable industry.

What is Kenya like?

Kenya is located on the Equator where it crosses central Africa. Photograph **A** shows Africa taken from space. On it Kenya looks quite a small country but in fact it is two and a half times **bigger** in area than the UK. However, its total population is two and a half times **smaller** than that of the UK.

Although Kenya is, economically, one of the poorer countries in the world, in terms of scenery and wildlife it is one of the richest. Its spectacular scenery includes vast lakes, high mountains, numerous volcanoes, huge stretches of sandy beaches, and even a snow-capped peak. Its natural vegetation includes desert, grassland and tropical trees. Kenya has a wealth of wildlife which includes many of the world's largest, and some of the rarest, animals and birds. It also has a population which has considerable differences in colour, religion and language.

What, if anything, do you already know about Kenya? Some of you may have seen Kenyan long distance runners winning many of the world's top athletic events (photo **B**). Others may have heard of the Maasai (photo **C**). Many more of you are likely to have watched travel programmes about Kenya on television. These programmes usually show holiday makers either relaxing in large, modern coastal hotels (photo **D**) or taking a wildlife safari (photo **E**).

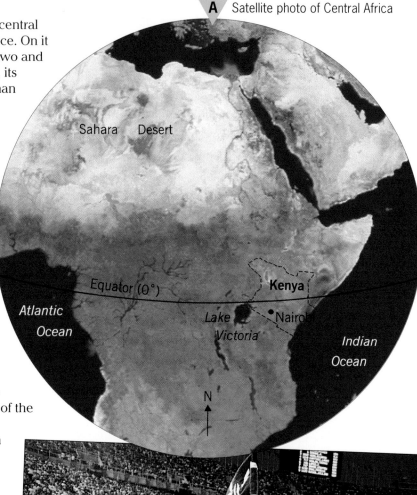

A Satellite photo of Central Africa

Sahara Desert

Equator (0°)

Kenya

Atlantic Ocean

Lake Victoria

•Nairobi

Indian Ocean

N

B Another gold medal for Kenya

C Maasai in their traditional red cloaks

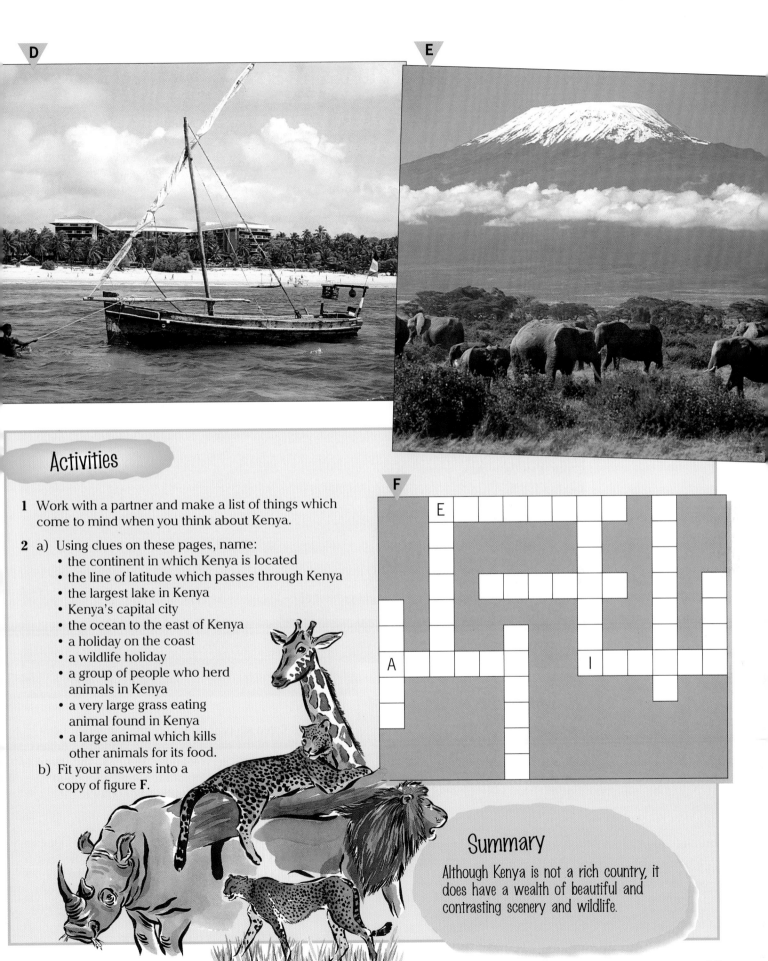

D

E

F

Activities

1 Work with a partner and make a list of things which come to mind when you think about Kenya.

2 a) Using clues on these pages, name:
- the continent in which Kenya is located
- the line of latitude which passes through Kenya
- the largest lake in Kenya
- Kenya's capital city
- the ocean to the east of Kenya
- a holiday on the coast
- a wildlife holiday
- a group of people who herd animals in Kenya
- a very large grass eating animal found in Kenya
- a large animal which kills other animals for its food.

b) Fit your answers into a copy of figure **F**.

The crossword grid cells show the following starting letters: E, A, I.

Summary

Although Kenya is not a rich country, it does have a wealth of beautiful and contrasting scenery and wildlife.

43

Physical features in Kenya

Kenya is part of a large continental **plate** that was once a flat, barren plain. This plate, like other plates, moved slowly across the earth's surface. In time it **collided** with a neighbouring plate. This collision pushed the land upwards causing it to buckle – like when a car crashes into a brick wall. One result of this buckling was the formation of huge cracks in the earth's surface. Two of the largest cracks ran side by side, not just through Kenya, but almost the whole length of Africa.

In Kenya, the land between the cracks collapsed to leave a very deep, steep-sided **rift valley** (photo **A**). Molten rock, known as the **magma**, was able to force its way upwards through the cracks to the earth's surface. Where it reached the surface, as **ash** or **lava**, it formed large volcanoes. These volcanoes have formed a line of mountains on either side of the rift valley They have also produced smaller **cones** on the flat valley floor (photo **B**). Later, water flowing into the valley was trapped and formed numerous lakes.

The Rift Valley in Kenya **A**

Volcano with secondary cone

B

Diagram **C** is a section drawn across Kenya to show the position of the rift valley and the landforms linked with it. Notice the old volcano of Mount Kenya. Even although it lies on the Equator it is high enough to have snow lying on its summit all year round (photo **D**).

Diagram **C** also shows how the land gradually slopes downwards to the sea. Along almost the whole length of Kenya's coast there are **sandy beaches** and a **coral reef** (photo **E**). The reef is one kilometre from the shore and protects the beaches from large storm waves. The only gap in the reef large enough for ships to sail through is opposite the port of Mombasa.

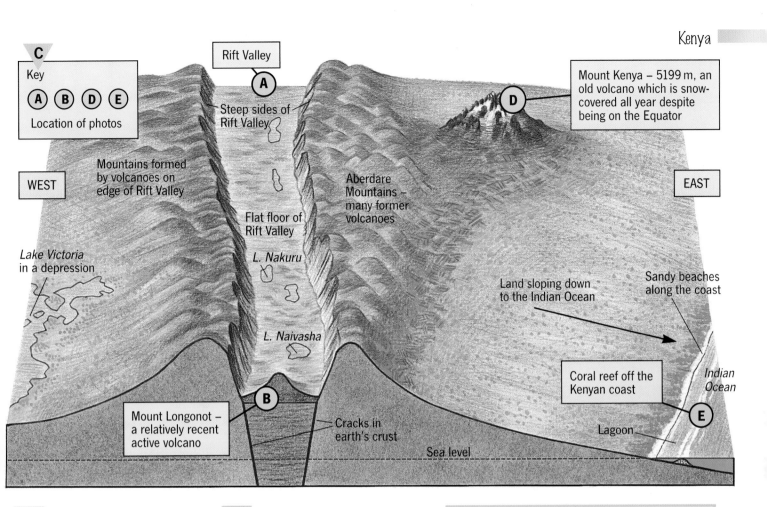

C Key
Ⓐ Ⓑ Ⓓ Ⓔ
Location of photos

Rift Valley **A**

Steep sides of Rift Valley

Mount Kenya – 5199 m, an old volcano which is snow-covered all year despite being on the Equator **D**

WEST

Mountains formed by volcanoes on edge of Rift Valley

Aberdare Mountains – many former volcanoes

EAST

Flat floor of Rift Valley

L. Nakuru

Lake Victoria in a depression

L. Naivasha

Land sloping down to the Indian Ocean

Sandy beaches along the coast

Coral reef off the Kenyan coast

Indian Ocean

B Mount Longonot – a relatively recent active volcano

Cracks in earth's crust

Lagoon

Sea level

D Mount Kenya

E Coral reef off the Kenyan coast

Activities

1 Make a copy of diagram **F**.
a) Label two places with:
   ● mountains formed by volcanoes
   ● lakes
   ● cracks in the earth's crust.
b) Label one place where there is:
   ● a rift valley
   ● a coral reef.

2 a) What is a rift valley? How does a rift valley form?
b) Why are volcanoes found along a rift valley?
c) Why do lakes form on the floor of a rift valley?

Summary

Many of Kenya's most attractive landforms can be seen along either the rift valley or the coast.

F

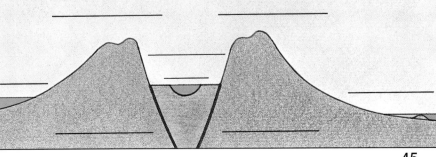

45

People in Kenya

The earliest of man's ancestors lived in parts of the rift valley in Kenya. More recently, people have moved into the country from several directions. This has resulted in many groups of people living together and sharing their different ways of life.

The movement of people into Kenya
Over 98 per cent of the present inhabitants of Kenya are Africans. They come from over 30 different **ethnic groups**. Each group has its own language and way of life. They arrived in Kenya from three different directions (map **A**). Although most Kenyans still identify themselves with one specific group, their way of life has been changed through marriages and contact with people from other groups.

Most of the remaining 2 per cent have come from Asia. They are usually either Arabs or Indians. The Arabs tend to live along the coast while most Indians live in Nairobi. A small group of Europeans, mainly British, also live in Kenya.

Where do people live in Kenya?
The population of Kenya, as in most other countries, is not evenly spread out. Some places are very crowded while others have very few people living there. This spread, or **distribution**, of people is shown on map **A**. The map also gives some of the reasons for the uneven distribution.

How is Kenya's population changing?
The total population of Kenya is increasing very rapidly (graph **B**).

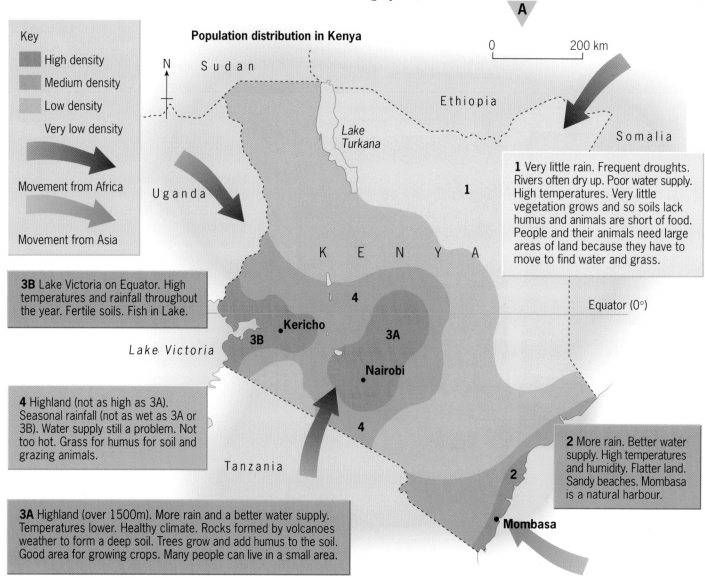

Population distribution in Kenya

A

0   200 km

Key
- High density
- Medium density
- Low density
- Very low density

Movement from Africa

Movement from Asia

S u d a n

N

Ethiopia

Lake Turkana

S o m a l i a

U g a n d a

K E N Y A

1 Very little rain. Frequent droughts. Rivers often dry up. Poor water supply. High temperatures. Very little vegetation grows and so soils lack humus and animals are short of food. People and their animals need large areas of land because they have to move to find water and grass.

Equator (0°)

3B Lake Victoria on Equator. High temperatures and rainfall throughout the year. Fertile soils. Fish in Lake.

•Kericho

3B

Lake Victoria

4

3A

•Nairobi

4 Highland (not as high as 3A). Seasonal rainfall (not as wet as 3A or 3B). Water supply still a problem. Not too hot. Grass for humus for soil and grazing animals.

4

T a n z a n i a

2 More rain. Better water supply. High temperatures and humidity. Flatter land. Sandy beaches. Mombasa is a natural harbour.

2

3A Highland (over 1500m). More rain and a better water supply. Temperatures lower. Healthy climate. Rocks formed by volcanoes weather to form a deep soil. Trees grow and add humus to the soil. Good area for growing crops. Many people can live in a small area.

•**Mombasa**

B

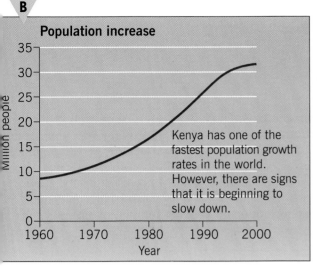

Population increase

Kenya has one of the fastest population growth rates in the world. However, there are signs that it is beginning to slow down.

C

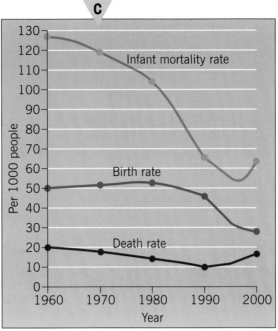

D

The life expectancy for a Kenyan man was 39 in 1960 and 45 in 2000.

The life expectancy for a Kenyan woman was 43 in 1960 and 45 in 2000.

In fact Kenya's population doubled in size between 1970 and 2000. Graph **C** shows that this increase was mainly due to
- a very high **birth rate** (one of the highest in the world)
- a falling **death rate** (graph **C**).

When birth rates are higher than death rates there is a **natural increase** in population.

Other reasons why Kenya's population is likely to continue to grow include:
- The rapid decline in **infant mortality** which means that fewer

babies die in the first year of their lives (graph **C**).
- Half of Kenya's population are aged 15 or under. This suggests that in a few years there will be even more people of child-bearing age.
- At present only a small proportion of the population is aged over 60. However, as life expectancy steadily increases, then more of

the population are likely to live longer (diagram **D**).

- During the 1990s, life expectancy actually decreased and both infant mortality and the death rate increased due to AIDS.

The rapid growth of Kenya's population means that the country's raw materials and natural resources have to be shared among a greater number of people.

Activities

E

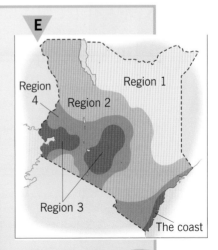

1 a) Which of the regions numbered on map **E** is the least crowded?
   b) Give three reasons why few people live in this region.
   c) Give three reasons why many people live along the coast.
   d) Which of the regions numbered on map **E** is the most crowded?
   e) Give three reasons why so many people live in this region.

2 Make a copy of table **F**. Use the information given in diagrams **B**, **C** and **D** to complete table **F**.

F

		1960	2000	Trend (rising or falling)
Total population		(million)	(million)	
Birth rate		(per 1000)	(per 1000)	
Death rate		(per 1000)	(per 1000)	
Infant mortality rate		(per 1000)	(per 1000)	
Life expectancy	Males			
	Females			

Summary

Kenya's population is very uneven in its distribution and is one of the fastest growing in the world.

Holidays in Kenya

There are few countries in the world that can offer the tourist the variety of scenery and wildlife that Kenya can. Inland there are mountains, lakes, grassy plains and a wealth of wildlife. On the coast there are sandy beaches and coral reefs. Tourism has become Kenya's fastest growing industry and largest earner of money from overseas.

To encourage tourism and to protect its scenery and wildlife, Kenya has set up over 50 **National Parks** and **game reserves**. Many visitors choose to visit some of these parks on organised tours known as 'safaris' (advert **A**). They are taken around in minibuses by drivers who are also expert local guides. The 7- or 9-seater minibuses have roofs and windows which open for viewing and photography.

A

Safari

Day 1 **Nairobi/Samburu (310 km)**
After breakfast drive north, cross the Equator and pass Mt Kenya, to Samburu Lodge. After lunch there will be a game drive when you should see elephant, buffalo, lion, giraffe, zebra, crocodile and many species of bird. Overnight at Samburu Serena Lodge right on the river.

Day 2 **Samburu**
Early morning game drive. Relax at mid-day around the swimming pool or watch the Samburu perform traditional dances. Late afternoon game drive. Overnight at Samburu Serena Lodge.

Day 3 **Samburu/Lake Nakuru (200 km)**
After early morning game drive, drive to the Thomson's Falls, and down into the Rift Valley to Nakuru for lunch. An afternoon drive will let you see vast flocks of flamingos and the endangered Rothschild giraffe. Overnight at Nakuru Lodge.

Day 4 **Lake Nakuru/Maasai Mara (340 km)**
Drive through the Rift Valley passing Lake Naivasha on the way to the Maasai Mara game reserve. Afternoon game drive. Overnight at Keekorok Lodge.

Day 5 **Maasai Mara**
The huge Mara plain provides some of the best game-viewing in East Africa. During early morning and late afternoon game drives you are likely to see huge herds of wildebeest and zebra, as well as lion, elephant, cheetah, leopard, giraffe, and hippo. An option is the early morning Balloon Safari. Overnight at the Keekorok Lodge.

Day 6 **Maasai Mara/Nairobi (260 km)**
Early morning departure arriving at Nairobi for lunch. Afternoon flight to Mombasa to continue your holiday at a beach hotel.

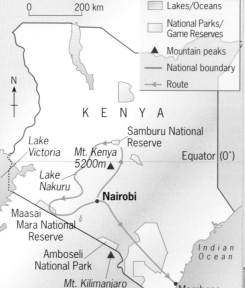

0   200 km

Lakes/Oceans
National Parks/ Game Reserves
▲ Mountain peaks
— National boundary
← Route

N

K E N Y A

Lake Victoria
Mt. Kenya 5200m ▲
Samburu National Reserve
Equator (0°)
Lake Nakuru
Nairobi
Maasai Mara National Reserve
Amboseli National Park
Mt. Kilimanjaro 5895m ▲
Indian Ocean
Mombasa

Not every visitor to Kenya goes on safari. Many tourists take advantage of the coastal climate. Because Kenya lies on the Equator, the climate is usually hot and sunny throughout the year. These visitors, who are often joined by weary safari travellers, prefer to relax at one of many beach resorts (advert **B**). The resorts have clean, sandy beaches. The warm sea, protected from storms by the coral reef, is ideal for water sports. The beach resorts extend along most of the coast either side of Mombasa.

B

Nyali Beach

One of Kenya's best known hotels is managed by Block Hotels and is situated four miles north of Mombasa in delightful grounds leading directly to a palm-fringed beach.

A good choice of restaurants and bars and regular evening entertainment and daytime activities are arranged. There are three swimming pools, including one for children. Nyali also boasts a Jacuzzi, snooker table, shops, hairdresser and beauty salon. Children have their own club with a supervised activities programme which leaves you free to be as lazy or as active as you choose. There is free use of pedaloes, canoes and minisails. Other watersports include waterskiing, windsurfing, sailing, scuba diving and glass bottom-boat rides.

Activities

1 Draw two star diagrams, like the ones on the right, to show at least four attractions of a safari holiday and four attractions of a beach holiday.

2 Design a poster for Kenya's Tourist Office. The poster should show the attractions of **either**
   a) a 'Safari holiday', **or**
   b) a 'beach resort holiday'.
   Try to include a map, a labelled photo or a collage of several photos, and a short written description.

C

Safari holiday

Beach holiday

Summary   Kenya has a wide variety of scenery and wildlife. Large numbers of overseas tourists are attracted there either for a safari or a beach holiday.

The benefits and problems of tourism

Kenya realises the importance of its spectacular scenery and wildlife as a major tourist attraction. The growth of tourism can bring many benefits to a country such as Kenya (diagram **A**). It can also create many problems. Large numbers of people now go on **safaris** or stay at **beach resorts** (diagrams **B** and **C**). However, their numbers can damage the very environments which attracted them there in the first place. Tourism puts pressure upon **fragile environments**, wildlife and local people.

A Advantages of tourism

> Tourism can create lots of new jobs. We are very short of work.

> Money from tourism has helped to improve our roads and to build more houses

> Tourism brings a lot of overseas money into Kenya

> Farmers have a larger market for their produce

> We can make souvenirs to sell to the tourists

> I hope to become a tourist guide or a safari driver when I leave school

> Money from tourism can be used to build schools and hospitals

B Problems created by safaris

The environment

Minibuses are meant to keep to well defined tracks but drivers often take short cuts to get as near to the animals as possible. This can cause tracks to be widened, to turn dusty in the dry season and marshy in the short rainy season. Both increase soil erosion.

Wildlife

Minibuses should not go within 25 metres of the animals. Drivers often ignore this rule as their passengers are more likely to give them good tips if they get very close to the animals. This may prevent the animals from feeding, drinking and mating.

Hot air balloons have gas burners which make a loud noise from time to time. Conservationists think this, and the balloons' moving shadows, can also disturb wildlife.

People

Apart from people working at safari lodges, nobody can live in the National Parks. We were forced to leave our homes and traditional grazing grounds when the National Park was opened. Most of the money which tourists spend goes to the government, not to us local people.

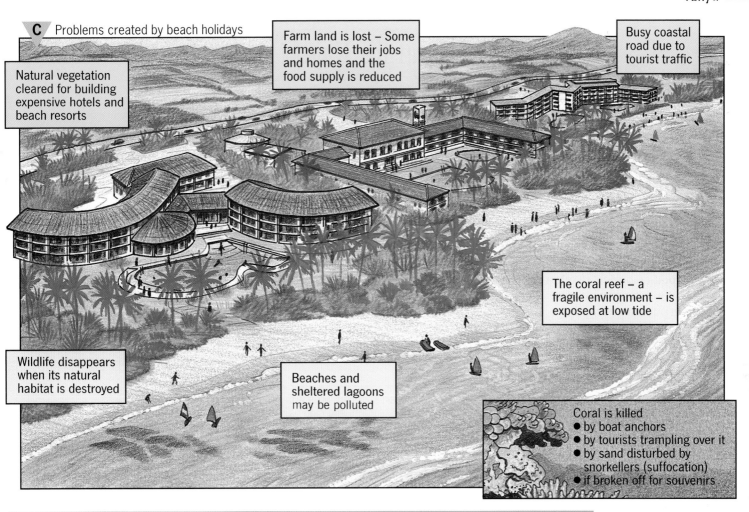

C Problems created by beach holidays

Farm land is lost – Some farmers lose their jobs and homes and the food supply is reduced

Busy coastal road due to tourist traffic

Natural vegetation cleared for building expensive hotels and beach resorts

The coral reef – a fragile environment – is exposed at low tide

Wildlife disappears when its natural habitat is destroyed

Beaches and sheltered lagoons may be polluted

Coral is killed
● by boat anchors
● by tourists trampling over it
● by sand disturbed by snorkellers (suffocation)
● if broken off for souvenirs

Activities

1 With the help of diagrams **A** and **D**:
  a) Give two reasons why an increasing number of tourists visit Kenya.
  b) Give two pieces of evidence to show that this increase has been rapid.
  c) Give three ways by which tourism can help local employment.
  d) Give three uses of the income (money) received from tourists.

2 a) What is meant by the term 'fragile environment'?
  b) Make a copy of table **E**. Give it the title 'Problems created by safari and beach holidays'. List the problems under these headings:
     ● environment
     ● wildlife
     ● local people.

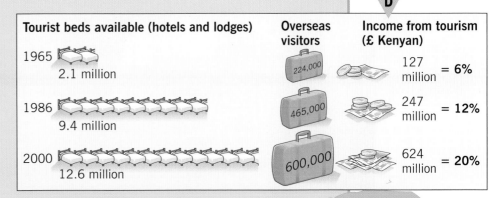

D

Tourist beds available (hotels and lodges)	Overseas visitors	Income from tourism (£ Kenyan)	
1965 — 2.1 million	224,000	127 million	= 6%
1986 — 9.4 million	465,000	247 million	= 12%
2000 — 12.6 million	600,000	624 million	= 20%

E

	Problems	
	Safari holidays	Beach holidays
Environment		
Wildlife		
Local people		

3 On balance, do you think that tourism is a good or a bad thing for Kenya? Write a short paragraph to explain your answer.

Summary

Tourism can bring jobs and earn money for countries such as Kenya. However, it can also cause problems for people and wildlife and can harm the environment.

Urban life in the Nairobi region

Nairobi is the capital city of Kenya. As in many large cities in developing countries the people who live and work in Nairobi are usually either well-off or very poor. The gap between the few who are rich and the majority who are poor is much larger than in economically more developed countries. In other words the rich are very rich and the poor are very poor.

Kip and Krista come from well-off families. They live, like most other well-off people, near to the city centre. Their parents have jobs which are full time and well paid. The best jobs are in the city centre, especially in various government buildings, tall office blocks and banks (photo A). Kip and Krista can afford the cost of travel into the city centre. They often make this journey to visit either the more expensive shops or the best places of entertainment.

Their houses are large and contain modern amenities such as air-conditioning, electricity and a bathroom with a shower. Each family has its own car, TV and video, and many modern gadgets. However, the houses need to be protected by good security systems. Kip and Krista both attend nearby private schools and hope eventually to go to Nairobi University.

Nairobi – the city centre **A**

- Location of Mathare Valley (shanty settlement)
- Main banks and financial buildings
- Inner ring road
- Main shopping area with hotels, restaurants and cinema
- Kenyatta International Conference Centre
- Parliament buildings
- Uhuru (Freedom) Park and sports arena

Activities

1 Make a list of the features found in the centre of Nairobi that:
   a) may also be found in your local town or nearest city centre;
   b) would not be found in your local town or nearest city centre.

2 Diagram **B** is a simplified map of Nairobi. Make a copy of the map and put these labels in their correct place:
   - large houses with many amenities;
   - shops and offices;
   - shanty settlements;
   - small houses with very few amenities;
   - well paid jobs;
   - small workshops.

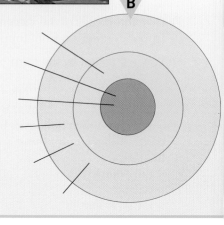
B

The well-off are, however, relatively few in number. Most people who live in Nairobi are poor and are forced to live in **shanty settlements** (photo **D**). Shanty settlements grow on land which had previously not been used. This might have been because it flooded regularly or because it was a long way from the shops and better jobs in the city centre.

Julius and Marietta come from families who live in a shanty. Most houses in a shanty settlement are small and often only have one room. They are built so close together that it can be difficult to squeeze between them. The walls are usually built from mud and the roofs from corrugated iron. Very few homes have electricity or water. Sewage runs down the tracks between houses. The tracks are muddy in the rainy season and dusty in the dry season. Uncollected rubbish lies everywhere. Shanty settlements often lack shops, schools, medical facilities and jobs.

It is almost impossible to find a permanent or a well paid job in a shanty. Some people may have stalls from which they sell food. Others find work in small workshops which they have either built by themselves or with friends. Some people may tour the local area collecting scrap and other waste materials which others will then melt down. It can then be hammered into various shapes producing objects which can be used in the home (photo **C**). These jobs are said to be **sustainable** because they involve the recycling of waste materials and they use the skills of local people.

Jua Kali workshops, recycling metal in Nairobi

C

Inside a shanty settlement – Nairobi **D**

3 Make a larger copy of table **E**. Give it the title 'Differences between well-off and poor families living in Nairobi'. Complete the table by listing some of the differences.

E

Nairobi		Kip and Krista – well-off families	Julius and Marietta – poorer families
Distance from city centre			
Houses	Size		
	Amenities		
Schools, shops, entertainment			
Jobs			

Summary

Well-off people live in pleasant areas near to the city centre where there are shops, good jobs and places of entertainment. Poorer people often have to live and find work in less pleasant shanty settlements.

Rural life in the region south of Nairobi

Like many cities in the developing world, Nairobi is increasing rapidly in size. This is mainly due to

- the country's high birth rate and rapid increase in population,
- the movement of people from the surrounding rural areas who are looking for a better way of life.

As Nairobi's population increases, so too does the demand for jobs and somewhere to live. The need for jobs and houses puts more and more pressure on any land near to the city.

Before this increase in pressure on the land, much of the area to the south of Nairobi was used by animals for grazing. Herds of domestic cattle and goats belonging to the Maasai (photo **A**) grazed together with wild animals such as rhino, gazelle, zebra and, where there were more trees, giraffe.

In 1945, an area of land touching the southern edge of Nairobi became Kenya's first National Park. Today, grazing rhino and giraffe or a lion catching a gazelle can be photographed with Nairobi in the background (photo **B**). Although the Nairobi Park protects animals and brings in money, the land there cannot be used either for farming or for settlement.

To the south of the Nairobi National Park are the grazing lands of the Maasai. For centuries the Maasai have followed a **semi-nomadic** way of life. They are **pastoralists** who have to move during the long dry season in order to find grass and water for their cattle and goats. The Maasai rely upon these animals for their daily food supply.

A Maasai herding their animals

Nairobi National Park
B

C Traditional Maasai village

Until recently, most Maasai lived in small villages which consisted of between 20 to 50 huts. The huts were arranged in a circle and built from local materials. The frame consisted of wooden poles. Cow dung was mixed with river mud for the walls, and with grass for the roof (photo **C**). Each hut had a narrow tunnel like entrance. There were no windows or chimneys – just a small hole in one wall. The inside, which was partitioned into small 'rooms', was dark and full of unhealthy smoke from the fire. Cowskins were laid on the floor to act as bedding.

A thick thorn hedge surrounded each village. Its purpose was to keep out wild animals such as lions, leopards and hyenas. An opening in the hedge allowed people to pass through and was large enough for the Maasai to drive their animals through at night.

In recent times, the Maasai way of life has been changing (diagram **D**). Some of these changes have been forced upon them; others have been made through choice. The biggest changes have resulted from the loss of grazing land. As the Maasai become less free to move around with their cattle, many have made their houses more permanent. Others have decided to move away from the countryside and to live in small towns. Although many of the older Maasai still keep their traditional values and way of life, the younger generation appear to welcome the changes.

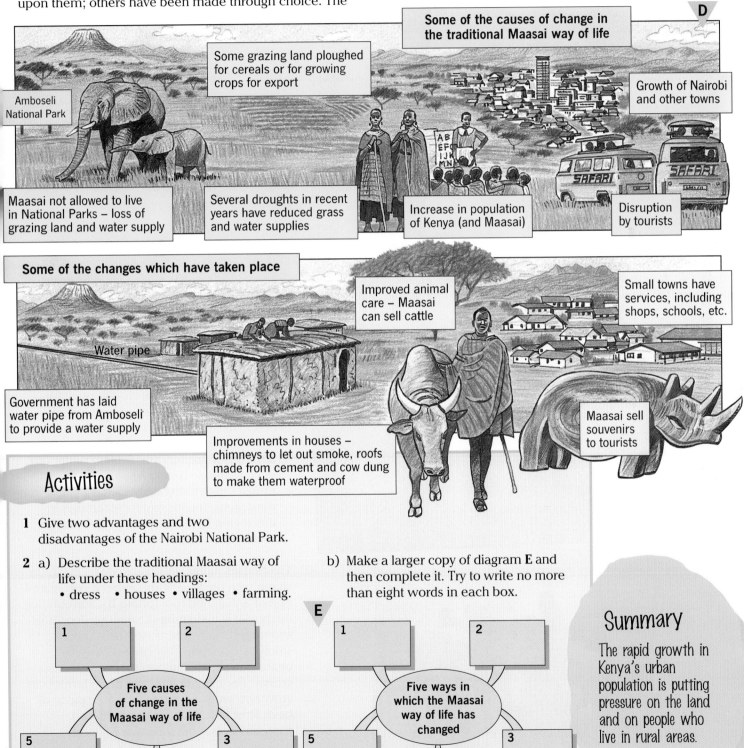

D

Some of the causes of change in the traditional Maasai way of life

Amboseli National Park

Some grazing land ploughed for cereals or for growing crops for export

Growth of Nairobi and other towns

Maasai not allowed to live in National Parks – loss of grazing land and water supply

Several droughts in recent years have reduced grass and water supplies

Increase in population of Kenya (and Maasai)

Disruption by tourists

Some of the changes which have taken place

Improved animal care – Maasai can sell cattle

Small towns have services, including shops, schools, etc.

Water pipe

Government has laid water pipe from Amboseli to provide a water supply

Improvements in houses – chimneys to let out smoke, roofs made from cement and cow dung to make them waterproof

Maasai sell souvenirs to tourists

Activities

1 Give two advantages and two disadvantages of the Nairobi National Park.

2 a) Describe the traditional Maasai way of life under these headings:
   • dress   • houses   • villages   • farming.

   b) Make a larger copy of diagram **E** and then complete it. Try to write no more than eight words in each box.

E

1	2

Five causes of change in the Maasai way of life

| 5 | 3 |
| 4 | |

1	2

Five ways in which the Maasai way of life has changed

| 5 | 3 |
| 4 | |

Summary

The rapid growth in Kenya's urban population is putting pressure on the land and on people who live in rural areas.

55

Subsistence farming to the west of the Rift Valley

The land to the west of the Rift Valley is highland. In many places it rises to over 2500 metres. The scenery consists of gentle ridges with a natural covering of forest. The area is ideal for both farming and settlement.

- The land, being both high and lying on the Equator, receives heavy afternoon rainfall nearly every day of the year.
- Because it is highland, the temperature is cooler and the climate healthier than in other parts of Kenya.
- Since it is on the Equator, temperatures are warm enough for crops to grow throughout the year.
- The soils, originally formed by volcanoes, are deep. They have been made even more fertile by the addition of **humus** from the natural forest.

A Shambas on a hillside in Kericho

B House and shamba

Most people who live in this highland region of Kenya are **subsistence** farmers. Subsistence farming is when farmers and their families produce only just enough for their own needs. There is rarely much left over for sale, despite having to work hard for most of each day. This is because

- Most farms are very small, often under one hectare in size (photo **A**).
- Kenya's high birth rate, which is highest in rural areas, means that most families in this region have at least six children all of whom need to be fed.

The houses in this region are often circular in shape with mud walls and either a corrugated iron or a thatched roof (photo **B**). Surrounding the house is a **shamba** or small garden. Most shambas grow maize under the shade of small banana trees. Vegetables, such as beans and yams, and tropical fruits are also grown. The climate and soils allow farmers to grow two crops a year on the same piece of land. Most farmers keep chickens and, sometimes, one or two cows. No land is wasted.

C Overcrowded local transport

Any surplus food is sold in local open air markets (photo **D**). These markets are open most mornings and are very noisy and colourful events. From early morning onwards, the sides of the rough tracks leading to the markets are packed with people. The majority have to walk, sometimes for several kilometres. Others will take advantage of any available transport (photo **C**). By mid-day, however, the heat is sufficient for people to retreat indoors and everything closes down (photo **E**). The end of the afternoon will be spent working in the shamba or, for many women, collecting fuelwood to be used in cooking stoves.

D

E

Activities

1 Draw a star diagram to show why this region is ideal for farming. Use these headings:
   - height of land;
   - rainfall;
   - temperatures;
   - soils;
   - shape of land.

2 a) What is subsistence farming?
   b) Give two reasons why subsistence farming takes place in this region.

3 Diagram **F** is sketch based on photo **B**. Make a copy of the sketch and complete it by adding the following labels:

   - thatch roof • circular house
   - mud walls • banana trees • maize
   - vegetables • shamba

F

4 Write a diary entry to describe the life in the day of a subsistence farming family. Use the information on these pages and diagram **G** to help you.

G

MONDAY 15 MAY	Male members	Female members
Early morning		
Mid-morning		
Midday		
Early afternoon		
Late afternoon		

Summary

The region west of the Rift Valley is ideal for farming. Subsistence farming is where most of the produce is needed by the farmer's family. There is very little left over for sale.

Commercial farming to the west of the Rift Valley

The cooler, damper, healthier climate of the region around Kericho also attracted European settlers (map **A** page 46). When the first settlers arrived they found much of the land still covered in forest. These settlers began clearing large areas of trees and replacing them with tea bushes. Today the area consists of ridge after ridge of bright green bushes (photo **A**). Tea is grown as a **cash crop** on a **commercial** scale. Commercial farming is when crops are grown, or animals are reared, for a profit. A cash crop is one that is usually grown for export. Tea is now Kenya's most valuable export.

Brooke Bond have several huge tea estates. The largest, at Kericho (map **E**), produces 12 per cent of Kenya's tea. Young tea plants are grown in the shade for five months and are only slowly exposed to the sun and rain. The bushes are then planted in long rows. The leaves of mature bushes are still plucked (picked) by hand (photo **C**). This means that the cultivation and collection of tea takes a lot of labour (see fact file). Each plucker is given his or her own section. They start at 0700 hours and work, with two breaks, until 16.30 (or longer if they wish). The text with photos **B** and **C** describes how the leaves are plucked, and how the workers are paid and live. Diagram **D** explains what happens in the tea processing factory.

A tea estate ▶ **A**

The pluckers put the leaves into bags and are paid according to the weight of the leaves picked. The plucker returns to each bush every 17 or 18 days. This keeps the height of the bush to one metre which is ideal for later plucking. Plucking goes on throughout the year.

B ▼

The pluckers work a nine hour day for the equivalent, in Britain, of 45p per day. They and their families are given free accommodation, education and medical care. Each tea estate has its own schools and hospital as well as shops and other amenities (map **E**). The houses have electricity, water and sewerage.

C ▼

D In the processing factory

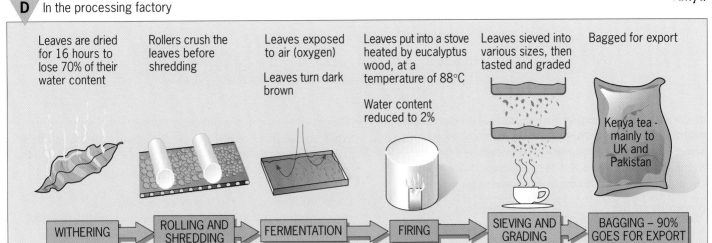

Leaves are dried for 16 hours to lose 70% of their water content

Rollers crush the leaves before shredding

Leaves exposed to air (oxygen)

Leaves turn dark brown

Leaves put into a stove heated by eucalyptus wood, at a temperature of 88°C

Water content reduced to 2%

Leaves sieved into various sizes, then tasted and graded

Bagged for export

Kenya tea - mainly to UK and Pakistan

WITHERING → ROLLING AND SHREDDING → FERMENTATION → FIRING → SIEVING AND GRADING → BAGGING – 90% GOES FOR EXPORT

Apart from tea, eucalyptus trees are also grown on the estate. These trees mature in seven years. They are used as fuel in the drying rooms of the tea-processing factory and in staff houses.

Despite the clearance of the natural forest, there is hardly any soil erosion. This is because the tea plants and the eucalyptus trees protect the ground from the heavy afternoon rains while their roots hold the soil together.

Activities

Fact file

Total area	20,000 hectares
Bushes per hectare	18,000
Number of workers' houses	9,900
Number of workers	16,000
Number of workers and families	100,000

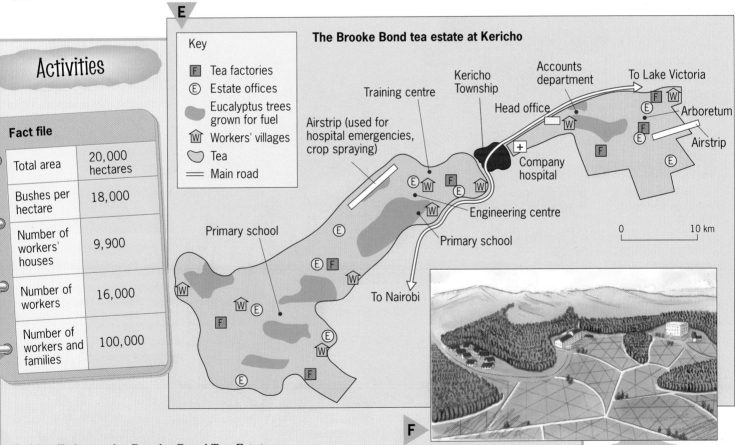

E The Brooke Bond tea estate at Kericho

Key
- F Tea factories
- E Estate offices
- Eucalyptus trees grown for fuel
- W Workers' villages
- Tea
- Main road

1 Map **E** shows the Brooke Bond Tea Estate at Kericho.
a) Write a short paragraph to describe the following:
- the climate of the area,
- jobs done before the tea is planted,
- how tea is collected,
- jobs in the factory,
- the workers' village,
- other amenities provided for the workers,
- why there is very little soil erosion.
b) Make a larger copy of sketch **F** and add these labels:

- highland • eucalyptus trees • tea bushes
- workers village • factory • estate office

Summary

Tea is Kenya's most valuable export and is grown commercially on large estates.

Sustainable development in Kenya

In the last few years the term '**sustainable development**' has become popular in geography. It is not, however, an easy term to explain and it can be used in different ways (diagram **A** and pages 16–17). Sustainable development should lead, ideally, to an improvement in people's:

● **quality of life** – how content they are with their way of life and the environment in which they live;
● **standard of living** – how well off they are economically.

This improvement should be achieved without wasting the earth's resources or destroying the environment. In other words, improvements should not just benefit people living today, they should be shared with future generations.

Diagram **A** also gives examples of sustainable development already described in this chapter. The next section looks in more detail at one of these examples within Kenya – energy.

A

Sustainable development means...

. . . using natural resources without spoiling the environment

. . . developing local skills, and passing these skills on to future generations, e.g. training village people to be vets, or townspeople to make stoves

. . . developing materials/utensils which will use fewer resources, e.g. improved cooking stoves need less fuelwood.

. . . thinking about resources and the three 're's:
● **re**newable resources such as wind and solar power
● **re**cycling resources as in Nairobi workshops
● **re**placing resources such as replanting eucalyptus trees on Brooke Bond's tea plantations

. . . using materials which will last for much longer, e.g. Maasai permanent houses where cement is added to cow dung to make roofs.

. . . protecting the environment, both landscapes and wildlife, so that they can be enjoyed and be useful to other generations, e.g. protecting coral reefs by creating marine reserves, and protecting rhinos and elephants in National Parks.

. . . developing technology appropriate to the skills, wealth and needs of local people

. . . allowing economic development to happen at a pace which a country can afford – giving a country too much finance means it can fall into debt

Cooking stoves

In rural Kenya, fuelwood is used by most families for cooking. Charcoal is used as a fuel in shanty settlements and in Nairobi's workshops. As Kenya's population increases so too does the demand for wood. More and more trees are cut down and not replaced. This means that

- people in rural areas have further to walk each day to find enough wood upon which to cook;
- it costs people living in towns more to buy charcoal;
- soil is eroded as there are fewer trees left to protect it from the wind and rain.

One way to save fuelwood is to design cooking stoves which are more efficient. This has been done, mainly by women, in several parts of Kenya. As traditional potters, women know that the best clay is found in river banks. Earth from termite mounds, sand, ash and water are added to the clay and the mixture is poured into a mould. It is left to dry for several days before the stove is baked in a kiln (photo **B**). By enclosing the fire, most of the heat is directed to the stove (photo **C**).

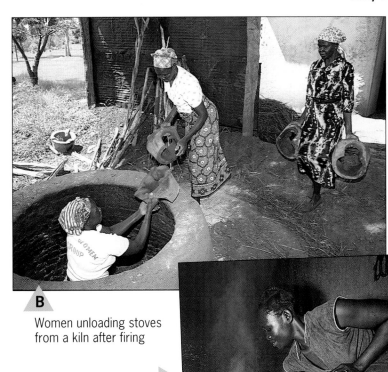

B
Women unloading stoves from a kiln after firing

The Upesi stove **C**

D

Less time is spent collecting wood and in cooking, leaving more time for other activities.

Less fuel is used. Fewer trees need to be cut down in rural areas. This saves money for people needing charcoal in urban areas.

Money can be made from selling the stoves.

Less smoke is given off, reducing air pollution and improving health.

Improved cooking stoves are, therefore, an example of sustainable development.

- In their **making** they use local, renewable resources and local skills, they do not spoil the environment and cost very little.
- In their **use** they save fuel, improve people's health and save time.

Activities

E

1 a) What do you understand by the term 'sustainable development'?
   b) Why is it important for development to be sustainable?

2 With the help of diagram **D**, explain how
   a) the making, and
   b) the use of cooking stoves in Kenya is a good example of sustainable development.

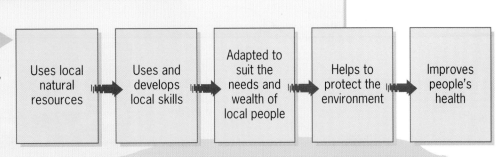

Uses local natural resources → Uses and develops local skills → Adapted to suit the needs and wealth of local people → Helps to protect the environment → Improves people's health

Summary Sustainable development should lead to an improvement in people's quality of life and standard of living without wasting natural resources or spoiling the environment.

How interdependent is Kenya?

No country has everything that its people want or need. To provide these things it has to exchange goods and materials with other countries. The exchange of goods and materials is called **trade**.

A country will buy (**import**) things which are in short supply or which can be made more cheaply elsewhere. These items may be either

- **primary goods**, such as foodstuffs and minerals which are often low in value, or
- **manufactured goods**, such as machinery, which are high in value.

In order to pay for these goods, a country has to sell (**export**) materials and goods of which it has a surplus. Ideally, a country hopes to have a **trade surplus**. This means it earns more money from its exports than it has to pay for its imports. A **trade deficit** is where imports are greater than exports.

Kenya's trade is typical of most developing countries (diagram **A**). Most of its exports are low value primary goods such as tea and coffee.

Most of its imports are higher value manufactured goods such as machinery and vehicles. The result is that Kenya has a trade deficit (graph **B**). Countries with a trade deficit have to borrow money which often leads to them falling into debt.

Most of Kenya's trade passes through the port of Mombasa (photo **C**). The exception are some exports, l..e fresh flowers and vegetables, which go through Nairobi airport. Kenya's most important **trading partner** is the United Kingdom (diagram **D**).

This is because Kenya was once a British **colony**. Colonies used to provide raw materials for colonial powers. The colonial powers then either used the raw materials or turned them into manufactured goods. These goods were then sold, at a profit, back to the colony.

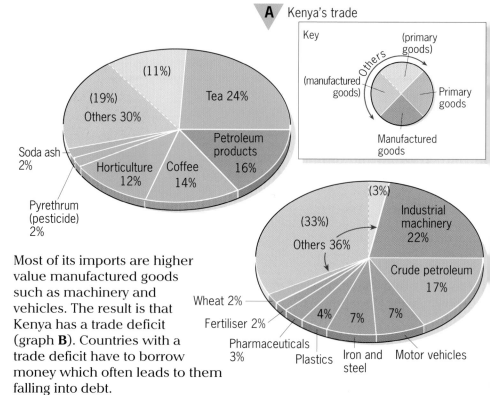

A Kenya's trade

Tea 24%
(11%)
(19%) Others 30%
Soda ash 2%
Horticulture 12%
Coffee 14%
Petroleum products 16%
Pyrethrum (pesticide) 2%

Key
Others
(manufactured goods)
(primary goods)
Primary goods
Manufactured goods

(3%)
Industrial machinery 22%
(33%)
Others 36%
Crude petroleum 17%
Wheat 2%
Fertiliser 2%
Pharmaceuticals 3%
4%
7%
7%
Plastics
Iron and steel
Motor vehicles

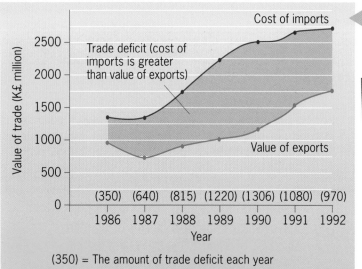

B Value and cost of Kenya's foreign trade

Cost of imports
Trade deficit (cost of imports is greater than value of exports)
Value of exports

Value of trade (K£ million)

(350) (640) (815) (1220) (1306) (1080) (970)
1986 1987 1988 1989 1990 1991 1992
Year

(350) = The amount of trade deficit each year

C The port of Mombasa

Although Kenya has been independent since 1963, most of its trade is still with economically more developed countries and the oil producing Gulf States (diagram **D**). To try to develop trade with other developing countries,

Kenya has joined the **Preferential Trade Area for Eastern and Southern African States** (**PTA**). Although Kenya has a trade surplus within PTA, the amount of trade between members is small.

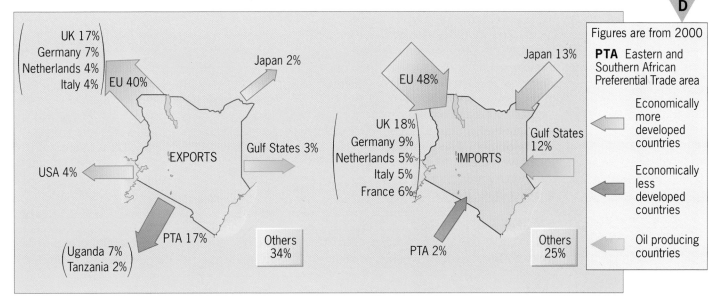

D

Figures are from 2000

PTA Eastern and Southern African Preferential Trade area

Economically more developed countries

Economically less developed countries

Oil producing countries

Kenya has other international links.
- It was the first developing country to become the headquarters of several United Nations agencies.
- It receives financial aid from overseas countries (mainly Germany, Japan and the United Kingdom) and international agencies (World Bank).

- Several large multinational companies, such as Brooke Bond, have invested money in developing the country's resources.
- It has also developed strong sporting and cultural links.

Activities

E

Trade	Things which are made from primary goods
Imports	Buying goods or materials from another country
Exports	Raw materials such as foodstuffs and energy resources
Trade surplus	Cost of imports is greater than money obtained from exports
Trade deficit	The exchange of goods and materials between counties
Primary goods	Money from exports is more than money paid for imports
Manufactured goods	Selling goods made in or obtained from a country

1 Complete the definitions in table **E** by matching the beginnings on the left with the correct ending from the list on the right.

2 Copy and complete table **F** which describes the major features of Kenya's trade. Do not use the 'Others' section from diagram **A**.

F

Trade (2000)	Exports (in order)	Imports (in order)
Primary goods	1 ___ 2 ___ 3 ___	1 ___
Manufactured goods	1 ___	1 ___ 2 ___ 3 ___
Value	£Kmn	£Kmn
Main countries	1 ___ 2 ___ 3 ___	1 ___ 2 ___ 3 ___
% with developed countries	%	%
% with developing countries	%	%

Summary

Countries need to be interdependent if they are to share in the world's resources. Countries like Kenya which export primary goods do not develop as quickly economically as those which export manufactured goods.

How developed is Kenya?

By now you should be aware that there are many differences between living in Kenya and in other countries such as the United Kingdom. These differences may include ethnic groups, dress, housing, religion, language, jobs and wealth. You should also be aware that countries are at different levels of development. The term development is not, however, easy to define. The most common meaning, though not always the most accurate, is based upon wealth.

To make comparisons between countries easier, the wealth of a country is given by its **gross national product** (GNP). Remember that GNP is the amount of money earned by a country divided by its total population.

Diagram **A** is based on GNP. It shows that Kenya is one of the poorest countries in the world although it is about average for Africa. Based on wealth, therefore, Kenya is considered to be one of the least developed countries in the world. What diagram **A** does not show, however, are the differences in wealth within Kenya itself. There are many Kenyans who are wealthy and have a high standard of living. Unfortunately the majority of people, especially those living in urban shanty settlements or isolated rural areas, are very poor (pages 52–53). The gap between the rich and the poor is a major problem in Kenya as it is in other developing countries.

Wealth is not the only way to measure, or describe, development. Development can be measured by differences in population, health, education, jobs and trade (diagram **B**). Yet each of these measures can be linked to wealth. Without wealth a country is unlikely to have enough money to spend on such things as schools, health care and birth control.

When applying most of these measures to a developing country such as Kenya it is easy to build up a negative and often incorrect picture of that place. More important than wealth should be the **quality of life**. Many Kenyans, especially those living in shanty settlements in Nairobi, are very poor. Yet the majority appear to be cheerful, relaxed and are nearly always prepared to help visitors or their neighbours (photo **C**). Socially they appear more developed and less selfish than many people in so-called 'richer' countries. Quality of life is hard to measure, in comparison to wealth, birth rates and trade.

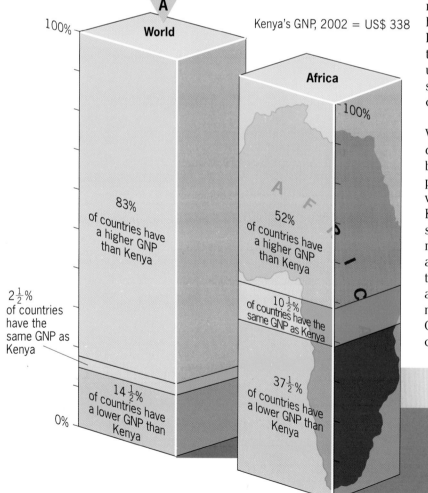

Kenya's GNP, 2002 = US$ 338

A

World: 100% / 83% of countries have a higher GNP than Kenya / 2½% of countries have the same GNP as Kenya / 14½% of countries have a lower GNP than Kenya / 0%

Africa: 100% / 52% of countries have a higher GNP than Kenya / 10½% of countries have the same GNP as Kenya / 37½% of countries have a lower GNP than Kenya / 0%

64

B

Jobs	Trade	Population	Health	Education
		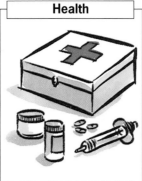		
Most Kenyans are farmers, or are involved in primary activities. Relatively few are employed in manufacturing or services (apart from tourism).	Kenya's main exports are primary goods (raw materials) which it sells at a low price. Its main imports are manufactured goods which it has to buy at higher prices.	Kenya has one of the highest birth rates in the world. It also has more young children dying (high infant mortality), adults dying at a younger age (shorter life expectancy) and a faster population increase than a developed country.	Kenya has relatively little money to spend on training doctors and nurses, and in providing hospitals and medicine.	Half of Kenya's population are of school age. Despite a lot of money spent on education, fewer people can read than in a developed country (low literacy rate). Girls do not receive the same education as boys.

One of the first photos in this unit (photo **B**, page 42) shows victorious Kenyan athletes. The unit ends by reminding you that when it comes to long distance races, as just one example, Kenyans are the world's best and **most** developed.

C

Activities

1 a) Name the seven measures shown in diagram **D** which can be used to describe a country's level of development.

b) Explain how each one can be used to measure development.

c) Which ones of the seven suggest that Kenya is still a developing country?

d) Why is GNP not always a good measure of development?

D

How developed is Kenya?

Summary

Despite its social and cultural development, Kenya is seen as a developing country. This is due to its limited economic development, lack of wealth and rapid population growth.

4 Italy

What is Italy like?

Most of us have a mental picture or image of what a country is like. A group of geography pupils were asked what pictures came to mind when they thought about Italy. The most popular ones that they came up with are shown in drawing **A** below. Look carefully at the drawing. How many of the pictures can you put names to? What other ones would you have thought of?

Italy, in fact, is one of Europe's best-known countries. It is often in the news and an increasing number of people have visited the country on holiday. The Italian passion for fashion, fast cars and football is well known throughout the world.

Look at drawing **B** which compares Italy with the United Kingdom. Notice that in many ways Italy is very similar to the UK. If you look closely however, you will see that there are also some quite important differences.

It is easy to find us on a map. We are situated in southern Europe. Our country is long and narrow and is almost surrounded by the Mediterranean Sea. The islands of Sicily and Sardinia are also part of Italy.

A

UK

Italy

Mediterranean Sea

Sardinia

Sicily

Italy and the United Kingdom compared

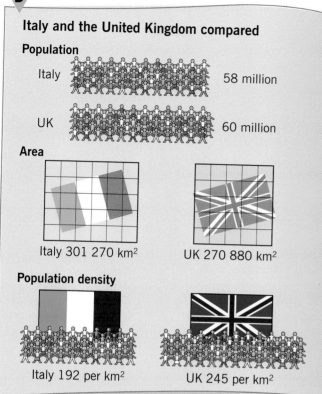

Population

Italy — 58 million

UK — 60 million

Area

Italy 301 270 km²

UK 270 880 km²

Population density

Italy 192 per km²

UK 245 per km²

	Italy	UK
In secondary education	74%	48%
Cars (per 100 people)	62	48
Televisions (per 100 people)	53	52
Tractors (in millions)	1.3	0.4
Tourists (in millions)	63	64
Urban population	67%	92%
Life expectancy (in years)	79	78

Activities

1 a) Captions for six of the pictures in drawing **A** are given below. Match the beginnings with the correct endings to find them.

b) Write down a caption for each of the other four pictures.

c) Work with a partner and make a list of any other things that come to mind when you think of Italy.

C

Rom...   Wi...

...ice   Op...

...c ream   ...ta

...era   Ice..   ...ans

...ne   Pas...

Ven...

2 Copy four pieces of information from drawing **B**. Next to each one explain what you think it tells you about Italy.

3 a) Give four pieces of information that show Italy to be similar to the UK.

b) Give four pieces of information that show Italy to be different to the UK.

4 Draw a poster to show what Italy is like. Use a sheet of A4 paper or a double page in your exercise book. Try to include:
- some drawings
- some captions
- some factual information

Make your poster as eyecatching, interesting, and colourful as you can.

Summary Italy is a beautiful country with a long and interesting history. Italians have developed their own customs and way of life.

What are Italy's main physical features?

Headlines like the ones above are quite common in Italy. As map **A** shows, there have been four major **earthquakes** in the last 25 years. There have also been several minor ones. Volcanic activity is even more frequent. Italy has Europe's only **active volcanoes** and eruptions happen every year. Problems like this are called **natural hazards**.

Earthquakes and volcanic eruptions are caused by movements of the **earth's crust**. These movements also help to build mountains. Over three quarters of Italy is hilly or mountainous.

Geologically, the country is quite young and most mountain building activity happened between 40 and 20 million years ago. This has left Italy with some spectacular scenery as the landscape has not yet been worn away and rounded off as much as it has in older places like Britain.

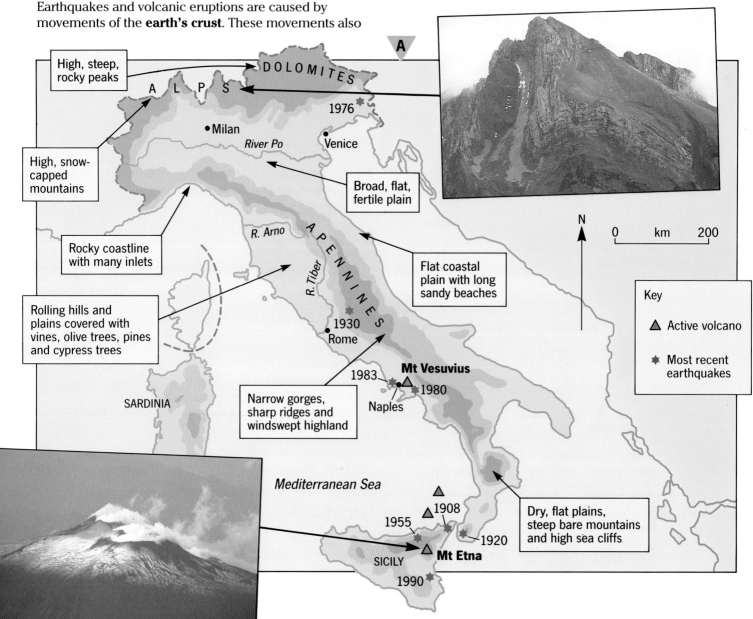

A

High, steep, rocky peaks

DOLOMITES

ALPS

1976

• Milan

Venice

River Po

High, snow-capped mountains

Broad, flat, fertile plain

Rocky coastline with many inlets

R. Arno

A P E N N I N E S

R. Tiber

Flat coastal plain with long sandy beaches

Rolling hills and plains covered with vines, olive trees, pines and cypress trees

1930
Rome •

N

0 km 200

Key

△ Active volcano

✶ Most recent earthquakes

Mt Vesuvius

1983 △ 1980

Narrow gorges, sharp ridges and windswept highland

Naples

SARDINIA

Mediterranean Sea

△
△ 1908
1955

1920

Dry, flat plains, steep bare mountains and high sea cliffs

△ **Mt Etna**

SICILY

1990

The earth's crust is broken into several enormous sections called **plates**. The boundaries and movement of plates near to Italy is very complicated and is not yet fully understood. Diagram **B** shows their probable movement. Scientists believe that as the plates move towards each other, heat from the friction between them makes the rock melt. The liquid rock rises upwards and erupts through holes in the earth's surface as volcanoes. Etna and Vesuvius are two such volcanoes.

The force of the two plates coming together puts tremendous pressure on the rock layers. This pressure causes them to bend and **fold**. The Apennines and Alps are **fold mountains** caused by rock being pushed upwards and folding. The movement of plates scraping together also makes the ground shake and sets off earthquakes.

B How some of Italy's physical landscape may have been formed.

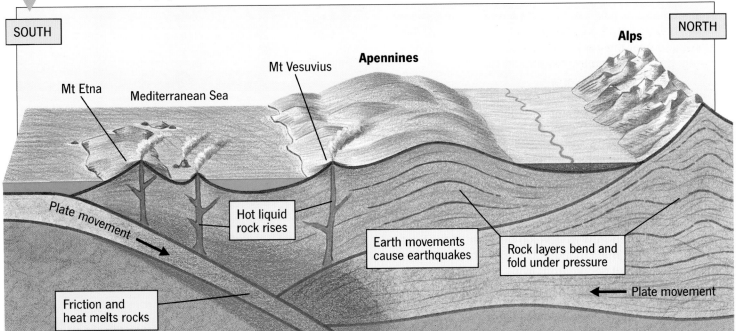

SOUTH · NORTH

Alps

Apennines

Mt Vesuvius

Mt Etna

Mediterranean Sea

Plate movement

Hot liquid rock rises

Earth movements cause earthquakes

Rock layers bend and fold under pressure

Plate movement

Friction and heat melts rocks

Activities

1 Why are earthquakes and volcanic eruptions called natural hazards?

2 Describe how the Alps were formed by sorting out the boxes below into the correct order. Link your boxes with arrows and add a title.

Pressure causes rocks to bend and fold

Two plates move toward each other

Rock layers put under pressure

Upward movement causes Alps to form

3 a) What are the dates of the four most recent earthquakes?
   b) Describe how earthquakes happen.

4 a) Make a copy of cross section **C**.
   b) Add labels to the boxes to show how Mount Etna erupts.
   c) Give your drawing a title.

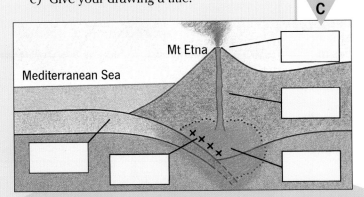

C

Mt Etna

Mediterranean Sea

Summary Italy is a mountainous country with little flat land. The landscape is mainly a result of earth movements happening in recent times.

Where do people live in Italy?

As we have seen, Italy and the United Kingdom are similar in many ways. They have populations of a similar size (58 and 60 million). They are a similar size in area, and in both countries, the population is unevenly spread out.

Map **A** shows where people live in Italy. It is easy to see that some areas have a lot of people and some have very few. The most crowded places seem to be toward the north and near the coast. The least crowded are the south, the centre and the extreme north.

There are good reasons for this **population distribution**. On the North Italian Plain, for example, the land is flat and ideal for farming. Building is easy and big industrial centres such as Milan and Turin have grown up. The availability of food, jobs and other facilities have encouraged people to live here so the area has become **densely populated**. On the other hand, life in many parts of the south of Italy is very difficult. The area is hot and dry and very rugged. Farming is not easy and industry has been slow to develop because of the long distances to the main markets of the north. Conditions have discouraged people from living here and the area is **sparsely populated**.

Some of the things that affect where people live are shown in drawing **B** below. Look at the photos on the opposite page. Their locations are shown on the map. For each one in turn try to work out why the area is likely to be densely populated or sparsely populated.

More than three quarters of the Italian people live in towns and cities. Rome, the capital and largest city, has nearly 3 million inhabitants. Like most cities in Italy it has magnificent buildings and a rich and interesting history. It is also nearly always crowded, noisy and congested.

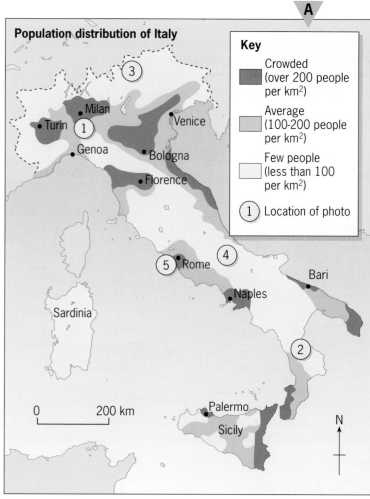

A

Population distribution of Italy

Key

Crowded (over 200 people per km²)

Average (100–200 people per km²)

Few people (less than 100 per km²)

① Location of photo

Milan · Turin · Venice · Genoa · Bologna · Florence · Rome · Naples · Bari · Sardinia · Palermo · Sicily

0   200 km

N

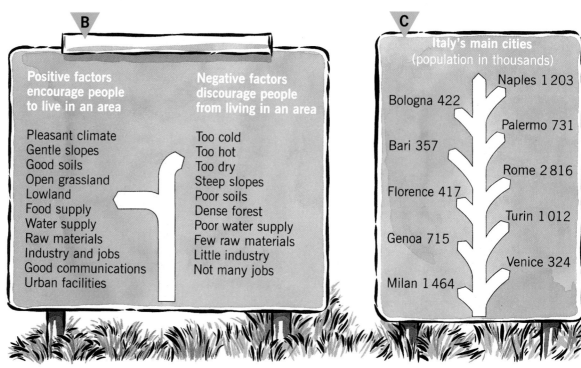

B

Positive factors encourage people to live in an area	Negative factors discourage people from living in an area
Pleasant climate	Too cold
Gentle slopes	Too hot
Good soils	Too dry
Open grassland	Steep slopes
Lowland	Poor soils
Food supply	Dense forest
Water supply	Poor water supply
Raw materials	Few raw materials
Industry and jobs	Little industry
Good communications	Not many jobs
Urban facilities	

C

Italy's main cities (population in thousands)

Naples 1 203
Bologna 422
Palermo 731
Bari 357
Rome 2 816
Florence 417
Turin 1 012
Genoa 715
Venice 324
Milan 1 464

1 Milan on the North Italian Plain

2 Campania in South Italy

3 Alps

5 Rome

4 Apennines

Activities

1 a) Is the population of Italy evenly or unevenly distributed?
   b) Where are the most crowded places?
   c) Where are the areas that are least crowded?

2 For each of the five photos above:
   a) Name the area shown in the photo.
   b) Say if it is crowded or sparsely populated.
   c) Suggest reasons for your answer. Drawing **B** will help you.

3 a) List the cities from diagram **C** in order of size. Give the biggest first.
   b) Which of the cities are on the coast?
   c) Which of the cities are on the densely populated North Italian Plain?

4 a) What is the population of Italy?
   b) What proportion of Italians live in cities?
   c) What are the advantages of living in a city like Rome?
   d) What are the disadvantages of living in a city like Rome?

Summary

People are not spread evenly through Italy. Some areas are very crowded whilst others are almost empty. Most Italians live in cities.

Wish you were here?

Italy is one of Europe's top tourist destinations. Over 63 million people visit the country each year. Most of them come from Germany, France, the UK and the USA. Most Italians also go on holiday in their own country. The majority of them go to the seaside or mountains.

A

B

There are three main reasons for Italy's popularity with tourists.

Firstly, Italy has a long and fascinating history. The country is full of archeological sites and historic remains. The ruins of ancient Roman buildings such as imperial palaces, temples, arches and simple villas are to be seen in many places.

The second reason is the landscape. Italy is a beautiful country with very varied scenery. There are snow-capped mountains, thickly wooded hills and spectacular volcanoes. Along the coast there are miles of sandy beaches, steep cliffs and rocky islands.

Thirdly, and perhaps most important of all, is the weather. Almost all of Italy enjoys a **Mediterranean climate**. This gives hot summers, warm winters and long hours of sunshine throughout the year. Only in winter is there enough rain to worry about.

C Some attractions of Italy

Glaciers
Lovely islands
Peaceful countryside
Interesting cities
Magnificent architecture
Coastal cliffs
Art galleries
Museums
Football
Sport

Watersports
Wine
Good food
Ski–ing
Mountaineering
Thermal springs
Fine hotels
Holiday entertainment
Good shopping

Plenty of sunshine
Warm temperatures
Little rain
Good climate
Fine beaches
Warm seas
Fascinating history
Spectacular mountains
Volcanoes
Lakes

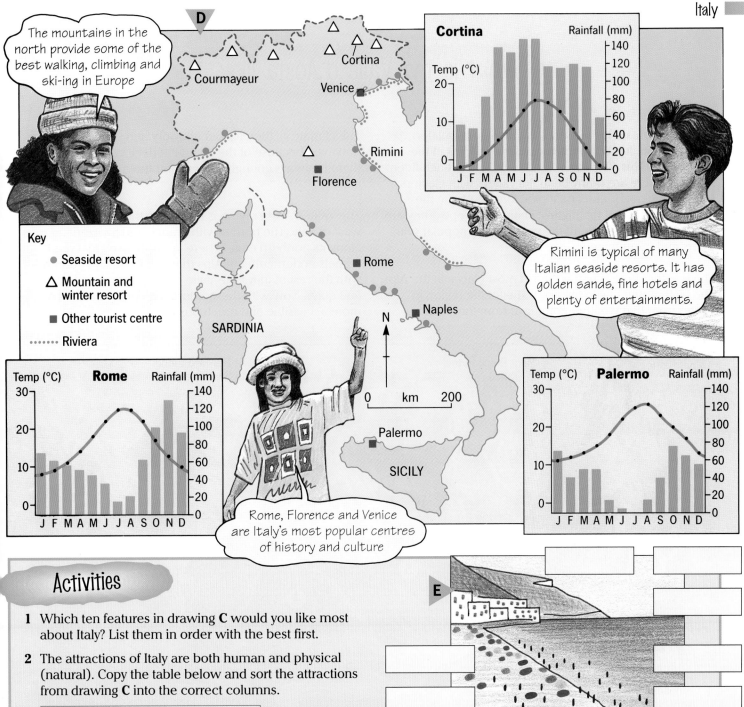

D

The mountains in the north provide some of the best walking, climbing and ski-ing in Europe

Courmayeur
Cortina
Venice
Rimini
Florence
Rome
Naples
SARDINIA
Palermo
SICILY

Key
- ● Seaside resort
- △ Mountain and winter resort
- ■ Other tourist centre
- ····· Riviera

Cortina Rainfall (mm) / Temp (°C)

Rimini is typical of many Italian seaside resorts. It has golden sands, fine hotels and plenty of entertainments.

Rome Temp (°C) / Rainfall (mm)

Palermo Temp (°C) / Rainfall (mm)

Rome, Florence and Venice are Italy's most popular centres of history and culture

N
0 km 200

Activities

1 Which ten features in drawing **C** would you like most about Italy? List them in order with the best first.

2 The attractions of Italy are both human and physical (natural). Copy the table below and sort the attractions from drawing **C** into the correct columns.

Attractions of Italy	
Human	Physical

3 Match the following areas of Italy with the correct climate decriptions. Use the climate graphs on map **D** to complete the temperature and rainfall figures for July.

Mountains of the north	**Summers:** hot (__ °C), dry (__ mm) **Winters:** warm with some rain
Rome and the coastal plain	**Summers:** hot (25 °C), very dry (__ mm) **Winter:** very warm, a little rain
Sicily and the south	**Summers:** warm (__ °C), some rain (15mm) **Winters:** cold (-2 °C) with rain or snow

E

4 Sketch **E** is a drawing based on photo **A**.
a) Make a larger copy of the sketch.
b) Add colour to make it clearer and more attractive.
c) Label ten features from drawing **C** that are likely tobe found at the resort which make it attractive to tourists.

Summary Tourists are attracted to Italy for many reasons. These include an interesting history, beautiful and varied scenery, and a very pleasant climate.

73

What is the Valle d'Aosta like?

The Valle d'Aosta is the smallest and least populated Italian region. It is a mountainous area and lies in the heart of the Alps. The region is famous for its magnificent scenery. There are many beautiful valleys with glaciers, fast-flowing rivers, and fine alpine forests. Above the valleys are some of the highest peaks in Europe. They are snow-covered throughout the year and are popular with skiers and mountaineers.

The weather here is better than in most places in the Alps. The high mountains to the north shelter the region in winter from bad weather coming in from the Atlantic.

The climate is, therefore, mainly dry and sunny. In winter, however, because of the high altitude, it can be cold and there is always enough snowfall for the many ski-ing resorts.

The Valle d'Aosta region is located in the extreme north-west of Italy. The border with France and Switzerland runs along its northern edge. There are now two great road tunnels underneath the Alps that link these two countries with the rest of Italy. The Valle d'Aosta was once isolated and quiet. Now with these improved communications it is more accessible and much busier.

A Valle d'Aosta region

Mont Blanc

Mont Blanc tunnel to France

St Bernard tunnel to Switzerland

Courmayeur

Aosta

Motorway in main valley

1. Smaller valleys very narrow and steep-sided
2. Little flat land even in bigger valleys
3. Little space for major industrial developments
4. Most valley sides densely forested

B Vineyards and mountains in the Valle d'Aosta region

74

C Map of the Valle d'Aosta region

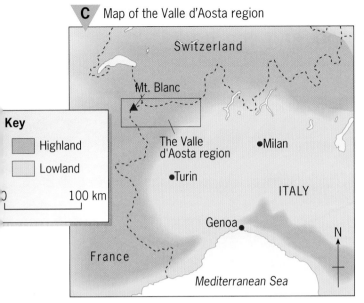

Key

Highland
Lowland

0   100 km

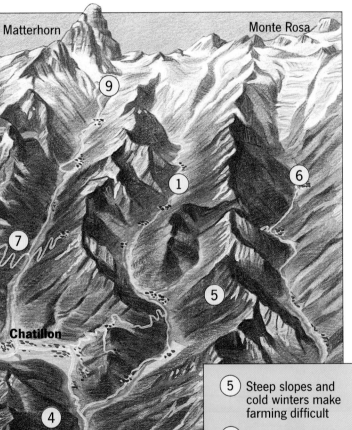

Matterhorn   Monte Rosa

Chatillon

Pont St Martin

5 Steep slopes and cold winters make farming difficult

6 Many very small villages scattered along the valleys

7 Steep slopes make communications difficult

8 High mountains provide all year round ski-ing

9 Many large ski-ing developments

Activities

1 Look at sketch **A** which shows some features of the Valle d'Aosta region. Find seventeen of these features in the word spiral. Sort them under the headings in a copy of table **D** below. Read the spiral from the centre outwards.

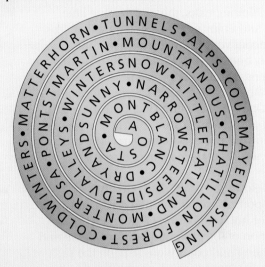

D

Towns and villages	Mountains	Weather	Other features

2 What improvements in communications have helped make the region more accessible and busier?

3 Why is the area good for ski-ing? Give at least four reasons.

4 Draw a simple sketch map to show the location of the Valle d'Aosta region. Drawing **A** on page 68 and map **C** will help you. Mark on and name:
   a) France, Switzerland and Italy,
   b) Aosta and three other towns,
   c) The Alps, Apennines and Mediterranean Sea,
   d) River Po, North Italian Plain and Mont Blanc.
   Add a key, scale line, north point and two road tunnels.

5 What is the distance from Aosta to:
   a) Milan,
   b) Mediterranean Sea?

Summary   The Valle d'Aosta region is a mountainous part of north-west Italy. The area is sparsely populated and there are few towns.

Winter sports: the good and the bad

Over the years, the Valle d'Aosta region has become increasingly popular with tourists. Most visitors come to see the beautiful snow-capped Alpine peaks, the picturesque little villages and enjoy peace, quiet and clean fresh air. In recent years, however, ski-ing has gradually become a main attraction. The high mountains, good winter snowfall and generally fine weather make the area perfect for winter sports. Once quiet centres like Courmayeur at the foot of Mont Blanc, and Cervinia below the Matterhorn have become bustling little towns that attract skiers from all over the world.

The development of tourism, and especially winter sports, has changed the region in many ways. For hundreds of years the main occupation of the area was farming. Cattle and some sheep and goats were kept on the high pastures in summer and brought down to the valley floor in winter. Alpine communities were close-knit, self-contained and slow to accept modern technology. Out-migration increased as many young people left the region in search of work and the attractions of city life. With the building of the tunnels and new roads, however, the area became much easier to get to. As the tourist boom began, new facilities had to be built to cater for their needs.

As photo **B** shows, these developments have brought many benefits to the area. Tourism has become an important source of wealth and standards of living for most local people have improved.

Unfortunately there have also been problems. Many people are concerned that winter sports facilities, in particular, are spoiling the countryside and permanently damaging the environment. Cartoon **C** shows some of these problems.

A

B Some benefits of tourism

More jobs

Fewer people leave the area

Money comes into area

Better paid jobs

New tourist amenities which locals can use

Improved roads

More people to meet – more interesting life

Better quality of life

C Some problems of tourism

Ugly ski-ing facilities spoil mountainside
· Danger from falling rocks
· New building work a nuisance
· Increased chance of floods
· Hotels spoil landscape
· Traffic jams
· Forests cleared
· Wildlife frightened away
· Plant life damaged

The ski-ing's great but is it worth all the damage?

Activities

1 a) What five reasons make the Valle d'Aosta popular with tourists?
  b) What three reasons help make the region good for winter sports?

2 Describe three features of life in the Valle d'Aosta before the arrival of large scale tourism.

3 Which benefits from photo **B** do you think would be most useful to a teenager about to leave school?

4 Match each of the labels from the notice board with the correct number from cartoon **C**.

5 a) Make a copy of table **D**.
  b) Tick the boxes for each effect of tourism.
  c) Colour the benefits in green and the problems in red.
  d) Choose any two problems and suggest what could be done to reduce them.

6 Do you think that winter sports developments should be encouraged or discouraged? Give reasons for your answer. Write about half a page or work with a partner for this question and present your arguments in a debate.

D

Effect	People	Environment
Increased wealth		
People to meet		
Traffic jams		
New jobs		
Deforestation		
Flooding		
Things to do		
Loss of wildlife		
Reduced out-migration		

Summary The Valle d'Aosta region is very popular with tourists particularly in winter. Tourism has brought many benefits but it has also caused problems.

Italy's Industrial Triangle

A

United Colors of Benetton.

You probably recognise the names on the left. They belong to well-known Italian companies that sell their products all around the world. These companies have their factories and main offices in an area that is called the Industrial Triangle.

The Industrial Triangle is located just south of the Valle d'Aosta region. It lies at the western end of Italy's largest area of lowland, the North Italian Plain. The cities of Milan, Turin and Genoa are at the three corners of the 'triangle'. Milan is the commercial and business centre of the region. Turin is an industrial city and the home of Fiat, one of the world's largest companies. Genoa is a major port on the Mediterranean Sea and an outlet for exports to foreign countries.

Industry developed in this area much later than in most other countries in Western Europe. It was not until the late 1900s that industrial development really took off in the region. This was largely because Italy has few natural resources. A lack of coal, in particular, caused problems until other forms of energy were developed. Now, energy for the region comes mainly from hydro-electric power stations, natural gas and a small number of nuclear power stations. Even now, some electricity has to be imported from France because these power sources are not sufficient to meet Italy's growing needs.

In the last 50 years industrial growth has been very rapid. Italy is now one of the seven richest nations in the world and the Industrial Triangle has become the wealthiest region in the whole country.

Look carefully at map **B**. It shows the main features of Italy's Industrial Triangle. See how many reasons you can find for the area being so attractive to industry.

Industry in Italy

Fashion · Shoes · Cars · Machinery · Textiles · Steel · Food · Ceramics · Chemicals

Activities

1 Draw a simple sketch map of the region shown in map **B**. Follow these instructions.
   a) Draw in the coastline and name the Mediterranean Sea.
   b) Mark the areas of highland and name the Alps and Apennines.
   c) Mark with a red dot and name Milan, Turin and Genoa.
   d) Draw in and name the Industrial Triangle.
   e) Shade the highland brown, the lowland green and the sea blue.
   f) Add a title and key to your map.

2 Give three facts about the location of the Industrial Triangle.

3 a) Why was Italy slower to industrialise than other countries in Western Europe?
   b) What main sources of energy are now used in the Industrial Triangle?

4 Make a larger copy of diagram **C** and complete it using information from map **B**.

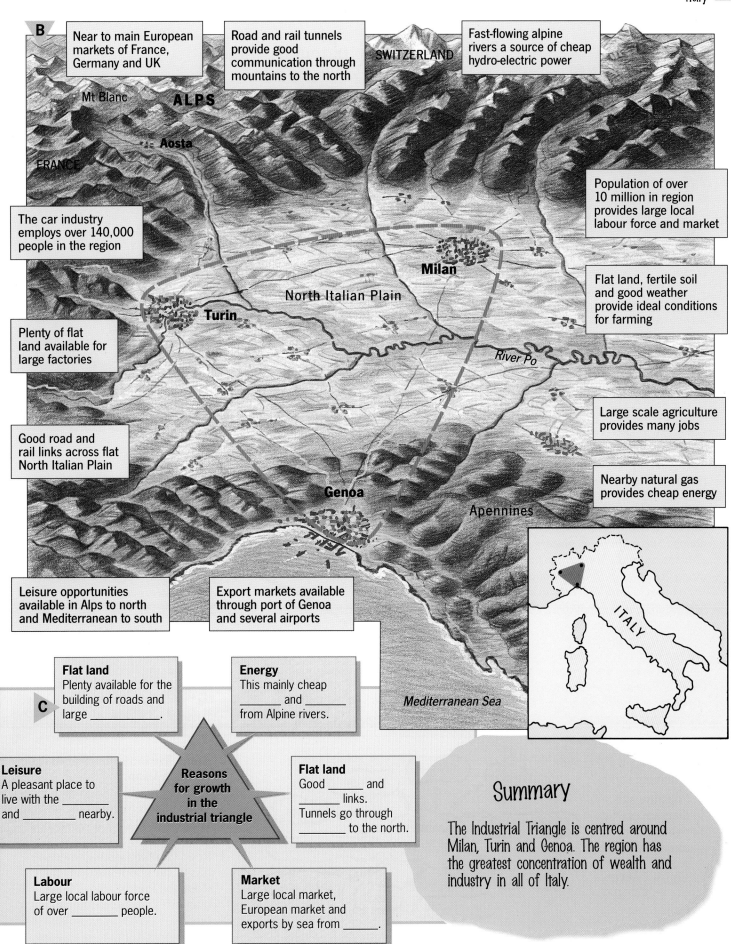

B

Near to main European markets of France, Germany and UK

Road and rail tunnels provide good communication through mountains to the north

SWITZERLAND

Fast-flowing alpine rivers a source of cheap hydro-electric power

Mt Blanc

ALPS

Aosta

FRANCE

The car industry employs over 140,000 people in the region

Population of over 10 million in region provides large local labour force and market

Milan

North Italian Plain

Turin

Flat land, fertile soil and good weather provide ideal conditions for farming

Plenty of flat land available for large factories

River Po

Large scale agriculture provides many jobs

Good road and rail links across flat North Italian Plain

Genoa

Nearby natural gas provides cheap energy

Apennines

Leisure opportunities available in Alps to north and Mediterranean to south

Export markets available through port of Genoa and several airports

Mediterranean Sea

ITALY

C

Flat land
Plenty available for the building of roads and large _____.

Energy
This mainly cheap _____ and _____ from Alpine rivers.

Leisure
A pleasant place to live with the _____ and _____ nearby.

Reasons for growth in the industrial triangle

Flat land
Good _____ and _____ links.
Tunnels go through _____ to the north.

Summary

The Industrial Triangle is centred around Milan, Turin and Genoa. The region has the greatest concentration of wealth and industry in all of Italy.

Labour
Large local labour force of over _____ people.

Market
Large local market, European market and exports by sea from _____.

Milan: a good place to live?

Buon giorno,

my name is Gennaro and I live with my family on the northern outskirts of Milan. We all like living in Milan. It's very big, very busy and there is always plenty to do.

Where we live is quite industrial but the city centre around the Piazza del Duomo is beautiful with many fine buildings. The cathedral is really spectacular. It has a hundred spires, a thousand statues and can hold 40 000 people. Next to it is the Galleria Vittoria Emmanuelle which is a glass-roofed arcade with lovely shops and restaurants. My parents like to go to the nearby La Scala theatre, one of the world's great opera centres.

My favourite place in Milan is the San Siro Stadium. It is the home of two of the world's top football teams. The World Cup final was held there in 1994 but unfortunately Italy lost! My sister came with me to the final but she really prefers night-clubs. There are plenty of them in Milan.

Milan is Italy's most important industrial and financial centre so I should have a good choice of jobs when I leave school. There are big engineering, chemical and food processing factories not far from where we live. I think I would like to work for Alfa Romeo making cars. My sister is trying to get into the fashion industry. Milan is famous for fashion clothing. Benetton, Armani and Gucci all have their headquarters in the city.

The roads around here are very good. Within a couple of hours we can be into the Alps for ski-ing or down to the Mediterranean to enjoy the beaches. That makes Milan an even better place to live.

A Milan cathedral and city centre

I ♥ Milan

B San Siro Stadium

Activities

C

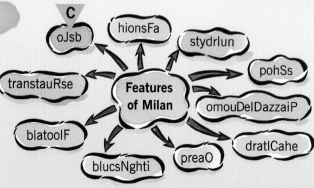

oJsb
hionsFa
stydrlun
transtauRse
Features of Milan
pohSs
blatoolF
omouDelDazzaiP
blucsNghti
preaO
dratlCahe

1 Copy the star diagram on the right and unscramble the words to give ten features of Milan.

2 Name five industries that may be found in Milan.

3 What places might easily be visited from Milan at weekends?

4 Read carefully what Francesca has to say about living in Milan. Copy the four headings from diagram **E** and add notes to each one.

Buon giorno,

my name is Francesca. I live with my parents in Gorgonzola just 18 kilometeres west of Milan's city centre.

Gorgonzola is famous for its cheese. When my parents moved here it was a quiet and pretty little town with vineyards and lovely countryside around it. Now we are just about part of Milan and the place is crowded and noisy.

The traffic around here is bad enough but in Milan centre it is even worse. At peak times they have traffic grid lock and it is almost impossible to cross the city. The cars also combine with industry to cause air pollution. Conditions are worst in winter. The cold, still air from the mountains traps the exhaust fumes and factory smoke. It produces a choking smog which often sits over the city for days.

Like every other big city, Milan has its problems. We think that many of our problems are because the city has grown too quickly. There doesn't seem to have been enough time to plan carefully and we have lost much of what was good and attractive about Milan. A lot of open space and parkland has gone in the last few years. This has mostly been replaced by huge blocks of flats, ugly estates and even more

congested roads. Industry is also on the decline in the Milan area. There is much more unemployment than there used to be and I am worried about getting a job when I leave school.

We are thinking of moving away from Milan soon. My parents are looking for work and a place to live in the lovely Valle d'Aosta region just north-west of here. We think that is a better place to live than Milan.

D Traffic congestion and pollution in Milan city centre

E

Traffic

Air pollution

Planning

Problems in Milan

Jobs and industry

5 If you lived in Milan would you
  a) prefer to stay there or
  b) prefer to move away to somewhere like the Valle d'Aosta region?
Give reasons for your answer.

Summary Milan is one of Italy's largest and most interesting cities. In recent years, rapid growth has caused problems for the people living there.

Two regions compared

Both the Valle d'Aosta region and the Industrial Triangle are located in north-west Italy. Whilst being located almost next to each other, they are different in many ways.

The Valle d'Aosta region is mountainous and mainly rural. The area is **sparsely populated** and most of the settlements are small and crowded along narrow, steep-sided valleys. **Communications** have improved recently with the building of new roads and tunnels through the Alps. Many places however, remain very **isolated**.

The weather here is usually dry and sunny although in winter there is much snow and it can be very cold. Tourism – especially winter sports – has become a major industry in the area. Some people are concerned that the development of winter sports facilities is spoiling the area.

The Industrial Triangle is different altogether. The area is mainly flat and low-lying. It has hot and sunny summers but winters can be wet and foggy.

There are good communications, many towns, and the region is **densely populated**. Although conditions are ideal for farming, it is manufacturing industry that has developed most in recent years. The area has become Italy's industrial heartland and the wealthiest region.

Growth in the Industrial Triangle has been very rapid and there have been difficulties with traffic congestion and pollution in recent years.

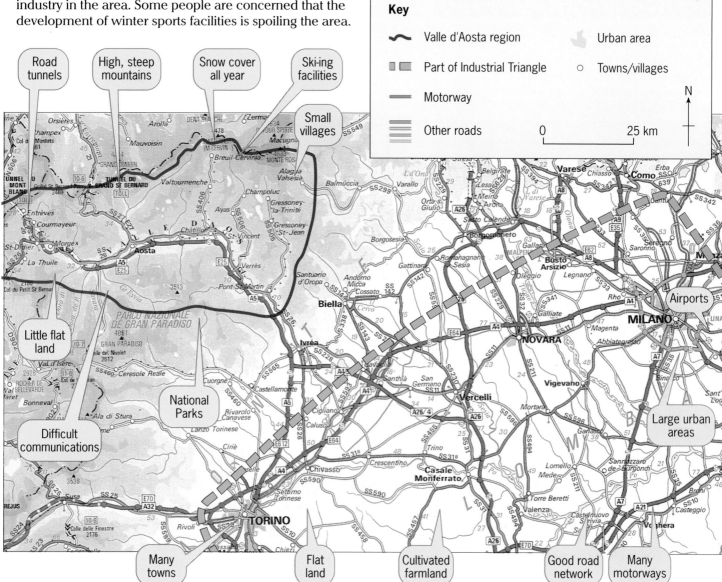

A

Key

~ Valle d'Aosta region

◾ ◾ Part of Industrial Triangle

— Motorway

≡ Other roads

Urban area

○ Towns/villages

0   25 km

N

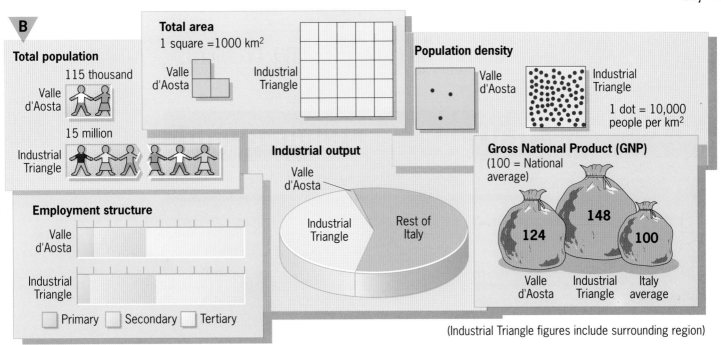

B

Total population

Valle d'Aosta — 115 thousand

Industrial Triangle — 15 million

Total area
1 square =1000 km²

Valle d'Aosta

Industrial Triangle

Population density

Valle d'Aosta

Industrial Triangle

1 dot = 10,000 people per km²

Employment structure

Valle d'Aosta

Industrial Triangle

☐ Primary ☐ Secondary ☐ Tertiary

Industrial output

Valle d'Aosta

Industrial Triangle

Rest of Italy

Gross National Product (GNP)
(100 = National average)

124 — Valle d'Aosta
148 — Industrial Triangle
100 — Italy average

(Industrial Triangle figures include surrounding region)

Activities

1 Use map **A** to answer these questions.
   a) What features have made industry difficult in the Valle d'Aosta region?
   b) What features help industry in the Industrial Triangle region?
   c) What features in the Valle d'Aosta region do you think would help to attract tourists?

2 a) Make a larger copy of Fact File **C**.
   b) Write the correct word from the bracket in each box.
   c) Give figures for each box.

3 a) Make a copy of table **D**.
   b) Complete the employment structure figures.
   c) Give an example of an industrial activity for each one. Choose from:
   Car making • Ski-ing • Banking and finance • Quarrying • Farming.

4 Explain what the GNP information shows about the wealth of the two regions.

5 Write a decription of each of the two regions.
   • Use the headings given below.
   • Write about 100 words for each one.

   • **Physical features** (relief and climate)
   • **Human features** (population, towns, communications)
   • **Economic features** (industry, jobs)
   • **Problems**

C

Fact File

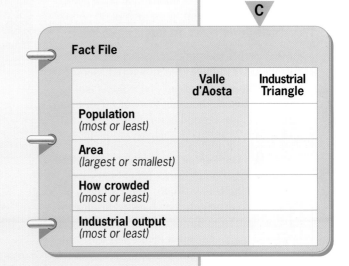

	Valle d'Aosta	Industrial Triangle
Population (most or least)		
Area (largest or smallest)		
How crowded (most or least)		
Industrial output (most or least)		

D

Region	Primary	Secondary	Tertiary
Valle d'Aosta			60%
Example		High-tech	
Industrial Triangle		42%	
Example			

Summary The Valle d'Aosta and Industrial Triangle regions are two important but different regions of Italy.

Does Italy have a flooding problem?

A

Italy battles floods again

Tuesday, 18 October 2000

Torrential rain, flooding and mudslides have once again hit northern Italy. At least 30 people have been killed and an estimated 3000 made homeless. The disaster comes just six years after the devastating 1994 floods which left over 100 people dead and several thousand without homes.

In the mountainous Valle d'Aosta region, bridges have been swept away, whole villages destroyed and farmland covered in a thick layer of mud. Up to 30 000 people have been without electricity and more than 8000 people evacuated over concerns for their safety.

Further south, the main industrial centres of Turin and Milan have also suffered. Essential services have been cut off and schools and factories closed. The giant Fiat car factory was forced to close as road and rail links were cut and flood waters swept through the plant.

One of the worst-hit areas has been the fertile Po valley. Emergency crews using boats and helicopters helped evacuate whole villages as the River Po overflowed its banks. Farming in the area has been devastated, with huge areas of wheat, maize and soya beans laid waste by flood water.

Prime Minister Giuliano Amato's cabinet has made £50 million immediately available to help the regions cope with their emergency needs. Early estimates have put the total cost of damage caused by flooding at over £4 billion.

Most of the flooding was caused by weeks of heavy rain in the Alps. Small streams in the Valle d'Aosta area quickly became raging torrents which washed away everything in their path. Further downstream the rivers Ticino and Po reached record levels, burst through existing flood defences and flooded the surrounding countryside.

Flooded farmland in the Po Valley

Families evacuated from their homes in Pavia near Milan

Whilst heavy rain was obviously the main cause of flooding in northern Italy, many people blame developers for making the disaster worse. After the 1994 floods, Adriano Sansa, the Mayor of Genoa, complained that:

❝ For decades we have encouraged building programmes and destroyed the forests and countryside without any thought for the environmental effects. In the last 25 years over 8000 square miles of our woodland and countryside has been destroyed. During that time the number of landslides a year have doubled to more than 4000 and 'serious' flooding has become a yearly occurrence. ❞

The point that the Mayor is making is very important. The aim of development, whether it be in the form of new ski-ing resorts or new factories, should be to bring about an improvement in conditions for people. In doing that, however, it should not harm or destroy the environment either now or in the future. Development like this is called **sustainable development**.

Sustainable development does not waste resources or damage the environment. It is progress that can go on for year after year. It helps improve our quality of life today but does not spoil our chances in the future.

Since the 1994 disaster, there has been much discussion in Italy on how to reduce the damaging effects of development. Most people agree that there is a need for much better planning if sustainable development is to be achieved. However, the steps taken to improve the quality of development have not yet been entirely successful. It will be interesting to see what happens in the years ahead.

B How development can increase flooding

More industrial development in the lowlands

Demand for more ski-ing facilities in the mountains

More land needed

Trees chopped down and buildings put up in the countryside

Unprotected soil washed into rivers – rivers fill up with silt

Less rainfall absorbed by vegetation – more water goes into rivers

Rivers overflow and cause flooding

Activities

1 Complete a flood Fact File using the headings shown on the right.

 C

Fact File

Place		Dead	
Date		Homeless	
Main towns		Damage	
Main rivers			

2 Complete these three sentences:
- Sustainable development is…
- Sustainable development should…
- Sustainable development should not…

3 What building developments have there been in northern Italy
a) in the mountains,
b) in the lowland areas?

4 Explain the two newspaper headings on the right. Write about 50 words for each one.

Skiers blamed for flood disasters

New industries bring problems not benefits

Summary

Flooding is a serious problem in northern Italy. Rapid and sometimes poorly planned development has been blamed for making the problem worse.

How interdependent is Italy?

When countries work together and rely on each other for help, they are said to be **interdependent**. Being interdependent can help a country progress and improve its standards of living.

One of the main ways that countries become interdependent is by selling goods to each other. They buy things that they need or would like to have. They then sell things to make money to pay for what they have bought. The exchanging of goods and materials like this is called **trade**.

For many years Italy has realised the importance of being a trading nation and has developed links with countries all around the world. Nowadays, as graph **A** shows, her most important trading partners are countries of the **European Union (EU)**.

Italy joined the EU as one of the six founder members in 1957. Since then, membership has grown to 25 countries, and the total market population to over 454 million people. This has provided Italy with a large and accessible market for her imports and exports. It has also enabled the country to benefit from being a member of one of the world's richest and most important groups of nations.

A Italy's trading partners

Italy's trading partners

Imports / Exports

EU countries 60% / 54%
USA 9% / 9%
Japan 2% / 6%
Rest of world 29% / 31%

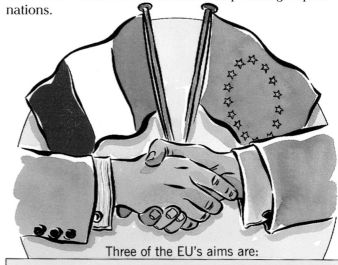

The European Union (EU) **B**

Three of the EU's aims are:

| To develop trade between member states | To provide help and support for each other | To develop a united Europe through interdependence |

C Italy's imports and exports

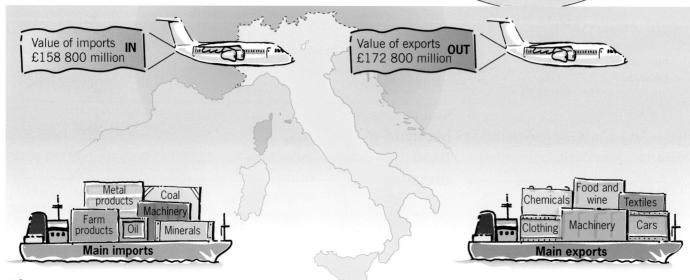

Value of imports **IN** £158 800 million

Value of exports **OUT** £172 800 million

Main imports: Metal products, Coal, Machinery, Farm products, Oil, Minerals

Main exports: Chemicals, Food and wine, Textiles, Clothing, Machinery, Cars

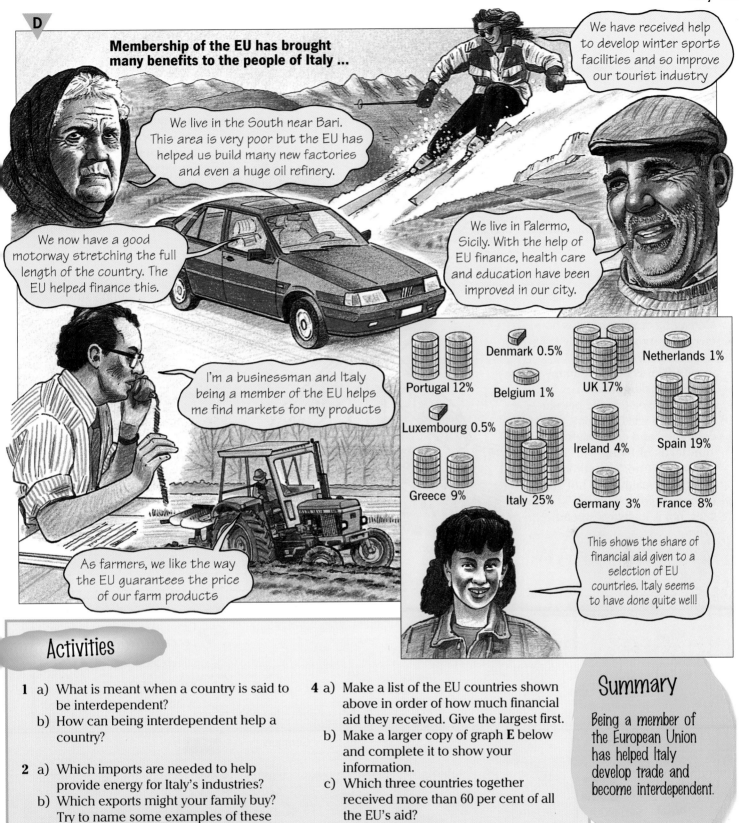

D

Membership of the EU has brought many benefits to the people of Italy ...

We have received help to develop winter sports facilities and so improve our tourist industry

We live in the South near Bari. This area is very poor but the EU has helped us build many new factories and even a huge oil refinery.

We now have a good motorway stretching the full length of the country. The EU helped finance this.

We live in Palermo, Sicily. With the help of EU finance, health care and education have been improved in our city.

I'm a businessman and Italy being a member of the EU helps me find markets for my products

Denmark 0.5%

Netherlands 1%

Portugal 12%

Belgium 1%

UK 17%

Luxembourg 0.5%

Ireland 4%

Spain 19%

Greece 9%

Italy 25%

Germany 3%

France 8%

As farmers, we like the way the EU guarantees the price of our farm products

This shows the share of financial aid given to a selection of EU countries. Italy seems to have done quite well!

Activities

1 a) What is meant when a country is said to be interdependent?
   b) How can being interdependent help a country?

2 a) Which imports are needed to help provide energy for Italy's industries?
   b) Which exports might your family buy? Try to name some examples of these products.

3 a) Give five ways in which membership of the EU has helped Italy's industry.
   b) What other benefits has EU membership brought?

4 a) Make a list of the EU countries shown above in order of how much financial aid they received. Give the largest first.
   b) Make a larger copy of graph **E** below and complete it to show your information.
   c) Which three countries together received more than 60 per cent of all the EU's aid?

0%   100%

E

Summary

Being a member of the European Union has helped Italy develop trade and become interdependent.

87

How developed is Italy?

The study of **development** is important in geography. Development is about progress and improving the quality of life for people. Progress and improvement should not, however, be at the expense of other people and it should not be damaging to the environment. In a word, development should be **sustainable**.

Measuring development is not easy. The most commonly used method is to look at wealth. This is because many people consider that if a country is wealthy, the people living there will be happy, contented and enjoy high **standards of living**. This is not always true. Sometimes a country's wealth does not go towards bettering people's lives, nor is it always spread evenly.

A Development is about...

More wealth

Longer life expectancy

Better education

Better health

The measurement of wealth by itself, therefore, is not always a good indicator of development. Other factors should also be considered. Some of these are shown in diagram **A**.

Whatever methods are used to measure development, most people agree that Italy is one of the world's most developed countries. Look at diagram **B** below which compares Italy with three other countries in the European Union (EU).

All of these countries are very well-off. As members of the EU they belong to one of the richest and most developed groups of nations in the world. Yet Italy in most cases, is equal to the best of them. Certainly by world standards, Italy is a modern, wealthy and highly developed nation.

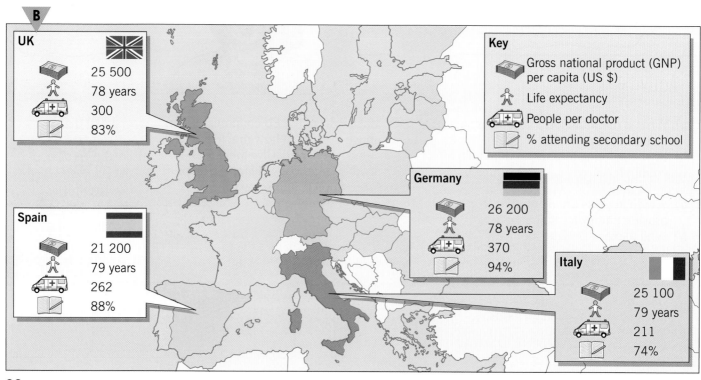

B

UK
25 500
78 years
300
83%

Spain
21 200
79 years
262
88%

Germany
26 200
78 years
370
94%

Italy
25 100
79 years
211
74%

Key
Gross national product (GNP) per capita (US $)
Life expectancy
People per doctor
% attending secondary school

The statistics for Italy as a whole, however, hide some problems. Maps **C** and **D** below show that wealth and quality of life are not evenly spread across the whole country. The North is mainly wealthy and has high standards of living. The South is less well developed. Many people there live in difficult conditions and have a much poorer quality of life.

Considerable effort has been put into improving living standards in the South. Over the past 40 years both the EU and the Italian government have invested enormous amounts of money in the region. Some progress has been made but the problem is proving to be a difficult one to solve.

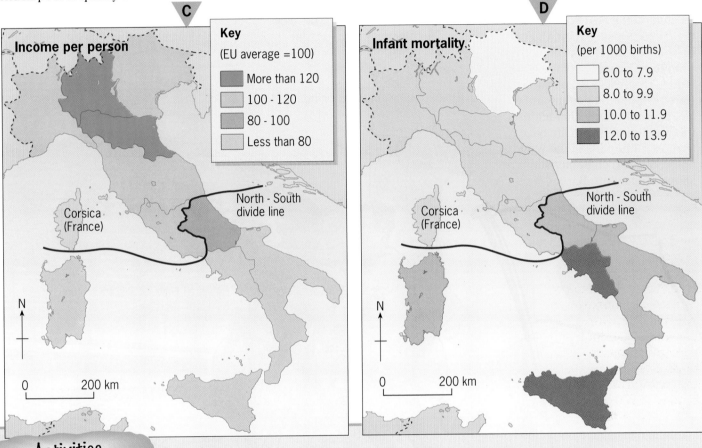

C

Income per person

Key
(EU average =100)

More than 120
100 - 120
80 - 100
Less than 80

Corsica (France)

North - South divide line

N

0   200 km

D

Infant mortality

Key
(per 1000 births)

6.0 to 7.9
8.0 to 9.9
10.0 to 11.9
12.0 to 13.9

Corsica (France)

North - South divide line

N

0   200 km

Activities

1 a) Make a larger copy of table **E** below and complete it using information from diagram **B**.
   b) List the countries from your table in order of
   • GNP/capita (highest first)
   • Life expectancy (highest first)
   • Number of people per doctor (lowest first)
   • % attending secondary schools (highest first)
   c) Look carefully at your completed lists. In your opinion, which two countries are the most developed? Give reasons for your choice.

2 In which part of Italy are
   a) incomes highest,
   b) workers likely to earn most money,
   c) the lowest infant mortality rates,
   d) babies most likely to die early?

3 Write a report expressing your worries about the uneven spread of wealth and living conditions in Italy. Try to include the following.

poor health care

poorer

better standards of living

wealthier

less developed

earn more money

E

	UK	Spain	Germany	Italy
GNP/capita				
Life expectancy				
People per doctor				
% attending secondary schools				

Summary Italy is one of the most developed countries in the world. Development, however, is not spread evenly. Some areas in the South have very poor standards of living.

5 Japan

What is Japan like?

Japan consists of four large islands and over 1000 smaller ones. It is located off the east coast of Asia in the Pacific Ocean (map **A**). For much of its history Japan has been isolated from most countries of the outside world. This isolation has allowed it to develop a unique culture and way of life. Recently many characteristics of this traditional way of life have spread to most other parts of the world. Some of these characteristics are shown in diagram **B**.

A

Asia

Japan

Pacific Ocean

Australia

B

Origami

Kimono

Buddhist temple

Sumo wrestling

Chopstic
and s

Bonsai tree

Karate

The last fifty years have seen a dramatic change in the traditional way of life. By the mid-1990s Japan had overtaken the USA to become the world's richest country. Although less than 3 per cent of the world's population live in Japan, the country earns nearly 10 per cent of the world's money. This growth in wealth has been the result of a rapid growth in industry.

Most Japanese spend long hours at work and have few holidays. They are very loyal to their place of work and to their family. They are also highly educated and skilled. Leading Japanese companies, like Toyota and Sony, have become household names across the world. It is likely that many things made by these companies can be found in your own home. Some of these goods are shown in diagram **C**.

C

Activities

1 Work with a partner and make a list of things which come to mind when you think about Japan.

2 Diagram **B** shows several features of the traditional Japanese way of life. Following a class discussion, write a short description of each feature.

3 Diagram **C** shows several items which your family might own. These items are made by such Japanese companies as Canon, Casio, Hitachi, Honda, JVC, Mazda, Minolta, Mitsubishi, Nissan, Pentax, Ricoh, Sharp, Toshiba and Toyota. Try to match up the items with the firms which make them (some companies may make more than one item). Put your answers in a table like this one.

D

		Company
Cameras		
Motor vehicles (cars)		
TVs and videos		
Calculators and computers		

Summary

The Japanese live on a group of islands. Their isolation has allowed the development of a unique culture and way of life.

Japan – a land of volcanoes and earthquakes

The surface of the earth is not all in one piece. It is broken into several large sections called **plates**. Each plate can move several centimetres a year. The place where two plates meet is called a **plate boundary**. It is at plate boundaries that most of the world's major volcanic eruptions and earthquakes occur.

Japan is at the boundary of three plates (diagram **A**). It is located where the Pacific and Philippines Plates move towards the Eurasian Plate. As they meet the Eurasian Plate, they are pushed downwards. This movement has brought **life** to Japan. It has also resulted in **death**.

As part of the crust is pushed downwards, friction causes it to melt. The liquid rock (**magma**) rises to the surface where it forms volcanoes. Without the formation of volcanoes there would be no Japan – the country owes its existence and **life** to volcanoes. Some Japanese volcanoes are still **active**. This means that they still erupt (photo **B**). Occasionally this can cause loss of life (extract **C**). Other volcanoes are either **extinct** or many never erupt again, or they are **dormant** and have not erupted for many years.

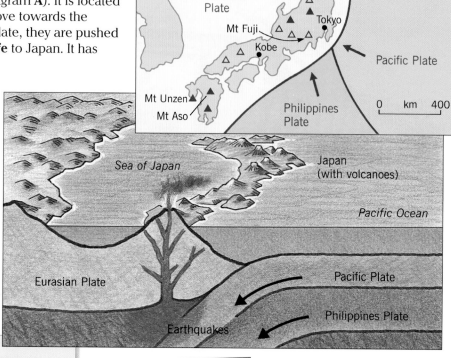

A

Key △ Dormant or extinct volcano
▲ Active volcano

Sea of Japan

Eurasian Plate

PACIFIC OCEAN

Mt Fuji
Kobe
Tokyo

Mt Unzen
Mt Aso

Philippines Plate

Pacific Plate

0 km 400

Sea of Japan

Japan (with volcanoes)

Pacific Ocean

Eurasian Plate

Pacific Plate

Philippines Plate

Earthquakes

C

Mount Unzen, on the southern island of Kyushu, had been dormant for almost 200 years until it erupted violently in June 1991.

Red hot lava rushed down the mountain-side at speeds of up to 120 km/hour. At the same time, clouds of poisonous gas were released into the air.

The eruption destroyed a small village, caused the death of 40 people and left many families homeless.

The last eruption in 1792 killed over 15 000 people.

B

Plates are not pushed downwards easily or smoothly due to friction. The pushing downwards of a plate often needs considerable force. This force comes from a build up of pressure. If this increase in pressure is released suddenly, then the plate may jerk forwards in a violent movement which is called an earthquake. Of 10 000 earthquakes in the world each year, over 1 000 occur in Japan. The majority are fairly gentle, but occasionally they can mean **death** for thousands of people and can destroy whole cities. An earthquake in 1923 resulted in 140 000 deaths in Tokyo and Yokohama. A more recent one in Kobe in 1995 killed over 5 000 people (photo **D**).

1.4 million people live in the prosperous port city of Kobe. Although earthquakes are frequently felt in the city, Kobe normally escapes any severe earth movements. That was until 17 January 1995! Early that day, fortunately before the morning rush-hour, an earthquake measuring 7.2 on the **Richter scale** devastated the city. It left over 5 000 dead, 10 000 injured and 250 000 homeless. Although it only lasted 20 seconds, the earthquake caused expressways and many buildings to collapse (photo **D**). Rescue work was hampered because of fears of further damage caused by 'after shocks', the total congestion of the road system, broken water mains, and hundreds of fires (photo **E**). Most fires resulted from broken gas pipes. Many fires lasted for several days, giving the sky an orange glow at night and leaving large areas of burned-out buildings and piles of ash. Many people were forced to camp on pavements in freezing temperatures either because they were homeless or because they were too afraid to go back into their homes.

D

E

Activities

1 a) Make a larger copy of diagram **F**.
   b) Add labels to show why volcanic eruptions and earthquakes occur in Japan.

2 Design a front page for a newspaper covering the Kobe earthquake. Try to include the following:
   - an eye-catching headline,
   - a simple map to show where the earthquake took place,
   - a paragraph describing the main effects of the earthquake,
   - two short paragraphs giving two eye-witness accounts of the scenes following the earthquake (one could be a night-time description),
   - a simple drawing to show one of the effects of the earthquake.

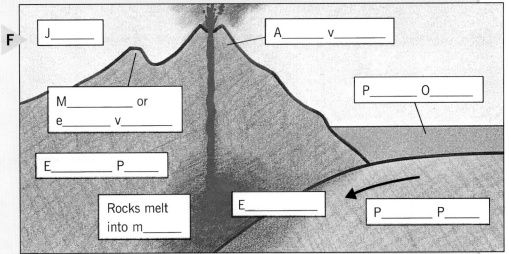

F

J_____

A_____ v_____

M_____ or
e_____ v_____

P_____ O_____

E_____ P____

Rocks melt into m_____

E_____

P_____ P____

Summary The movement of plates created Japan with its mountains and volcanoes. They also cause volcanic eruptions and earthquakes which can destroy cities and leave many people dead.

Where do people live in Japan?

The population of Japan, as in most other countries, is not evenly spread out. This spread, or **distribution**, of people is shown on map **A**. As 87 per cent of Japan is mountainous, there are large areas where few people live. Most Japanese live in large towns and cities which are crowded onto narrow strips of flat land that lie next to the sea. These coastal areas are among the most **densely** populated regions in the world (photos **B** and **D**). Parts of central Tokyo have the highest population densities in the world (diagram **C**).

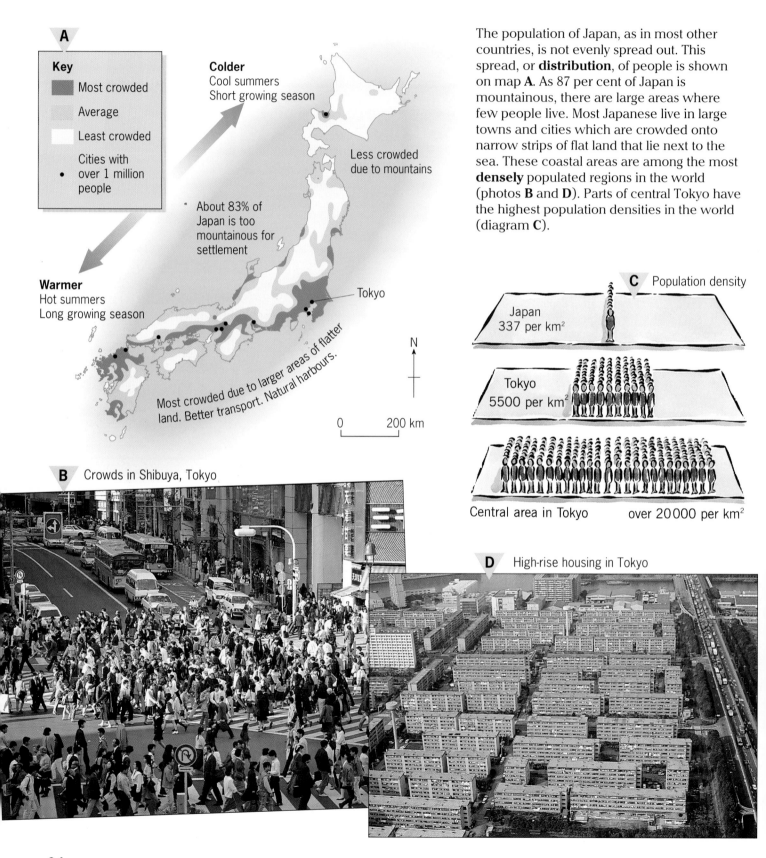

A

Key

- Most crowded
- Average
- Least crowded
- • Cities with over 1 million people

Colder
Cool summers
Short growing season

Less crowded due to mountains

About 83% of Japan is too mountainous for settlement

Warmer
Hot summers
Long growing season

Tokyo

Most crowded due to larger areas of flatter land. Better transport. Natural harbours.

N

0   200 km

C Population density

Japan
337 per km²

Tokyo
5500 per km²

Central area in Tokyo   over 20000 per km²

B Crowds in Shibuya, Tokyo

D High-rise housing in Tokyo

How is Japan's population changing?

The total population of Japan is increasing very slowly (graph **E**). In fact it is expected to decrease by the year 2020. Graph **F** shows that this slow increase was mainly due to a very low **birth rate** and an almost equally low **death rate**. Once birth rates fall below death rates then there will be a **natural decrease** in the population.

Japan's population problems

Japan's slow and declining increase in population is causing two major problems.

1 The low birth rate has resulted in small families. Small families are favoured because most Japanese houses are small and it is a very expensive country in which to bring up children. However, this means that Japan is becoming increasingly short of people of working age.

2 The falling death rate is producing an **ageing population**. Japanese people have the world's longest **life expectancy** (diagram **G**). This is mainly because they have the money to spend on health care and on healthy diets. Estimates suggest that one-quarter of Japanese people will be over the age of 65 by the year 2020. This is likely to put extra strain on the cost of health care.

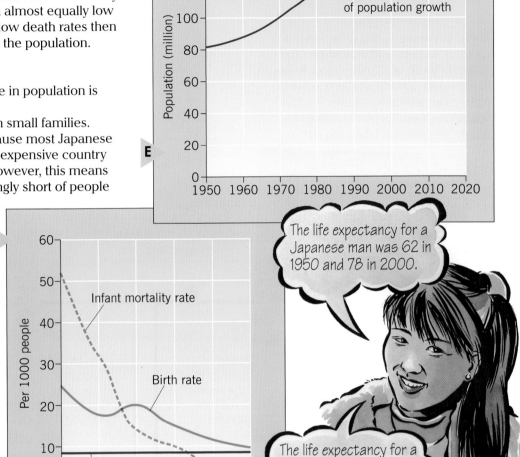

E Japan has a slow rate of population growth

F Infant mortality rate / Birth rate / Death rate

G The life expectancy for a Japanese man was 62 in 1950 and 78 in 2000.

The life expectancy for a Japanese woman was 66 in 1950 and 84 in 2000.

Activities

1 a) Which of the islands named on map **H** is the least crowded?
   b) Give three reasons why relatively few people live on this island.
   c) Why do many Japanese crowd into large cities?
   d) On which island are most of the largest cities?
   e) Give three reasons why most large cities are found on this island.

2 a) Make a copy of table **I**. Use the information given in diagrams **E**, **F** and **G** to complete it.
   b) Describe two problems caused by Japan's low birth rate and its increasing life expectancy.

H Hokkaido, Honshu, Shikoku, Kyushu

		1950	2000	Trend (rising or falling)
Total population				
Birth rate				
Death rate				
Infant mortality rate				
Life expectancy	males			
	Females			

I

Summary

Japan's population is uneven in its distribution and is one of the slowest growing in the world.

Japan — a land of contrasts

There are many contrasts in Japan's climate, scenery and way of life. The extreme south of Kyushu (map **A**) lies in the same latitude as Cairo in North Africa. This island has active volcanoes, tropical plants and a very warm, wet climate (diagram **B**).

The extreme north of Hokkaido lies in the same latitude as Milan in north Italy. The mountainous island has a cold climate (diagram **C**). Sapporo has an annual snow festival and hosted the 1972 Winter Olympics.

A

Hokkaido
Sapporo • **Nemuro**
Sea of Japan
Pacific Ocean
N
0   200 km
Honshu
Tokyo
Hiroshima   Osaka
Kyushu   **Kagoshima**
Shikoku

B

Coral islands off the south coast of Kyushu

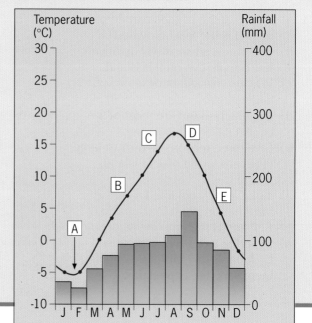

C

The snow-festival – Sapporo

Kagoshima (South Kyushu)
A Mild winters. Often clear skies.
B Cherry blossom (end of March). Early springs.
C Winds from Pacific Ocean.
D Typhoon season (September).
E Mild, pleasant autumns.

Nemuro (North Hokkaido)
A Very cold winters. Heavy snowfalls. Winds from Asia.
B Cherry blossom (mid-May). Late springs.
C Cool, relatively dry, summers.
D Typhoon season (September).
E Cool autumns. Often clear skies.

Honshu, the largest island, lies between Hokkaido and Kyushu. It has high mountains, large forests, many volcanoes and attractive lakes. Its climate is at its best during cherry blossom time in spring and when the leaves of trees change colour in autumn. Honshu is also the most populated island (page 94). It contains many traditional wooden castles, shrines and temples, as well as large modern cities such as Tokyo and Osaka.

D Mount Fuji and Lake Ashi

Itsukushima Shrine on Miyajima Island, near Hiroshima

E

Osaka Castle and high-rise office blocks **F**

G Central Tokyo

Activities

1 a) Copy and complete table **H** to show the differences in climate between Kyushu and Hokkaido.
  b) Why do cherry trees blossom in Kyushu six weeks before they do in Hokkaido?
  c) Give two reasons why Sapporo is a good place for Winter Olympics.

2 Imagine you are spending a few days on the Japanese island of Honshu. Write a postcard home describing
  a) the countryside,
  b) any traditional sites that you might have seen on your visit.

H

		Kyushu	Hokkaido
Temperature	January		
	July		
Rainfall	January		
	July		

Summary Japan is a land of contrasts. There are wide differences in the scenery and climate, and between the traditional and modern way of life.

The growth of Tokyo

Tokyo is one of the world's largest cities. Over 12 million people now live within Tokyo's city boundary, and 32 million within 50 kilometres of the city centre. It has grown so rapidly that is has become joined to several nearby urban areas.

Why was Tokyo a good site for a large settlement?

When we use the word **site** we mean the actual place where a town or city grew up. A site for a settlement was chosen if it had one or more natural advantages. The more natural advantages a place had the more likely it was to grow in size. As diagram **A** shows, Tokyo had many important natural advantages.

What are the functions of present day Tokyo?

For a small settlement to grow into a large city it had to have several specific purposes. Each of these purposes is known as a **function**. As shown in diagram **D**, Tokyo has several functions. It is a major port and industrial centre. It has many high-rise buildings (photo **B**). Most of these belong to big financial firms or are used by the government. Within Tokyo there are several large shopping centres (photo **C**), universities and places of entertainment.

A Growth of Tokyo

Tokyo (pale grey) built on the largest area of flat land in Japan

In early days several rivers (grey green) gave water supply

Much land (pale cream) has been reclaimed from the sea

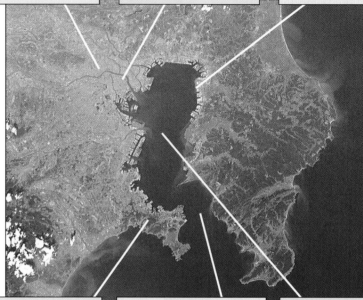

Highland (dark green) – difficult for settlement

Narrow entrance to bay gives protection from severe storms (typhoons)

Tokyo Bay (deep blue) – a deep harbour for large ships

C A busy shopping centre

High-rise government buildings **B**

98

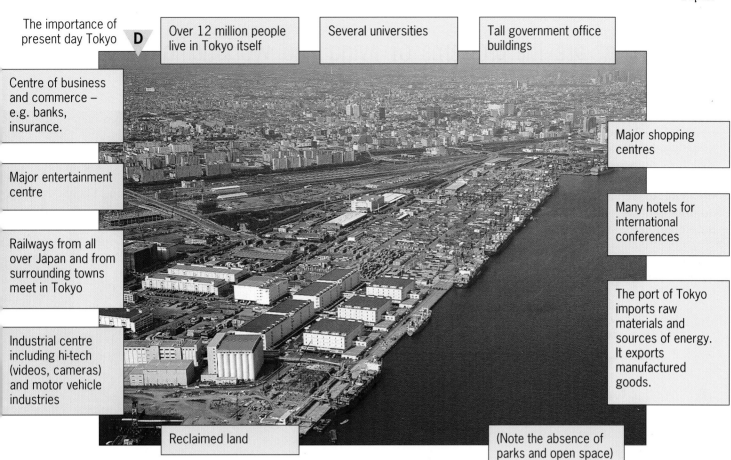

The importance of present day Tokyo **D**

Over 12 million people live in Tokyo itself

Several universities

Tall government office buildings

Centre of business and commerce – e.g. banks, insurance.

Major shopping centres

Major entertainment centre

Many hotels for international conferences

Railways from all over Japan and from surrounding towns meet in Tokyo

The port of Tokyo imports raw materials and sources of energy. It exports manufactured goods.

Industrial centre including hi-tech (videos, cameras) and motor vehicle industries

Reclaimed land

(Note the absence of parks and open space)

Activities

1 a) Write down the meaning of the word 'site'.
 b) Copy and complete diagram **E** by giving five reasons why Tokyo was a good site for a large city.

2 a) Write down the meaning of the word 'function'.
 b) List at least six functions of present day Tokyo.

3 Diagram **F** is a landsketch based on photo **D**. Make a copy of the diagram. Add to it the following labels:
 ● Tokyo
 ● Tokyo Bay
 ● Port
 ● Reclaimed land
 ● High-rise office buildings
 ● Main railways and roads.

4 Why do you think land in Tokyo Bay needs to be reclaimed?

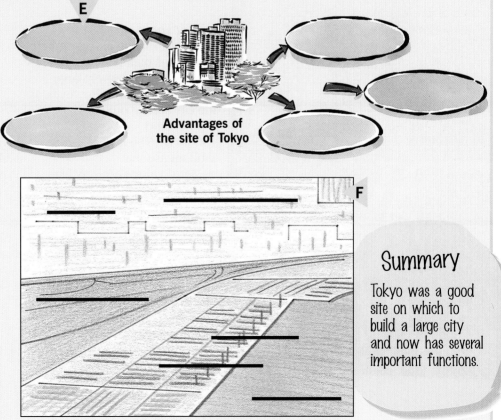

Advantages of the site of Tokyo E

F

Summary

Tokyo was a good site on which to build a large city and now has several important functions.

99

What are the problems of living and working in Tokyo?

Tokyo is the richest and one of the busiest cities in the world (photo **A**). Its well-paid jobs and exciting life-style have attracted large numbers of people from surrounding areas. However, wealth and the large number of new-comers to Tokyo have created major problems.

A

'Tokyo is a rapidly growing, rapidly changing city. It is exciting, stimulating and safe. Fast-paced, energetic and busy, the city rarely seems to rest.'
Tourist Guide for Tokyo

B The city of Tokyo

Lack of space

Flat land in Japan is very limited. Tokyo was built in one of the few places with a relatively large amount of flat land. However, as the city spread outwards, most of this flat land has been built upon (photo **B**). The lack of usable land means that

- **land values** are very high. High land values mean that it costs a lot of money to buy or rent a piece of land. In parts of Tokyo the price of land can double within a year. Central Tokyo has the highest land values in the world.
- smaller, older buildings have been pulled down and replaced by taller, modern buildings.
- most houses are small in size. Many only have one main room and lack gardens.
- land has to be **reclaimed** from Tokyo Bay for new factories, port facilities and housing (Fact File **D**).
- there is very little **open space**, apart from the area around the Imperial Palace.

Threat of earthquakes

In 1923 an earthquake, and the fires which followed, killed 140 000 people in Tokyo. For many years after this new buildings **had** to be less than 33 metres in height. This law no longer exists due to the rapid rise in land values and improvements in constructing earthquake-proof buildings.

The main government offices are in a building 233 metres in height. They have yet to be tested by a big earthquake. However, as Tokyo has had a major earthquake every 70 to 80 years, another big one is due at any time.

Congestion and pollution

Commuters are people who travel to work. Over 2 million people commute into central Tokyo each day. For many of them the journey can take up to two hours each way. Railway lines have often been built either underground or above existing roads. Railways and expressways become congested at peak times.

Tokyo's road traffic and factories create noise and air pollution. Its inhabitants produce huge amounts of waste. This waste is either burnt or is dumped in Tokyo Bay where it creates more land. Tokyo has several ambitious plans based upon the infilling of parts of Tokyo Bay. One such scheme is described in Fact File **D**.

Fact File - Tokyo Teleport Town

☑ **Plan** To form a new island of 400 hectares. The new area of flat land to be created from disposed waste and through dredging the sea-bed.

☑ **Transport** New road bridge. Ten minutes by subway train to central Tokyo.

☑ **On completion** An International Convention Park, Business Centre, 100 000 jobs (mainly in computers),

C Rush hour for Japanese commuters

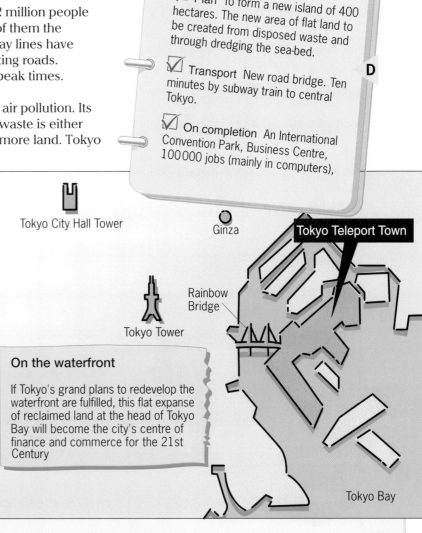

Tokyo City Hall Tower

Ginza

Tokyo Teleport Town

Rainbow Bridge

Tokyo Tower

On the waterfront

If Tokyo's grand plans to redevelop the waterfront are fulfilled, this flat expanse of reclaimed land at the head of Tokyo Bay will become the city's centre of finance and commerce for the 21st Century

Tokyo Bay

Activities

1 a) What do we mean by the term 'land values'?
   b) Why are land values in Tokyo the highest in the world?

2 Diagram **E** gives the results of a 'Public Opinion Survey on Urban Improvement in Tokyo'. Describe the **causes** of each of the five types of problem referred to in the survey.

3 Describe how the Teleport Town scheme aims to reduce Tokyo's problems of
   a) shortage of land,
   b) travel (commuting) to work,
   c) lack of housing.
   What type of jobs does the scheme hope to create?

E Public opinion survey on urban improvement in Tokyo

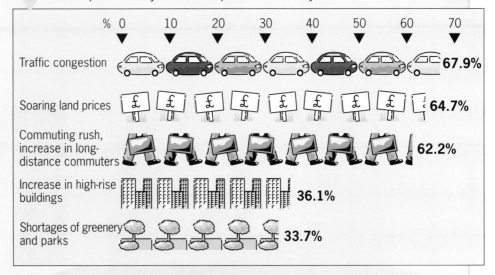

%	0	10	20	30	40	50	60	70	
Traffic congestion									67.9%
Soaring land prices									64.7%
Commuting rush, increase in long-distance commuters									62.2%
Increase in high-rise buildings									36.1%
Shortages of greenery and parks									33.7%

Summary Tokyo's rapid growth has created many problems. These include high land values, congestion, pollution and a lack of open space.

101

Life in rural Kyushu

Kyushu is the warmest of the main Japanese islands. It is also the one which is furthest away from Tokyo. Much of Kyushu is still mainly rural and many people still live in traditional houses (diagram **A**).

Farming
Akira and Chika, like many other people in rural Kyushu, live on a farm.

A

Konnichiwa, ogenki desula!

That is Japanese for 'Hello. How are you'. Our names are Akira and Chika. We live on a farm in Kyushu. Our house there is typical of many still found in rural areas of Japan.

The outside walls are made of wood while the roof is usually made either from tiles or thatch. The entrance hall has a wooden floor. We have to remove our shoes in the hallway and put on slippers before we enter the rest of the house. Apart from the kitchen, the floors of all our rooms are covered in **tatami**. Tatami are mats made of woven rushes. The inside walls of most rooms are usually sliding doors which we call **shoji**. They can be opened to make a larger room or to let in fresh air during the hot summers.

At meal times we sit cross-legged on floor cushions at a low table. Our main meal is in the evening and it often consists of several courses. Before we go to bed the room has to be cleared. We then lay large mattresses, or **futons**, on the floor ready for us to sleep on. In the morning these are rolled up and stored in large cupboards. Because many houses are small, we often have to use the same room for living, eating and sleeping. Fortunately, few Japanese families have more than two children and so our small houses do not seem to be too overcrowded.

kakejiku (hanging scrolls)

butsudan (family shrine)

Futons stored away during daytime

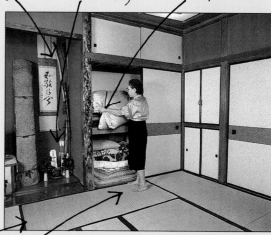

shoji (sliding doors)

Tatami (matting)

No shoes. Removed on entry to the house.

They are expected to help their parents at busy times of the year. However, like many others of their age, Akira and Chika want to find work in a city and do not want to have their own farm.

We have already seen that the amount of flat land in Japan is limited. Most farms are therefore small in size and have to be farmed **intensively**. Intensive farming is when the maximum use is made of the land and no space is wasted. By using fertiliser and modern machinery

Japanese farmers are able to grow as much as possible on each hectare of land. The warm, wet Kyushu climate also allows two crops to be grown in the same field every year. Rice has always been the most important crop in Japan (diagram **B**). However, the Japanese are now eating a wider diet, especially Western food. As a result rice production has fallen considerably. As most farmers grow less rice they now grow more fruit and vegetables.

B Rice Growing

1 Cultivators are used to plough the land

2 Tractors prepare the paddies (rice fields)

3 Seedlings are grown in greenhouses

4 Seedlings are planted in the paddies

5 Herbicides and fertilisers are spread

6 Binders harvest the rice

Rice fields

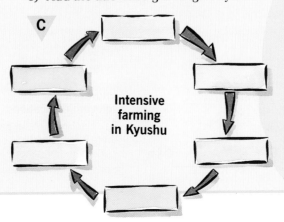

Harvesting rice

Activities

1 Imagine you are either Akira or Chika. Write a letter to a friend who lives in Tokyo. In your letter describe your house and explain how you try to save space within it.

2 a) What is meant by the term 'intensive farming'?
  b) Why is farming in Kyushu intensive?

3 a) Make a larger copy of diagram **C**.
  b) Complete it using information given in diagram **B**.
  c) Add the title 'Rice growing in Kyushu'.

C

Intensive farming in Kyushu

Summary

Most houses and farms in Kyushu, as elsewhere in rural Japan, are small in size. This means maximum use has to be made of space in the house and land on the farm.

103

Recent changes in Kyushu

Industry began to develop rapidly in Japan after 1950. The main industrial areas were around Tokyo and other large cities on the main island of Honshu. Places furthest away from Tokyo, like Kyushu, tended not to become industrialised. Even as late as the 1980s many people living on Kyushu were still farmers.

Since 1990 there has been a decline, or a **recession**, in industry across the world. Even Japan has been affected by this recession. Yet at this same time industry has developed rapidly in Kyushu causing a decline in the importance of farming. Diagram **A** gives some of the many reasons why industry has been attracted to Kyushu. For example,

- during the 1980s many of Japan's largest electronic firms built factories there;
- in the early 1990s car firms (Toyota and Nissan) opened assembly plants on the island.

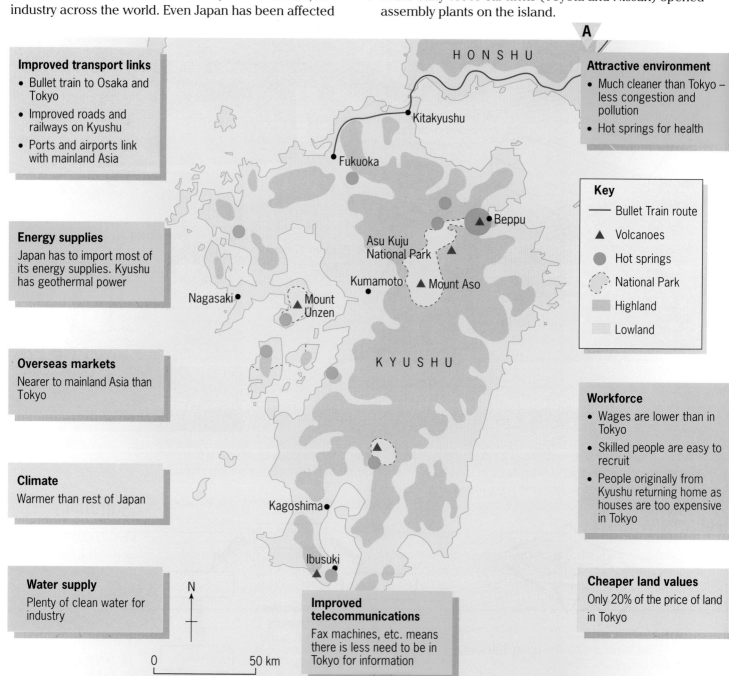

A

Improved transport links
- Bullet train to Osaka and Tokyo
- Improved roads and railways on Kyushu
- Ports and airports link with mainland Asia

Energy supplies
Japan has to import most of its energy supplies. Kyushu has geothermal power

Overseas markets
Nearer to mainland Asia than Tokyo

Climate
Warmer than rest of Japan

Water supply
Plenty of clean water for industry

Improved telecommunications
Fax machines, etc. means there is less need to be in Tokyo for information

Attractive environment
- Much cleaner than Tokyo – less congestion and pollution
- Hot springs for health

Key
- ——— Bullet Train route
- ▲ Volcanoes
- ● Hot springs
- National Park
- Highland
- Lowland

Workforce
- Wages are lower than in Tokyo
- Skilled people are easy to recruit
- People originally from Kyushu returning home as houses are too expensive in Tokyo

Cheaper land values
Only 20% of the price of land in Tokyo

HONSHU

Kitakyushu

Fukuoka

Beppu

Asu Kuju National Park

Kumamoto

Mount Aso

Nagasaki

Mount Unzen

KYUSHU

Kagoshima

Ibusuki

N

0   50 km

B Geothermal steam at Beppu

C

A hot sand bath at Ibusuki

A second change has been the growth of tourism. Diagram **D** suggests why people living and working in Tokyo might want to visit Kyushu.

D

I want to see the active volcanoes in the National Parks

The air is cleaner and the sky clearer than in Tokyo

I want to visit the health spas and bathe in the hot sands

I want to see the cherry blossom in early Spring and the changing leaves in Autumn

The climate is warmer in winter and more healthy all year than in Tokyo

Activities

1 Look at the captions in diagram **E**. Explain how each caption has helped to attract industry to Kyushu.

E

Overseas markets

Climate

Land values

Environment

Energy supplies

Transport

Workforce

2 Imagine you are having a short holiday in Kyushu. Write a postcard to a friend in Tokyo. Describe the weather, things you have seen and things you have done during your visit.

3 List some of the ways in which you think that living in Kyushu today is different to living there twenty years ago. You may need to refer to pages 98 to 101 to answer this question.

Summary

Kyushu has recently attracted many new industries and an increasing number of tourists.

Two regions compared

As we have seen, there are considerable differences between Tokyo and Kyushu. The Tokyo region is almost totally built up. It is an urban area with very little open space. Kyushu, in contrast, is mainly rural. There are, however, several cities in the north of the island which are now growing rapidly. As diagram **A** shows, for every person living in one square kilometre in Kyushu, there are 17.5 in Tokyo.

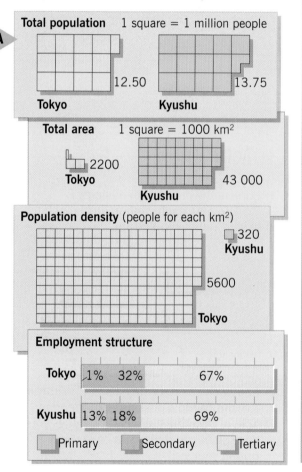

A

Total population 1 square = 1 million people

12.50 Tokyo   13.75 Kyushu

Total area 1 square = 1000 km²

2200 Tokyo   43 000 Kyushu

Population density (people for each km²)

320 Kyushu

5600 Tokyo

Employment structure

Tokyo 1% 32% 67%

Kyushu 13% 18% 69%

Primary Secondary Tertiary

B

Childhood years	Marriage

1 In Tokyo

With their father at work and rarely home, city children tend to spend most of their time with their mother. In homes in which both parents work, some children must look after the house until their parents come home.

Big cities are full of paved roads and have few parks. Few children have anywhere outside to play. As a result, video games and other indoor amusements are popular.

It is expensive to support a family in the big cities, where the prices of houses, food and clothes are high. The Japanese are having to marry later. In Tokyo it is usual for both husband and wife to have jobs.

2 In Kyushu

Because the parents in a farming household are extremely busy, the children are normally raised by the grandparents.

In farming communities, located in a rich natural environment, children swim in rivers, collect insects and amuse themselves. Few will stay closed up indoors.

The problem in Kyushu is a shortage of young women. This is because many move to big cities to study or to find work.

Activities

1 a) Make a larger copy of Fact File **C**.
   b) Write the correct word or number from the bracket in each box.
   c) Using your completed Fact File, write five sentences to show differences between the two regions.

C

Fact File

		Tokyo	Kyushu
Population	(most or least) (12.5 or 13.75)	.... million	.... million
Area	(larger or smaller) (2 200 or 43000)	.... km²	.... km²
Population density	(higher or lower) (5 600 or 320)	.... per km²	.... per km²
Primary jobs	(more or fewer) (1 or 13)	.... %	.... %
Secondary jobs	(more or fewer) (32 or 18)	.... %	.... %

The way of life in each region is very different (diagram **B**). Tokyo has many high-rise buildings, office blocks, factories, shops, places of entertainment, roads and railways. The people who live there have one of the highest standards of living in the world. Despite recent industrial growth, Kyushu has relatively few large urban areas. It has mountains, active volcanoes, hot springs, an attractive coastline and several National Parks. Although its standard of living is lower than Tokyo, it is still high compared with most other places in the world.

Children	Getting to work	At work	Retirement	Elderly years
The higher standard of living and the desire for an expensive house, car and holidays has led to a fall in the birth rate. An increasing number of couples are choosing not to have children.	Because the majority of business-people commute into Tokyo, the morning and evening rush hours are deadly to say the least. Many people use much of their energy just getting to work.	Most jobs in central Tokyo are in offices. Many companies expect people to work until late at night and to report to work in holiday time. Few people change jobs.	For businesspeople who put work before their private lives, retirement can be quite a shock. Many Japanese use retirement as an opportunity to begin a totally new lifestyle.	More elderly Japanese are choosing to spend their later years in retirement homes or in overseas resorts. An increasing number of senior citizens live apart from their children, passing lonely years in city apartments.
Farming communities continue to have a deep-rooted sense of 'the more children the better', and so the birth rate is comparatively high. Having a son who will take over the family farm is considered to be very important.	Many farmers are now employed in work other than agriculture. There is a vast number of such households in Japan today, where the grandparents and wife are now the main farmers.	Young people who remain in the country must help out with farm work. Most end up spending their entire lives in these communities. Eventually they will take over the family farm from their parents.	As long as there is land, there will be no such thing as 'retirement' on the farm. The movement of young people to the cities has caused middle-aged farmers to take other jobs to supplement their income, and farm work is increasingly being done by the elderly.	The main responsibility of elderly people on the farm is to take care of their grandchildren. However, as the children leave home, many older couples find themselves living lonely lives in country houses.

2 Describe the differences in the way of life between the following groups of people living in Tokyo and Kyushu.
  a) Children (under 15 years)
  b) Young couples (20–30 years)
  c) Middle aged people (30–60 years)
  d) Elderly people (over 60 years)

3 Imagine that you are a writer for a geographical magazine. Write two short articles of about 100 words each to describe the main features of
  a) Tokyo
  b) Kyushu.
You should refer to any information given in this unit.

Summary

Living and working in Tokyo is very different to living and working in Kyushu.

Sustainable development in Japan

In the last few years the term 'sustainable development' has become popular in geography. It is not an easy term to explain. If you refer back to pages 16 and 17 you will see that different people use the term in different ways. Ideally, sustainable development should lead to an improvement in people's:

- **quality of life** – how content they are with their way of life;
- **standard of living** – how well-off they are economically.

These improvements should be achieved without wasting the earth's resources or destroying the environment. They should not, therefore, just be of benefit to people living today, but also for future generations.

Energy supplies in Japan

Japan has become the world's richest industrialised country. Industry needs many raw materials and uses large supplies of energy. Strangely, Japan has very few raw materials of its own and has very limited energy supplies. This means that it has to rely upon other countries to provide **natural resources**. As diagram **A** shows, natural resources can be divided into two groups. Unfortunately, 87 per cent of Japan's energy comes from **non-renewable** sources, and that means non-sustainable sources. It would appear desirable, from a sustainable development point of view, that Japan should try to develop more of its **renewable** forms of energy such as **hydro-electricity** and **geothermal** (graph **B**).

The Nagara River

The Nagara River flows into the Pacific Ocean to the west of Nagoya (map **C**). In 1990, it was one of the last free-flowing rivers in Japan. Since then a construction company has been building a huge dam across the river. The dam is over 600 metres wide. It will create a huge reservoir of fresh water for nearby cities and industries. Although in many parts of the world the storage of water is seen as an example of sustainable development, the Nagara River scheme has become a major controversy within Japan.

Non-renewable resources are those which can only be used once. Non-renewable resources include coal, oil and natural gas. Many pollute the environment. In time these resources will run out. They are, therefore, non-sustainable.

Renewable resources can be used over and over again. Renewable resources include hydro-electricity and geothermal power. As they will not run out or pollute the environment, they are sustainable.

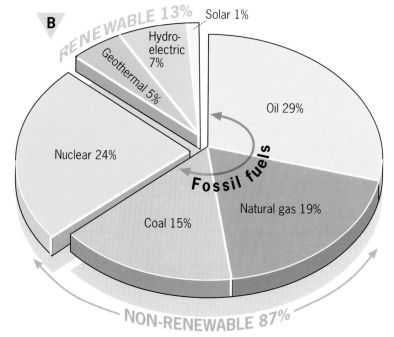

B

RENEWABLE 13%

Solar 1%

Hydro-electric 7%

Geothermal 5%

Oil 29%

Nuclear 24%

Fossil fuels

Natural gas 19%

Coal 15%

NON-RENEWABLE 87%

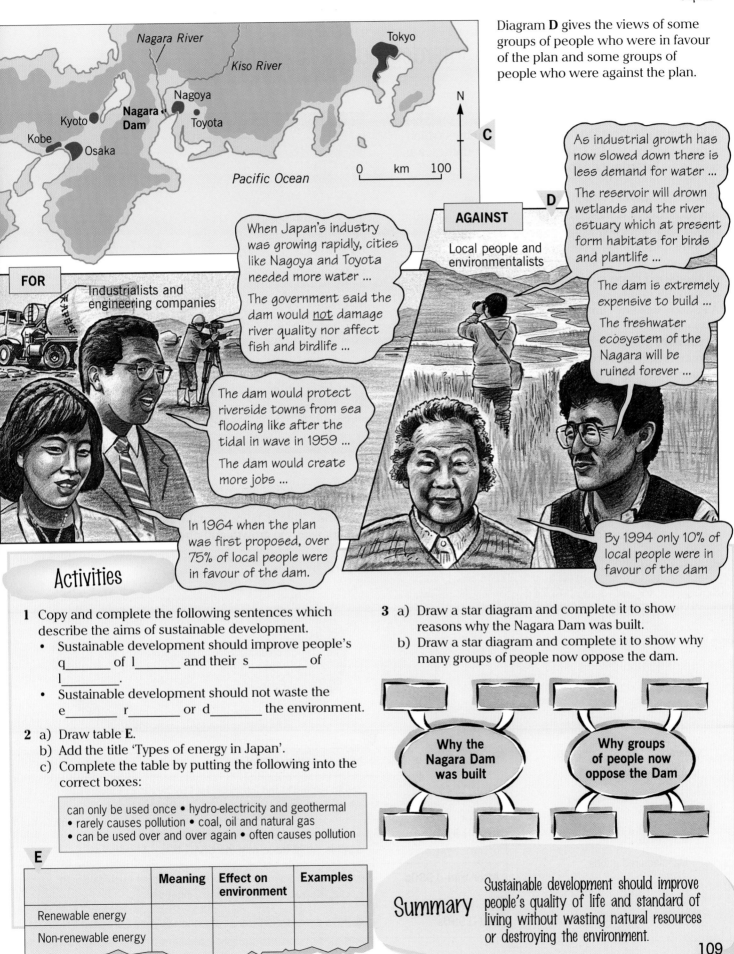

Diagram **D** gives the views of some groups of people who were in favour of the plan and some groups of people who were against the plan.

Activities

1 Copy and complete the following sentences which describe the aims of sustainable development.
- Sustainable development should improve people's q_____ of l_____ and their s_____ of l_____.
- Sustainable development should not waste the e_____ r_____ or d_____ the environment.

2 a) Draw table **E**.
  b) Add the title 'Types of energy in Japan'.
  c) Complete the table by putting the following into the correct boxes:

  can only be used once • hydro-electricity and geothermal • rarely causes pollution • coal, oil and natural gas • can be used over and over again • often causes pollution

3 a) Draw a star diagram and complete it to show reasons why the Nagara Dam was built.
  b) Draw a star diagram and complete it to show why many groups of people now oppose the dam.

E

	Meaning	Effect on environment	Examples
Renewable energy			
Non-renewable energy			

Summary Sustainable development should improve people's quality of life and standard of living without wasting natural resources or destroying the environment.

How interdependent is Japan?

Countries need to work together if they are to progress and improve their standards of living. Countries which work together, or which rely upon other countries, are said to be **interdependent**.

One of the ways in which countries become interdependent is by selling and buying from each other. No country has everything that its people want or need. To provide these things a country will have to exchange goods and materials with other countries. This exchange of goods and materials is called **trade**.

A country will buy (**import**) things which it lacks. These may either be
- **primary goods**, such as foodstuffs and minerals, which are often low in value, or
- **manufactured goods**, such as machinery, which are high in value.

In order to pay for these a country has to sell (**export**) goods of which it has a surplus. Ideally a country aims to have a **trade surplus**. This means that it earns more money from its exports than it spends on its imports.

Japan's trade surplus is one of the biggest in the world (graph **A**). Its trade is typical of many economically more developed countries (graph **B**). Most of its imports are relatively low value foodstuffs and minerals. Most of its

exports are higher value manufactured goods. Japan is therefore able to loan money to, and invest in, other countries. This all helps to make Japan richer. Table **C** summarises the growth and direction of Japan's trade.

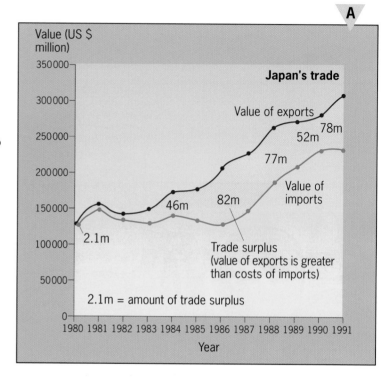

A

Japan's trade

Value of exports

78m
52m
77m

46m   82m

Value of imports

2.1m

Trade surplus (value of exports is greater than costs of imports)

2.1m = amount of trade surplus

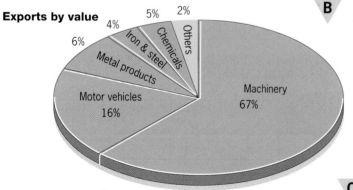

Exports by value

B

- Machinery 67%
- Motor vehicles 16%
- Metal products 6%
- Iron & steel 4%
- Chemicals 5%
- Others 2%

Others / Primary goods / Manufactured goods

Imports by value

- Others 13%
- Wood 3%
- Minerals 4%
- Textiles 4%
- Chemical products 7%
- Foodstuffs 15%
- Machinery 18%
- Energy supplies (fuels) 36%

C

Before World War II	Little trade with rest of world.
After 1945	Japan begins to industrialise; had to import raw materials which were used to make goods needed in Japan.
After 1970	Japan exports more than it imports – this is called a trade surplus. Most trade with the USA.
After mid–1980s	Increase in trade with 'Pacific Rim' countries such as South Korea, Taiwan, Hong Kong and Singapore.
Mid–1990s	World's third largest trader afterthe USA and European Union (EU)

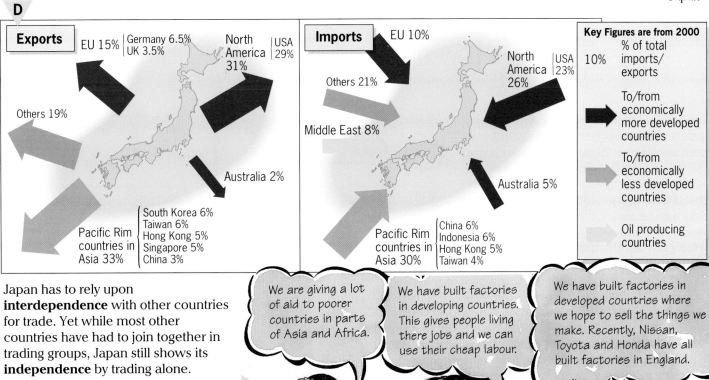

Japan has to rely upon **interdependence** with other countries for trade. Yet while most other countries have had to join together in trading groups, Japan still shows its **independence** by trading alone.

Japan's trade surplus has meant an increase in wealth. Some of this wealth is now being used overseas as shown in diagram **E**.

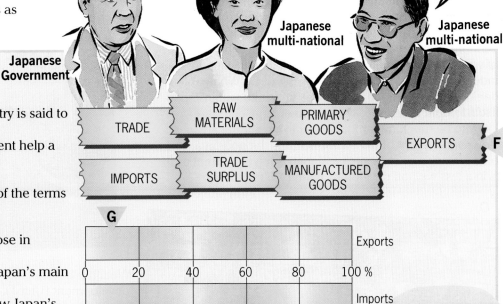

Activities

1 a) What is meant when a country is said to be interdependent?
  b) How can being interdependent help a country?

2 Explain what is meant by each of the terms in diagram **F**.

3 a) Draw two bar graphs like those in diagram **G**.
  b) Complete the first to show Japan's main exports.
  c) Complete the second to show Japan's main imports.
  d) On each graph colour raw materials (minerals and foodstuffs) in green and manufactured goods in red.
  e) How do your completed graphs account for Japan's trade surplus?

4 a) Make a copy of table **H**.
  b) Complete the table by ranking in order the countries to which Japan exports most goods and the countries from which Japan imports most goods.

Rank order	Exports to	Imports from
1		
2		
3		
4		
5		
6		

Summary

The need to import raw materials and foodstuffs and to export manufactured goods has made Japan increasingly interdependent.

How developed is Japan?

You should now be aware that there are many differences between living in Japan and in other countries such as the United Kingdom. These differences may include ethnic backgrounds, dress, housing, religion, language, jobs and wealth. You will also be aware that different countries are at different levels of **development**. However, development is not an easy term to define. To many people development means how rich a country is and how high a standard of living it has. To make comparisons between countries easier, the wealth of a country is given by its **gross national product (GNP)**. Remember that GNP per person is the amount of money earned by a country divided by its total population. Based upon wealth, countries are said to be either **economically more developed** or **economically less developed**.

Table **A** gives the GNP for several countries including those referred to in this book. Because Japan has the highest GNP it could, therefore, be described as the richest country and the one which is the most economically developed. Certainly, extremely high levels of wealth and technology can be seen in both Japanese industry and every day life (photos **B** and **C**). What table **A** does not show, are the differences in wealth within Japan itself. People living in Tokyo and other large cities are likely to be much richer than those living in rural areas. However, the gap between the rich and the poor in a well-off developed country such as Japan is never as great as it is in a less well-off developing country like Kenya.

A

Country	GNP (US$)	Country	GNP (US$)
Japan (Richest)	39 640	Brazil	3 640
USA	26 980	Kenya	280
Italy	19 020	India	340
UK	18 700	Mozambique (Poorest)	80

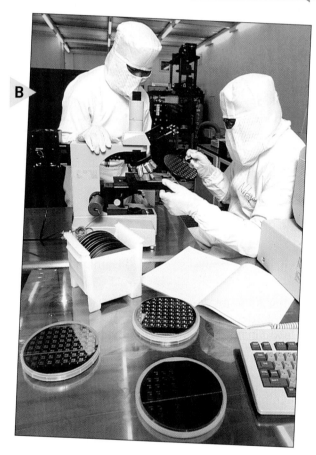

Wealth is not the only way to measure (or describe) development (Unit 1). Differences in development between countries can also be seen by looking at
- population measures such as birth rates, death rates, infant mortality rates and life expectancy;
- levels of health, education, jobs and trade (diagram **D**).

Yet each of these measures can in turn be linked to the wealth of a country. The richer a country the more money it will have to spend on such things as schools, universities, health care and birth control. It will also be more likely to have a modern transport system, high-tech industries, and to have become more interdependent.

D

Jobs	Trade	Population	Health	Education
Most Japanese are employed in manufacturing industries or in providing services. Very few are farmers or work in primary activities.	Japan has a large volume of trade. It imports foodstuffs and minerals at a low price. It exports large amounts of higher value manufactured goods.	Japan has a low birth rate, few young children dying (low infant mortality) and the longest life expectancy in the world. It has a very slow population increase compared with a developing country.	Japan has much wealth which it spends on training doctors and nurses, and in providing hospitals and medicines.	Japan also spends a lot of money on education. Children have to work hard to pass exams to get into better schools and to university. The literacy rate is 100%.

Although standards of living in Japan are very high, does the same apply to the quality of life? On the one hand levels of crime are very low and concern for the environment is now very high. On the other hand there are considerable pressures placed upon Japanese children and workers to succeed (diagram **E**).

Japan chose rapid industrialisation as the way to develop. This has brought wealth and economic success to the country and to most of its people. The Japanese have been prepared to sacrifice their quality of life in order to improve their standard of living.

E

Children, even under the age of 10, have lots of homework and often, in cities, have to attend extra classes at night. Older children have to work very hard to get to university. Workers work long hours, have few holidays and are expected to work when told.

Our crime rate is one of the lowest in the world. People are usually safe as is their property. We now have strong conservation laws protecting our scenery, forest and wildlife.

F

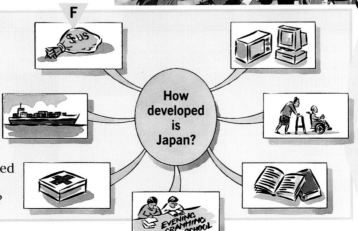

Activities

1 Explain how each of the seven measures shown in diagram **F** indicate that Japan is a rich and an economically well developed country.

2 How have the Japanese 'sacrificed their quality of life in order to improve their standard of living'?

How developed is Japan?

EVENING CRAMMING SCHOOL

Summary

The rapid industrial growth of Japan since 1945 has led to the country now being the most economically developed in the world.

6 The United Kingdom

What are the UK's main features?

First of all what is the **UK**? The UK is short for the **United Kingdom** a country made up of England, Wales, Scotland and Northern Ireland. This country is governed by the Parliament at Westminster in London which is attended by members from all four countries.

Within this system however, each country has a certain amount of self rule and is able to develop its own distinct characteristics. Scotland for example has its own education system, legal system and its own forms of local government. Wales has its own language and Northern Ireland separate laws and a distinct system of education.

A

The British Isles is made up of two large islands and many smaller ones.

Great Britain is the largest of the islands. It is sometimes just called Britain. It is divided into three parts – England, Wales and Scotland.

Ireland is the other large island. It is divided into two parts – Northern Ireland and the Republic of Ireland.

The United Kingdom is made up of England, Wales, Scotland and Northern Ireland.

The Republic of Ireland is a separate country with its own government. Until 1921 it was part of the UK.

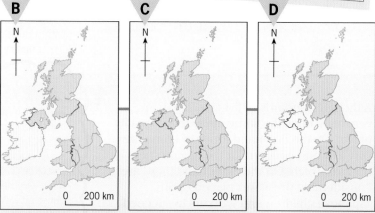

Activities

1 Give a title to each of the maps **B**, **C** and **D**. Choose your titles from box **A** above.

2 Complete the crossword using the clues below. All of the answers can be found on map **E** opposite.

  1 The Channel between England and France.
  2 A Scottish river that starts in the Southern Uplands.
  3 A capital city on the River Thames.
  4 An island off the south coast of England.
  5 A city on the River Clyde.
  6 The capital city of Northern Ireland.
  7 An island off the north coast of Wales.
  8 A river with its source in the Cotswolds.
  9 A city in the north east of Scotland.
  10 The ocean west of Scotland.
  11 A mountain range in Scotland.
  12 The sea to the east of Britain.
  13 A river flowing into the Bristol Channel.
  14 A city in north east England.
  15 A highland area of northern England.
  16 The sea between England and Ireland.
  17 The capital city of Wales.

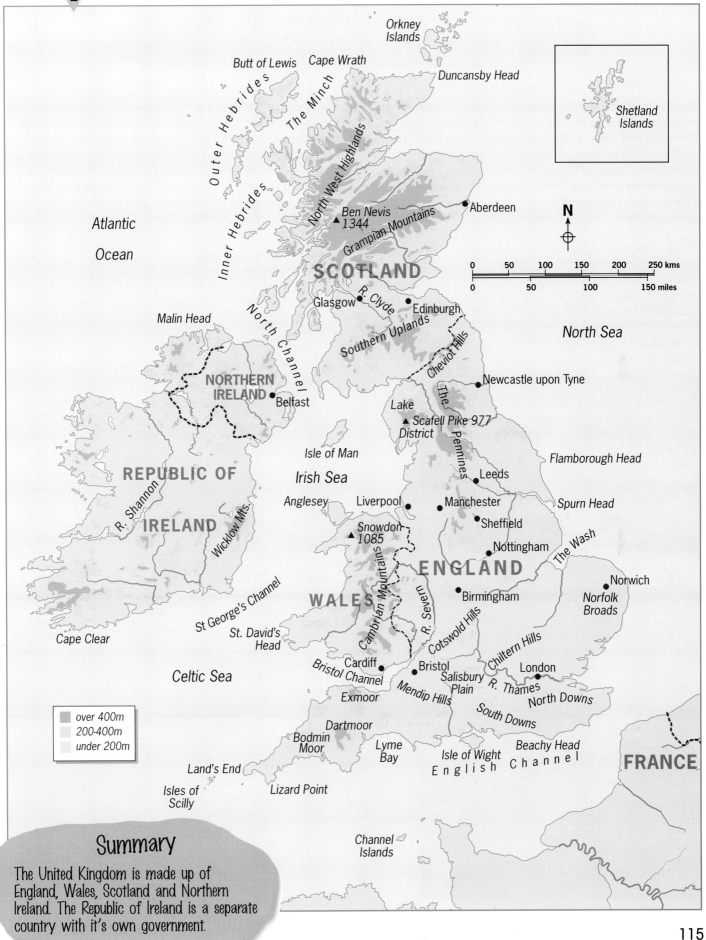

E

Orkney Islands

Butt of Lewis Cape Wrath Duncansby Head

Outer Hebrides

The Minch

Shetland Islands

Atlantic

Ocean

Inner Hebrides

North West Highlands

Ben Nevis ▲ 1344

Grampian Mountains

● Aberdeen

N

SCOTLAND

0   50   100   150   200   250 kms

0   50   100   150 miles

North Channel

Glasgow ● R. Clyde

● Edinburgh

North Sea

Malin Head

Southern Uplands

Cheviot Hills

NORTHERN
IRELAND

● Belfast

Newcastle upon Tyne

Lake
District

▲ Scafell Pike 977

The Pennines

REPUBLIC OF

Isle of Man

Irish Sea

Flamborough Head

IRELAND

R. Shannon

Leeds ●

Anglesey   Liverpool ●

Manchester ●

Spurn Head

Wicklow Mts.

● Sheffield

Snowdon
▲ 1085

Nottingham ●

The Wash

Cambrian Mountains

ENGLAND

Norwich ●

WALES

R. Severn

Birmingham ●

Norfolk
Broads

St George's Channel

Cotswold Hills

Chiltern Hills

Cape Clear

St. David's
Head

Cardiff ●   Bristol ●

London ●

Celtic Sea

Bristol Channel

Salisbury
Plain

R. Thames

North Downs

Exmoor

Mendip Hills

South Downs

Dartmoor

Beachy Head

Bodmin
Moor

Lyme
Bay

Isle of Wight

English   Channel

FRANCE

Land's End

Isles of
Scilly

Lizard Point

Channel
Islands

over 400m
200-400m
under 200m

Summary

The United Kingdom is made up of
England, Wales, Scotland and Northern
Ireland. The Republic of Ireland is a separate
country with it's own government.

What are the UK's main physical features?

The UK is a fairly small country yet it has a remarkable variety of **landscapes**. The most mountainous areas are in the north and west. The older rocks that are found here tend to be more resistant to **erosion** and so form widespread areas of highland. Over millions of years, this highland has gradually been worn away by water and ice. The resulting landscape is one of rugged mountain peaks and long, steep-sided valleys.

The south and east of the UK is very different. Most of this area was once covered by a shallow sea. Vast amounts of material were carried from the land to the sea and **deposited** on the sea floor along with the skeletons and remains of dead sea creatures. Gradually this material hardened to form layers of rock which were later raised above sea level. As these layers tilted and folded they formed the hills, valleys and rolling plains that are typical of this area.

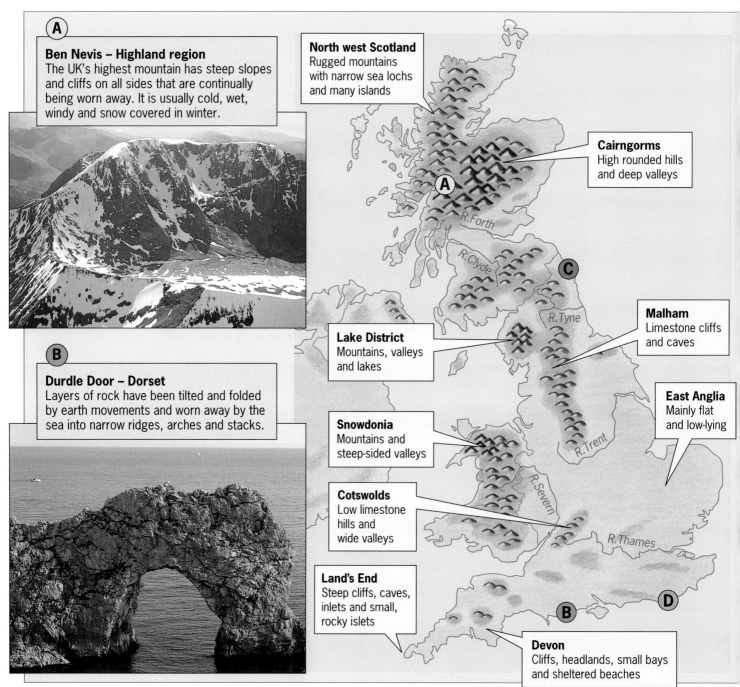

A

Ben Nevis – Highland region
The UK's highest mountain has steep slopes and cliffs on all sides that are continually being worn away. It is usually cold, wet, windy and snow covered in winter.

North west Scotland
Rugged mountains with narrow sea lochs and many islands

Cairngorms
High rounded hills and deep valleys

R.Forth

R.Clyde

C

R.Tyne

Malham
Limestone cliffs and caves

Lake District
Mountains, valleys and lakes

East Anglia
Mainly flat and low-lying

B

Durdle Door – Dorset
Layers of rock have been tilted and folded by earth movements and worn away by the sea into narrow ridges, arches and stacks.

Snowdonia
Mountains and steep-sided valleys

R.Trent

Cotswolds
Low limestone hills and wide valleys

R.Severn

R.Thames

Land's End
Steep cliffs, caves, inlets and small, rocky islets

B

D

Devon
Cliffs, headlands, small bays and sheltered beaches

116

The UK coastline is over 11,000 km long and has as great a variety of scenery as inland Britain. **Erosion** landforms such as **cliffs**, **caves**, **arches** and **stacks** are the most spectacular coastal features. Other attractive landforms are **beaches**, **sand dunes** and **spits**. These are examples of **deposition** landforms and are formed when material from one part of the coast has been **transported** and dropped somewhere else.

C

Northumberland coast
Long sandy beaches backed by sand dunes and outcrops of volcanic rock on which castles like this one at Bamburgh have been built.

D

The Seven Sisters – Sussex
A landscape of gently rolling hills and dry valleys with high chalk cliffs under constant attack by the sea at their base.

Activities

1 As a geographer you should be building up your geographical vocabulary. Write down the meaning of the following terms. The Glossary at the back of the book will help you.

   a) Physical features   f) Arch
   b) Landscape   g) Stack
   c) Erosion   h) Beach
   d) Deposition   i) Sand dune
   e) Transportation   j) Spit

2 Look at the map and photos **A**, **B**, **C** and **D**.
   a) List three features that have been caused by erosion.
   b) List three features that have been caused by deposition.

3 a) Name two features from the map and photos that are near to where you live.
   b) Name and describe another two physical features from your local area that you know about.

4 Look at photo **D**. Explain how this feature has been made by putting the following statements into the correct order.

   ● Layers of rock tilted and folded.
   ● Sea erodes and steepens cliff.
   ● Cliff collapses and coast worn away.
   ● Rock formed as deposits harden.
   ● Material deposited on sea bed.
   ● Rock pushed up above sea level.
   ● Rolling hills and valleys formed.

5 Look at photo **A**. Suggest why the mountains here are the highest in Britain and why the scenery is so rugged with many big cliffs.

Summary

The scenery of the UK is varied and attractive. Most of the physical features that make up the scenery are a result of erosion and deposition processes that have been going on for many millions of years.

What is the UK's climate?

Is the summer always like this or are we just lucky this year?

The word **climate** is used to describe the average weather of a place over many years. The climate of the UK is described as **temperate** with warm summers, mild winters and some rain throughout the year. It is rarely too hot or too cold, and although it does seem to rain a lot, it is not often too wet or too dry.

There are however, differences in climate between one place and another even in a small area like the British Isles. Some of these differences are shown on maps **C**, **D** and **E** on the opposite page. The maps also suggest how the UK may be divided into different climatic regions each slightly different in terms of temperature and rainfall from the others.

Activities

1 Make a larger copy of table **A**.
Complete the table using information from maps **C**, **D** and **E** opposite. Give the average figures for each climatic region.

A

Region	Summer temp	Winter temp	Rainfall
North west			
North east			
South west			
South east			

2 Which of the four climatic regions in your table is:
a) warmest in summer,
b) coldest in summer,
c) warmest in winter,
d) coldest in winter,
e) wettest,
f) driest?

3 Match the descriptions in **B** below to each of the four climatic regions.

4 Look at your completed table and maps **C**, **D**, **E**, and **F**. Which of the regions would be best for:
a) a summer beach holiday,
b) a winter skiing holiday?
Give reasons for your answers.

5 a) Describe the pattern of rainfall shown on map **E**.
b) Describe the pattern of relief shown on map **F**.
c) Describe the link between rainfall and relief.

6 a) Give the summer temperature, winter temperature and annual average rainfall for each of the highland areas marked 1, 2 and 3 on map **F**. Present your information in a table.
b) Describe the climate of the UK's highland areas.

Summary

The UK's climate varies from place to place. The north is different to the south and the east is different to the west. Highland areas are usually cooler and wetter than lowland areas.

B

It is dry here, with mild summers and cold winters

It is quite wet here, with warm summers and mild winters

This area is wet but we have mild summers and mild winters

The climate here is dry, with warm summers and cold winters

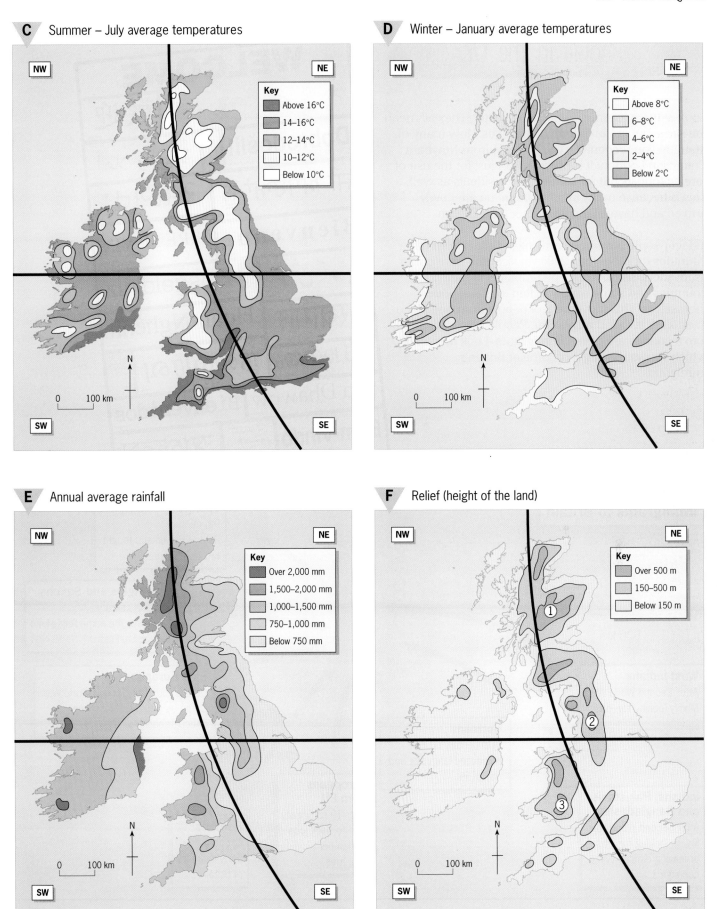

C Summer – July average temperatures

NW | NE

Key
- Above 16°C
- 14–16°C
- 12–14°C
- 10–12°C
- Below 10°C

N

0   100 km

SW | SE

D Winter – January average temperatures

NW | NE

Key
- Above 8°C
- 6–8°C
- 4–6°C
- 2–4°C
- Below 2°C

N

0   100 km

SW | SE

E Annual average rainfall

NW | NE

Key
- Over 2,000 mm
- 1,500–2,000 mm
- 1,000–1,500 mm
- 750–1,000 mm
- Below 750 mm

N

0   100 km

SW | SE

F Relief (height of the land)

NW | NE

Key
- Over 500 m
- 150–500 m
- Below 150 m

N

0   100 km

SW | SE

People in the UK

Look at the welcome signs on the poster. They all mean the same but are in different languages. How many of them do you recognise? The poster is from Newham Council in London. It is provided not just for the use of foreign tourists but for some of the residents as well. This is because many families in Britain are newly arrived and have a language other than English.

In fact people have been arriving in Britain from other countries for more than 2000 years. Some have come as invaders, some to escape problems in their own countries and some simply to find jobs and better themselves. This movement of people from one place to another is called **migration**. People who migrate into a country are called **immigrants**. Look at map **B** which shows the origin of some of Britain's immigrants.

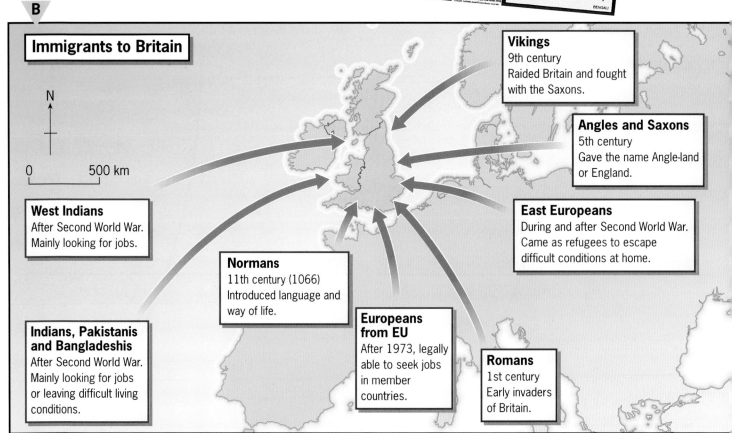

B

Immigrants to Britain

N

0   500 km

Vikings
9th century
Raided Britain and fought with the Saxons.

Angles and Saxons
5th century
Gave the name Angle-land or England.

East Europeans
During and after Second World War. Came as refugees to escape difficult conditions at home.

West Indians
After Second World War. Mainly looking for jobs.

Normans
11th century (1066)
Introduced language and way of life.

Indians, Pakistanis and Bangladeshis
After Second World War. Mainly looking for jobs or leaving difficult living conditions.

Europeans from EU
After 1973, legally able to seek jobs in member countries.

Romans
1st century
Early invaders of Britain.

Some of the largest groups of immigrants are from countries that were once part of the British Empire like India, Pakistan and the West Indies. After the war there were serious labour shortages in Britain. The government of the time invited people from these countries to come and fill job vacancies. Almost a million responded to the call. Most settled permanently in Britain, had families and along with their descendants became UK citizens.

The affect of migration into Britain has been considerable. It has caused an increase in numbers and altered the mix of people in the country. It has also produced a **multicultural society** where people of different race, religion, belief and tradition live and work together. Most people agree that this has added variety and interest to the UK.

C   Mixed races at Notting Hill Carnival

Activities

1 a) How many different languages are shown on poster **A**?
   b) Write out the welcome signs from three European countries and three non-European countries.

2 a) Make a list of where people in your class come from. Try to go back to previous generations.
   b) Plot the information on a world map.

3 Look at map **B**. List the groups of immigrants that have arrived in Britain over the past 2000 years. Start with the ones that arrived first. Add the information to your world map.

4 Look at graph **D**.
   a) From where did most immigrants come?
   b) Suggest why immigrants are now allowed into the UK from this area.
   c) Which group of immigrants are likely to have relatives in the UK already?
   d) Why did these relatives originally come to the UK?
   e) Add each of the places to your world map.

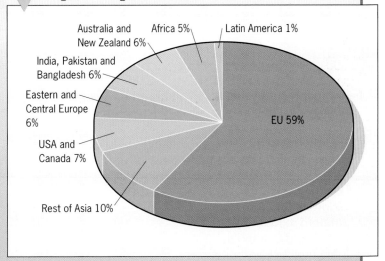

D   Origin of immigrants to Britain

Australia and New Zealand 6%
Africa 5%
Latin America 1%
India, Pakistan and Bangladesh 6%
Eastern and Central Europe 6%
USA and Canada 7%
Rest of Asia 10%
EU 59%

Summary

The UK is made up of people from many different countries. The differences in race, religion, language and culture have helped give rise to the country's distinctive characteristics.

The best of Britain

In 2003, 25 million overseas visitors arrived in the UK. They spent over £12 billion which helped support many businesses and jobs in the tourist industry. The visitors came from all over the world buy most were from the USA, France and Germany.

Britain has much to offer the visitor. It has fine scenery, pretty villages and interesting towns. Most foreign visitors however, are interested in the history and traditions that Britain has to offer. They like to see the castles, palaces, stately homes and historic features that make Britain different to other places in the world.

The holiday shown is taken from the brochure of a company based in California. It is a typical historic tour and is advertised as 'The best of Britain'.

A

Ashness Bridge near Keswick. The Lake District is quite a small area but it has the finest mountain and lake scenery in England.

Activities

1 List four features that make Britain an interesting holiday destination.

2 Use chart **C** to measure the distances between the tour stops. The first one has been done for you.

London to Oxford   =   91 km
Oxford to Stratford   =
Stratford to Keswick   =
Keswick to Edinburgh   =
Edinburgh to Cambridge =
Cambridge to London   =

3 Draw a star diagram like the one below to show at least six attractions of London.

B

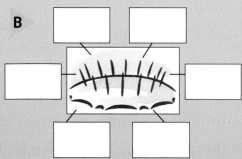

C

BIRMINGHAM								
181	CAMBRIDGE							
477	538	EDINBURGH						
317	413	205	KESWICK					
192	96	661	501	LONDON				
142	258	350	192	298	MANCHESTER			
109	160	592	434	91	258	OXFORD		
32	192	508	349	176	174	93	STRATFORD	
214	251	309	184	339	114	296	246	YORK

4 Imagine that you are at the end of Day 9 of your holiday. Write a postcard to a friend in California describing the Scottish part of your tour.

Summary

Britain's varied scenery, interesting towns and long history attract large numbers of tourists from all over the world.

D

Edinburgh is Scotland's capital and one of Europe's finest cities. It's history stretches back at least 1000 years. The view shows the castle, gardens and Princes Street shopping area.

E

Cambridge is home to one of the world's most famous universities. Some of Britain's most important research establishments are in this area. The view shows the River Cam and one of the ancient colleges.

Days 1 & 2 London
Half day tour visiting the Tower of London, Houses of Parliament and Buckingham Palace. Relaxing afternoon cruise on the River Thames.

Day 3 Oxford
Leave by air conditioned coach for Oxford. Visit Hampton Court Palace and Royal Windsor on route. Afternoon tour of Oxford Colleges.

Day 4 Stratford
Morning tour of Blenheim Palace, once home of Winston Churchill. Drive to Stratford in afternoon. Evening at leisure in Shakespeare's birthplace.

Day 5 Stratford
Morning walking tour of Stratford. Afternoon free for shopping and sightseeing. Shakespeare play at Memorial Theatre in evening.

Day 6 Keswick
Whole day drive to Lake District National Park. Overnight in old market town of Keswick situated beside Derwentwater. Evening talk by National Park Ranger.

Day 7 Keswick
Whole day tour of Lake District visiting Grasmere – where the poet Wordsworth once lived – Ambleside and Langdale. Afternoon boat trip on Lake Windermere.

Day 8 Edinburgh
Morning drive through the Border Country. Visit Floors Castle to view historic treasures. Arrive in Edinburgh late afternoon. Military display in Edinburgh Castle in evening.

Day 9 Edinburgh
Visit former Royal Yacht Britannia in morning. Tour of Hollyrood Palace and re-opened Scottish Parliament in afternoon. Time for late night shopping in Princes street.

Day 10 Cambridge
Whole day coach drive to Cambridge. Lunch in York and guided tour around the Mediaeval walls and castle. Optional visit to railway museum.

Day 11 Cambridge
Morning tour of Cambridge Colleges. Lunch at riverside pub. Leave in late afternoon by coach for London.

F

Day 12 London
Morning trip on London Eye. Rest of day free for shopping and sightseeing.

What is London like?

London is the UK's capital, largest city and biggest industrial centre. Its history can be traced back almost 2000 years to when the Romans built their settlement of Londinium on the banks of the River Thames. Since then, the city has developed into one of the largest and most important in the world.

Modern London is huge and very busy. It stretches some 50 km from one side to the other, is **densely populated** and has serious traffic congestion. Most people travel by tube, an underground railway that serves much of the city.

Many areas are now old and are being **redeveloped**. One such area is the East End.

Activities

1 Draw and name the symbols at these references Answer like this.

374803 = ⊖ = underground station

| 402805 | 381796 | 382776 | 363818 | 378780 |

2 Name the features at these locations.

| 391801 | 376803 | 378799 | 390816 | 363805 |

3 a) Give the references of three tunnels under the River Thames.
b) Name four underground stations.
c) Describe four means of transport that can be used to reach the Millennium Dome.

4 a) Four features have been labelled **A**, **B**, **C** and **D** on the photo. Find each one on the map and say what they are.
b) In which direction was the camera pointing when the photo was taken?

5 Copy and complete the following description using the correct words from the brackets.

The map and photo show part of London's (East or West) End. The River (Lea or Thames) is about (300 or 800) metres wide here and flows round (Greenwich or the Isle of Dogs) in a big bend.

The land is (hilly or flat) and very crowded with (few or many) buildings and (little or much) open space. There has been (little or much) change here. Some buildings have been knocked down or modernised. Others like Canary Wharf and the Millennium Dome have been recently (demolished or constructed).

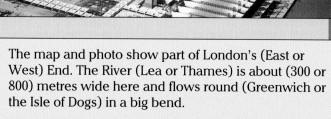

Summary   London is a large and interesting city that is crowded and always busy. Redevelopment schemes are helping improve conditions in the older areas.

Greenwich Meridian line

Bow Common

South Bromley

Canning Town

Limehouse

Lea Valley Walk

Thames Path

Thames Path

Limehouse Basin

Westferry Station

All Saints Station

East India Station

POPLAR

Blackwall

Royal Victoria Station

West India Quay Station

Billingsgate Market

Wharf

Pier

Wharf

Canary Wharf

Blackwall Tunnel

Jetty

Millennium Dome

Heron Quays Station

Wharf

Jetty

CITY FARM

Russia Dock Woodland

Wharf

FB South Dock Marina

Jetties

North Greenwich (Due to open mid 1999)

Wharves

Direction of photograph

South Quay Station

Wharves

Blackwall Reach

Industrial Estate

Jetties

West India & Millwall Docks

Wharves

Greenland Dock Marina

Pier

London Arena

Wharves

Jetty

Pier

Wharf

Millwall

Crossharbour Station

Hypermarket

Cubitt Town

Pier

Sports Ground

Lock Slipway

ISLE OF DOGS

CITY FARM

Jetty

Wks

A 102(M)

Mudchute Station

Millwall Park

Wharves

Wharf

A 1206

Landing Stages

Island Gardens Station

Thames Path

Park

BOAT TRIPS

Subway Tunnel

Royal Naval College Pier

GREENWICH

Hosp

Pleasaunce

DEPTFORD

Greenwich Reach

THE CUTTY SARK & GIPSY MOTH IV

The Queen's House National Maritime Museum

Fordham Park

LEISURE POOL

Old Royal Observatory

Greenwich Park

New Cross

South Building

Tumuli Resr

Metres 0 Kilometres

Feet 0 Miles

Scale: 1:25 000

- ⊖ Underground station
- Ⓜ Museum
- Ⓟ Parking
- 𝒊 Information centre, all year/seasonal
- ▦ English Heritage
- Ⓚ Recreation/Leisure/Sports centre
- 🚲 Cycle trail
- Ⓥ Visitor centre
- ❗ Walks/Trails
- ⛵ Water activities
- ☆ Viewpoint
- ☆ Other tourist feature

What is it like living in London?

Hello,

I'm Kirsty and I'm 14 years old. I live with my parents and brother at Stanmore in the outer suburbs of London some 18 km from the city centre. We have a semi-detached house with a garden and garage. There are a few shops nearby and a nice park where I walk the dog. The motorway is nearby and although it's always busy, we use it at weekends to get away from the city and into the countryside.

My Dad works in an office in the centre of London near Piccadilly. Everyday he drives to Stanmore station, leaves his car there and takes the underground to work. He hates the journey because it takes nearly an hour and is quite expensive. My brother is about to leave school and would like to find work near to home. Unfortunately there are not a lot of jobs in the suburbs where we live.

At the moment I like living in Stanmore. I have lots of friends here, it's only a short walk to school and there's one or two good discos nearby. When I grow up however, I think that I might prefer to live nearer to the city centre where it's not so far to travel to the shops and nightlife that London has to offer.

Activities

1 Make a copy of the Quizword and complete it to give nine facts about where Kirsty lives.

Quizword

Name of area
Entertainment
Nearby open space
House feature
Rail travel
Type of house
Road travel
House feature
Location in city

2 Write a paragraph of no more than 100 words to describe where Kirsty lives. Include all of the words from the Quizword.

3 What four things does Kirsty like best about where she lives?

4 What does Kirsty's family like least about where they live?

Hello,

My name is Robby and I live in Bethnal Green with my parents and sister. We are close to where TV's EastEnders is filmed so you probably know our area quite well. We have a terraced house that is over a hundred years old. It is very small and there is no back garden or garage so we don't have much space. It's a great place to live though because everybody around here knows each other and there is a good community spirit.

My Dad has a fruit and veg stall near Smithfield Market which is close to here. Mum often helps him on busy days as she can walk to the market which is just down the road. My older sister works in a Whitechapel travel agents. She can walk there but if it's raining gets the underground. We don't have a car. There really isn't much point having one around here as the roads are very busy and the underground is handy if we need to go elsewhere in London.

This area is changing a lot. Old buildings are being knocked down or modernised. New buildings like Canary Wharf and the Millennium Dome have been finished and an extension to the underground is now complete. This has all brought many new jobs to the area and generally improved the quality of life here.

These developments, good public transport, and the fact that we are close to the city centre with all its amenities, has made the East End a popular place to live. Unfortunately this has caused house prices to rise and young people have to leave the area because they can't afford the houses here.

5 Describe where Robby lives. Include information about the house, the work his family does and the area where they live. Try to write between 50 and 100 words.

6 Read carefully what Robby has to say about changes to the East End.
   a) Use the headings below to explain why newcomers are attracted to the area.
   b) How have these changes affected local people?

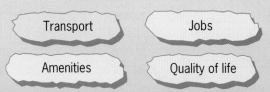

Transport   Jobs

Amenities   Quality of life

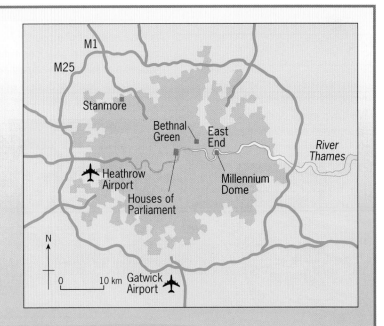

Summary London is a large and interesting city with many different places in which to live. Each place has both advantages and disadvantages.

What are South West England's main features?

South West England is one of Britain's most popular tourist areas. About one in six of all holidays in the UK are spent in this region.

Tourism is important to the South West. It supports over 11 000 businesses and helped create some 225 000 jobs. In 2003 the 24.1 million tourists and visitors to the area spent £5906 million. This money has been good for the area. It has helped provide facilities for local people and generally improved their quality of life.

A Blackpool Sands in Devon

B Tourist activities

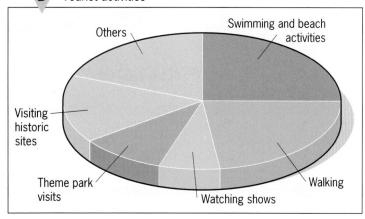

- Others
- Swimming and beach activities
- Visiting historic sites
- Theme park visits
- Watching shows
- Walking

C

Our weather is better than most other places in Britain. We have early springs, warm summers and high average sunshine totals.

We have some of the country's finest holiday resort locations. Our seaside towns have modern and highly developed entertainment facilities. There are also several theme parks and adventure centres.

Our countryside is superb. We have rolling hills, beautiful valleys, ancient forests and wild moorland. Along the coast there are miles of sandy beaches, steep cliffs and rocky islands.

We have a wealth of sporting and recreational opportunities here. There is walking, riding, sailing, fishing and water activities of all kinds. The sheltered coves and inlets are ideal places for pottering around in boats.

Some reasons for the South West's popularity with tourists

The South West has a long and fascinating history. There are remains from prehistoric days as well as abbeys, castles, stately homes and industrial sites from more recent times.

D South West England

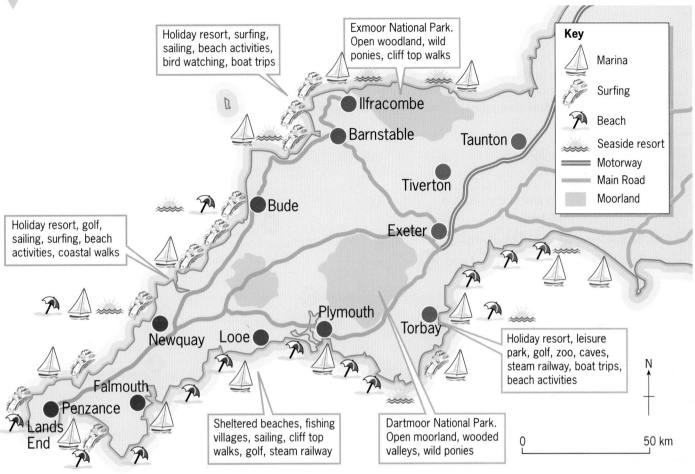

Holiday resort, surfing, sailing, beach activities, bird watching, boat trips

Exmoor National Park. Open woodland, wild ponies, cliff top walks

Key
- Marina
- Surfing
- Beach
- Seaside resort
- Motorway
- Main Road
- Moorland

Ilfracombe

Barnstable

Taunton

Tiverton

Bude

Exeter

Holiday resort, golf, sailing, surfing, beach activities, coastal walks

Plymouth

Torbay

Newquay   Looe

Holiday resort, leisure park, golf, zoo, caves, steam railway, boat trips, beach activities

N

Falmouth

Penzance

Lands End

Sheltered beaches, fishing villages, sailing, cliff top walks, golf, steam railway

Dartmoor National Park. Open moorland, wooded valleys, wild ponies

0   50 km

Activities

1 a) List the activities from graph **B** in order of popularity. Give the percentage for each one using the figures below.

(25) (23) (19) (16) (10) (7)

   b) List the activities in the order that you most like them.

2 The attractions of the South West are both human and physical (natural). Copy the table below and sort the attractions from drawing **C** into the correct columns. Two have been done for you.

Attractions of South West England	
Human	Physical
Abbeys	Rolling hills

3 Plan a ten day holiday for your family in South West England as follows.
- Prepare and itinerary as shown on page 123.
- State where you will be each day and say what you will be doing.
- Use the information in these two pages.
- A brochure from a travel agent would also be useful.
- If you have access to the Internet you could use the West Country Tourist Board website at www.wctb.co.uk
- Try to add photos, drawings and maps to your plan to make it more interesting and attractive.

Summary

Tourists are attracted to South West England for many reasons. These include fine scenery, attractive villages, an interesting history and plenty of things to do.

What is South West England like?

Geographers can obtain important information about places by using maps and photographs. The following activities will help you learn about part of South West England. They should also extend your ability to interpret maps and photos. Page 10 and Unit 7 in *New Foundations* will help you with this.

Activities

1 Look at the OS map and sketch map **A**. Name the following features
   a) The villages at Ⓐ Ⓑ Ⓒ and Ⓓ
   b) The headlands at Ⓔ Ⓕ Ⓖ and Ⓗ
   c) The woods at Ⓘ Ⓙ and Ⓚ
   d) The river at Ⓛ

2 Look at the OS map and photo **B**. Name the following features
   a) The island at ①
   b) The beach at ②
   c) The village at ③
   d) The river at ④
   e) The headland at ⑤
   f) The building at ⑥

3 a) What is the distance by road from the car park at Bigbury-on-Sea to Bigbury village?
   b) What is the distance by river from Avon Mouth to Doctor's Wood?

4 Give map references for two golf courses, a caravan park and a coastal walk.

5 Use the OS map and photo for this activity.
   Imagine that you live at Bigbury-on-Sea and have been asked to write about the area for a holiday brochure.
   ● You will need to describe both physical features – the river, beaches, coast, hills, etc. and human features – villages, accommodation, sports facilities, walks, etc.
   ● Present your work on a sheet of A4 and try to include a labelled sketch and simple map.

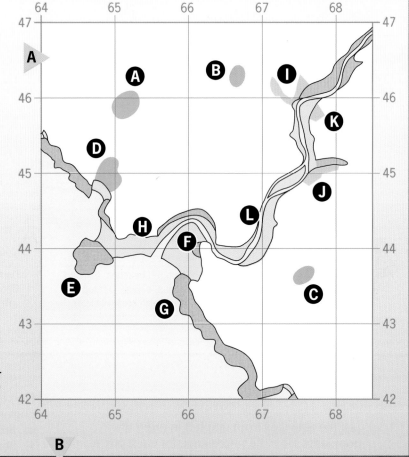

A

B

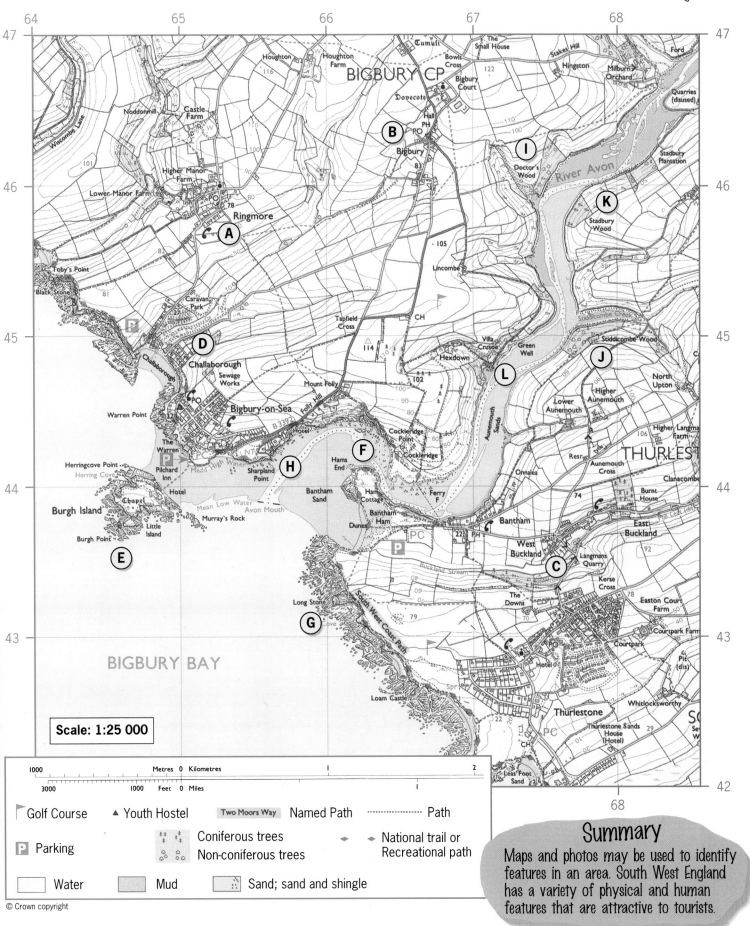

Scale: 1:25 000

Golf Course   ▲ Youth Hostel   Two Moors Way Named Path   ---------- Path

P Parking   Coniferous trees   ◆—— National trail or
                  Non-coniferous trees   Recreational path

Water   Mud   Sand; sand and shingle

© Crown copyright

Summary
Maps and photos may be used to identify features in an area. South West England has a variety of physical and human features that are attractive to tourists.

Sustainable development in the UK

The UK is one of the world's most industrialised countries. The development of industry has brought great wealth to the nation and helped provide most people with a very good standard of living.

Unfortunately, industrial growth has also brought problems. One of these problems is **acid rain**, a kind of air pollution which comes mainly from burning fossil fuels like coal, gas and oil. Acid rain can be very damaging to the environment and cause serious harm to forests, soils, lakes, rivers and the stonework of buildings.

Many people are concerned about acid rain and want to reduce the problem. They argue that the aim of development should be to bring about an improvement in conditions for people. In doing that, however, it should not harm or destroy the environment either now or in the future. Development like this is called **sustainable development**.

Sustainable development does not waste resources or damage the environment. It is progress that can go on for year after year. It helps improve our quality of life today but does not spoil our chances in the future.

The damage caused by acid rain can be stopped but it will be costly and, because the pollution is blown from country to country by the wind, will need international co-operation. These can be difficult problems to overcome.

A

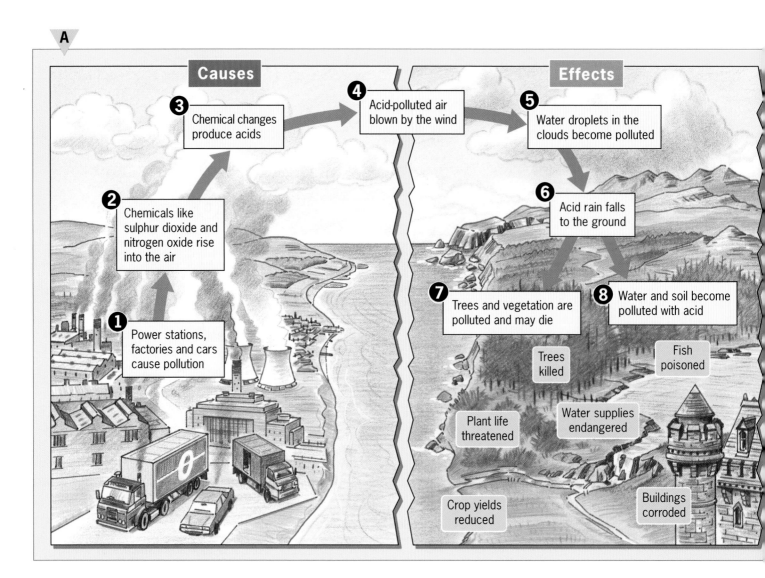

Causes

❸ Chemical changes produce acids

❹ Acid-polluted air blown by the wind

Effects

❺ Water droplets in the clouds become polluted

❷ Chemicals like sulphur dioxide and nitrogen oxide rise into the air

❻ Acid rain falls to the ground

❶ Power stations, factories and cars cause pollution

❼ Trees and vegetation are polluted and may die

❽ Water and soil become polluted with acid

Trees killed

Fish poisoned

Plant life threatened

Water supplies endangered

Crop yields reduced

Buildings corroded

Activities

1 Complete these three sentences.
   a) Sustainable development is…
   b) Sustainable development should…
   c) Sustainable development should not…

Acid rain – a threat to our future

2 Write a short article for a newspaper using the headline below. In your article say what acid rain is, explain its causes and describe its effects.

3 Look at map **B**.
   a) List the countries in order of the amount of sulpher deposited. Give the highest first.
   b) Which countries receive more than half of their deposits from elsewhere?
   c) Suggest where most of the sulpher deposits in northern Europe might come from. Explain your answer.
   d) Why is acid rain described as an international problem?

4 a) Explain how using energy more efficiently could reduce acid rain.
   b) Give two reasons why solving the acid rain problem may be difficult.

Summary

Sustainable development improves people's quality of life without damaging the environment. Acid rain is caused by burning fossil fuels and can harm our surroundings. It is an international problem.

Solutions

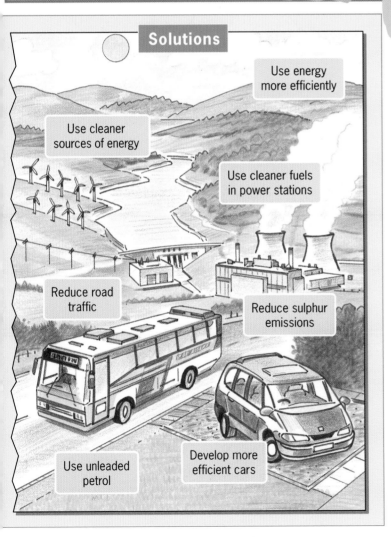

Use energy more efficiently
Use cleaner sources of energy
Use cleaner fuels in power stations
Reduce road traffic
Reduce sulphur emissions
Use unleaded petrol
Develop more efficient cars

B

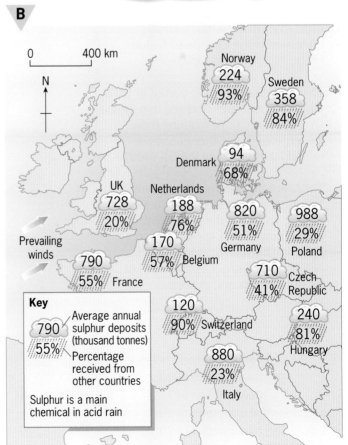

0   400 km

Norway 224 93%
Sweden 358 84%
Denmark 94 68%
UK 728 20%
Netherlands 188 76%
Germany 820 51%
Poland 988 29%
Belgium 170 57%
France 790 55%
Czech Republic 710 41%
Switzerland 120 90%
Hungary 240 81%
Italy 880 23%

Prevailing winds

Key
790 — Average annual sulphur deposits (thousand tonnes)
55% — Percentage received from other countries
Sulphur is a main chemical in acid rain

How interdependent is the UK?

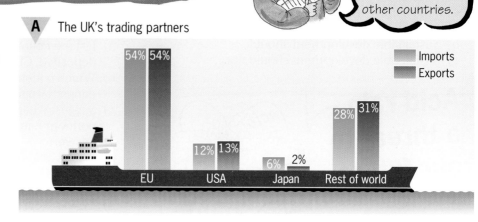

Imports are goods that are bought by a country. Exports are goods that are sold to other countries.

All countries need help from other countries if they are to make progress and improve their standards of living. Countries which work together, or rely on other countries are said to be **interdependent**.

One of the ways that countries become interdependent is by selling goods to each other. They buy things that they need or would like to have. They then sell things to make money for what they have bought. The exchanging of goods and materials like this is called **trade**.

The UK has always been a trading nation and has developed links with countries all around the world. Until recently, most of the trade was with countries of the British Commonwealth like Australia, Canada, India and New Zealand. Nowadays, as graph **A** shows, her most important trading partners are countries of the **European Union (EU)**.

The EU is like a club. It started in 1957 when six countries decided that they would benefit from working more closely together. Other countries joined later including the UK in 1973.

There are now 25 member countries. Together, they form one of the largest trading groups in the world with a population of over 454 million people. This has provided the UK with a large and accessible market for her imports and exports.

A The UK's trading partners

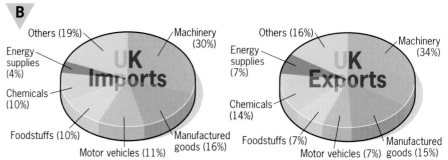

Imports
Exports

54% 54%
12% 13%
6% 2%
28% 31%
EU USA Japan Rest of world

B

Others (19%)
Machinery (30%)
Energy supplies (4%)
UK Imports
Chemicals (10%)
Foodstuffs (10%)
Motor vehicles (11%)
Manufactured goods (16%)

Others (16%)
Machinery (34%)
Energy supplies (7%)
UK Exports
Chemicals (14%)
Foodstuffs (7%)
Motor vehicles (7%)
Manufactured goods (15%)

C The growth of the European Union

Key	
	Founder members in 1957
	New members by 1981
	New members by 1991
	New members by 1995
	New members by 2004
	Applying in the future?

As the drawings below show, the EU has developed into more than just a trading group. Some people are pleased about that. They feel that increased interdependence and being a member of the richest and most important group of nations in the world can bring many benefits.

Other people are not so sure. They are concerned about the loss of independence and do not want other countries to interfere in their laws and way of life. They also worry that the UK may be putting more into the EU than it gets back. These problems may get worse as some of the poorer countries of eastern Europe join the EU.

D

" To develop a united Europe "
Agree on policies and issues affecting Europe and the world as a whole.

" To agree a common approach on important issues "
Agree guidelines on a range of issues including health, hygiene, pollution levels and transport.

" To develop trade between member states "
Introduce a common currency, the Euro, and allow goods to travel more freely across borders.

" To have freedom of movement and work "
Enable people to work, study and travel in other member countries.

" To help regions in economic difficulty "
Give support and aid to areas experiencing industrial decline.

" To develop and improve farming across the whole of the EU "
Ensure an efficient and reliable way of food production through the Common Agricultural Policy.

Activities

1 a) What is meant when a country is said to be interdependent?
   b) Why does a country have to trade?

2 Give three goods that the UK
   a) imports more than it exports,
   b) exports more than it imports.

3 a) Draw a timeline like the one below (**E**) to show the growth of the EU. Use the information on map **C** to mark when each country joined.
   b) How many countries are waiting to join the EU?
   c) What could be the total membership in the future?

4 Do you think membership of the EU is good or bad for the UK? Give reasons and actual examples to support your answer.

E

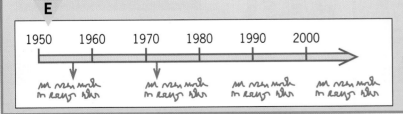

Summary

Being a member of the European Union has helped the UK develop trade and become more interdependent.

How developed is the UK?

All countries are different. Some are rich and have high **standards of living**. Others are poor and have lower standards of living. Countries that differ in this way are said to be at different levels of **development**.

There are many different ways of measuring development. Some of these are shown below and in table **C** opposite. Together they show the UK's level of development.

A

Wealth

In terms of wealth the UK is a rich and highly developed country. Not everyone is well-off however. Some people have low earnings and a poor standard of living.

Bank

Jobs

Most workers in the UK are employed in manufacturing industries or providing services. Very few are farmers or work in primary activities.

Trade

The UK is a major trading nation. It imports foodstuffs and minerals at a low price. It exports large amounts of high value manufactured goods.

Population

Population statistics show the UK to be a highly developed country. It has low birth rates, low infant mortality, long life expectancy and very slow population increase.

Health

The UK is a wealthy country and spends a considerable amount of money on training doctors and nurses, and in providing hospitals and medicines.

CITY HOSPITAL EMERGENCY

Education

The UK spends large amounts of money on education. Recent changes have brought about improvements in learning and higher standards. More students now attend university than ever before.

Whatever methods are used to measure development, most people agree that the UK is a modern, wealthy and highly developed nation. Like all other countries however, wealth and high standards of living are not shared equally between everyone. Most people are well off and live an enjoyable life but some are quite poor and live in difficult conditions.

B

We enjoy high standards of living and a good quality of life.

The UK is one of the most developed countries in the world.

Our country is developed but that doesn't mean that we're all well off.

Our country is as wealthy as most others in Europe.

C

	UK 🇬🇧	Italy 🇮🇹	Spain 🇪🇸	Brazil 🇧🇷	Kenya 🇰🇪
Wealth US $ (GNP per person)	25 500	25 100	21 200	7600	1100
TVs (sets per 1000 people)	521	528	409	223	26
Cars (number per 1000 people)	476	617	521	80	15
Health (people per doctor)	300	211	262	1000	10 130
Education (% attending school)	83	74	88	81	20

Activities

1 Give the meaning of the following terms. The Glossary at the back of the book will help you.
  a) Development
  b) Developed country
  c) Developing country
  d) Standard of living
  e) Quality of life
  f) Gross National Product

2 a) Make a larger copy of drawing **D** below and add labels to show some of the different ways of measuring development.
  b) Chose any two of the measures and explain in your own words how the show the UK to be a developed country.

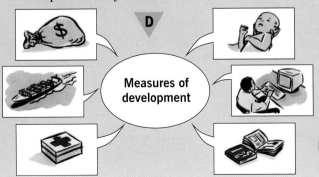

D

Measures of development

3 a) List the countries from table **C** in order of:
  • Wealth (highest income first).
  • TVs per person (highest first).
  • Cars per person (highest first).
  • Health (lowest first).
  • Education (highest first).
  b) Look carefully at your completed lists. In you opinion, which country is most developed? Give reasons for your choice.

4 If you have access to the Internet you could compare the UK's development with any other country in the world using the United Nations website at www.un.org/Pubs/CyberSchoolBus or the site at www.odci.gov/cia/publications/factbook

Summary

The UK is one of the most developed countries in the world. Development however, is not spread evenly. Some people still have poor standards of living.

What is China like?

China is, by area, the fourth largest country in the world (table **A**). It also has the world's largest population with, at present, more than one in five (21 per cent) of people living within this one country.

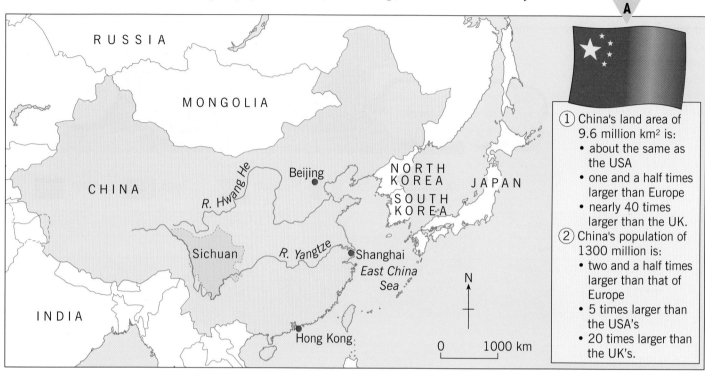

A

① China's land area of 9.6 million km² is:
- about the same as the USA
- one and a half times larger than Europe
- nearly 40 times larger than the UK.

② China's population of 1300 million is:
- two and a half times larger than that of Europe
- 5 times larger than the USA's
- 20 times larger than the UK's.

How much do you know about China? A group of Year 9 geography students were asked that same question. Their answers are shown in diagram **B**. What else can you add to this list?

B

Due to its size, China is very difficult to describe, It has a great variety of physical features, climate and types of vegetation (pages 140 and 141). There are also great variations in how the Chinese live from place to place and in their wealth and quality of life.

Since 1980, however, there has been a dramatic change in the traditional way of life in many parts of the country. In large cities such as Beijing and Shanghai, the rate of change has been as fast as anywhere in the world. In contrast, many rural areas remain extremely poor.

Activities

1 Make a larger copy of diagram **D**. Complete the diagram using information from diagram **A** and the inside back cover.

	Area (km²)	Population (millions)
China	9.6 million	
USA		
Europe		
UK		

D

2 a) Work with a partner and make a list of things that come to mind when you think of China.
  b) Describe six of the features shown in diagram **B**.

3 China has recently become a major exporting country. With the help of diagram **C**, list some things in your home that have been, or might have been, 'made in China'.

Summary

China is the fourth biggest country in the world and has the world's largest population.

What are China's main physical features?

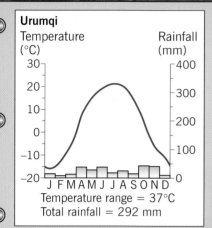

Urumqi

Temperature (°C) / Rainfall (mm)

Temperature range = 37°C
Total rainfall = 292 mm

North and west
- Mainly high mountains and inland drainage basins.
- Very cold winters and warm summers give a large annual range of temperature.
- Rainfall is light and spread evenly throughout the year.
- Snow may lie for over 100 days each year.
- Strong winds, especially in winter.
- Mainly desert and semi-desert.
- Hazards include extreme cold with a high wind chill in winter, strong winds causing dust-storms, and an annual drought.

Urumqi

Beijing

Shanghai

Sichuan
- A large, low-lying region.
- Winters are cold and quite dry.
- Summers are very hot and wet.
- Hazards include high humidity in summer and river flooding.

A

Hong Kong

South and west
- Includes the Himalayas (Mt Everest 8850 m) and the high Plateau of Tibet (over 4000 m).
- Winters are very cold.
- Summers are quite warm but the nights are very cold.
- Large annual range of temperature.
- Wet summers and dry winters.
- Limited vegetation cover.
- Hazards include snow and high wind chill in winter.

River Yangtze
- Third largest river in the world both in length (6380 km) and discharge.
- Has its source on the Plateau of Tibet and flows into the South China Sea near to Shanghai.
- It flows through deep gorges in its upper course and over a wide flood plain in its lower course.
- The only major natural routeway into central China.
- Hazards include river flooding and pollution.

The photos that make up this map of China were taken from an orbiting satellite. The colours have been altered slightly (**enhanced**) to show the relief features and drainage patterns more clearly. The red dashed line has been added to show China's border.

Dense forest and lush vegetation show up as green, drier regions are light brown or orange, mountains are dark brown, snow is white and water surfaces are blue.

North and east
- Includes the North China Plain and the valley of the Huang He, or Yellow, River.
- The Huang He flows, in parts, over a deep yellow, fertile, easily eroded soil known as loess.
- Very cold winters and very warm summers give a large annual range in temperature.
- Snow may lie for up to 150 days a year and rivers may freeze for up to six months.
- Winters are dry but summers are usually very wet.
- Forest nearer the coast with grassland inland.
- Hazards include very cold winters, high humidity in summer, soil erosion and occasional drought and river flooding.

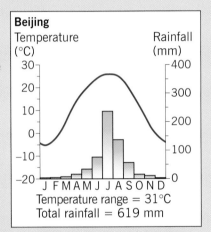

Beijing
Temperature (°C) — Rainfall (mm)
Temperature range = 31°C
Total rainfall = 619 mm

South and east
- Mainly low mountains (under 1000 m).
- Winters are warm and summers very hot, giving a low annual range of temperature.
- Winters are dry and summers very wet.
- Includes tropical rainforest.
- Hazards include typhoons (tropical storms) and high humidity in summer.

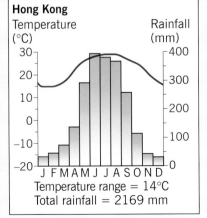

Hong Kong
Temperature (°C) — Rainfall (mm)
Temperature range = 14°C
Total rainfall = 2169 mm

Activities

1 Make a larger copy of map **B**. Complete the descriptions for each of the four regions by using information given on these two pages.

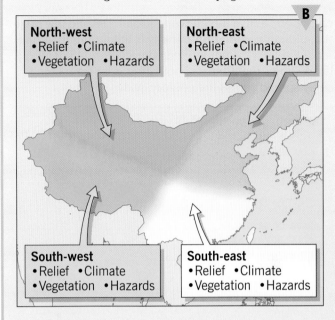

B

North-west
- Relief • Climate
- Vegetation • Hazards

North-east
- Relief • Climate
- Vegetation • Hazards

South-west
- Relief • Climate
- Vegetation • Hazards

South-east
- Relief • Climate
- Vegetation • Hazards

2 Using the three climate graphs shown on these two pages, which region has:
a) the warmest summer and the warmest winter?
b) the coolest summer and the coldest winter?
c) the lowest range of annual temperature?
d) the most rainfall?
e) the least rainfall?

3 Write out the following paragraph filling in the missing words.

The Yangtze River
The Yangtze is the .... longest river in the world (after the Nile and Amazon) and has the third largest discharge (after the Amazon and Congo). It flows ...... km from its source in .... to its mouth in the .... (near the city of ....). In its upper course it passes through deep .... while in its lower course it flows over a wide .... A large dam has just been built to stop the .... hazard and to improve transport and trade.

Summary

China is a huge country with high mountains and low-lying plains. Its climate includes places that are very hot, very cold, very dry and very wet. The Yangtze is China's largest river.

People in China

China's population in 2004 was 1.3 billion. This was 21 per cent, or one in five, of the world's total. Despite this huge total, China's **population density** is little more than half that of the UK (134 per km² compared with 245 per km²). Map **A** shows that China's population is far from being evenly spread across the country, with:

- 94 per cent living on only 40 per cent of the land area – mainly in coastal areas and the lower Yangtze basin
- 6 per cent living in the remaining area that coincides with the more mountainous and desert regions of the north and west.

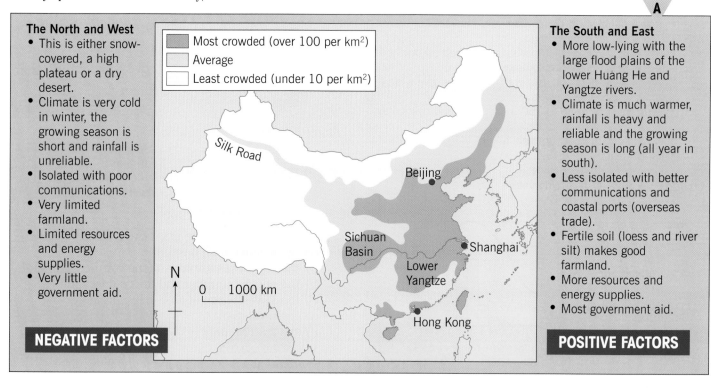

A

The North and West
- This is either snow-covered, a high plateau or a dry desert.
- Climate is very cold in winter, the growing season is short and rainfall is unreliable.
- Isolated with poor communications.
- Very limited farmland.
- Limited resources and energy supplies.
- Very little government aid.

NEGATIVE FACTORS

Most crowded (over 100 per km²)
Average
Least crowded (under 10 per km²)

Silk Road
Beijing
Sichuan Basin
Shanghai
Lower Yangtze
Hong Kong
N
0   1000 km

The South and East
- More low-lying with the large flood plains of the lower Huang He and Yangtze rivers.
- Climate is much warmer, rainfall is heavy and reliable and the growing season is long (all year in south).
- Less isolated with better communications and coastal ports (overseas trade).
- Fertile soil (loess and river silt) makes good farmland.
- More resources and energy supplies.
- Most government aid.

POSITIVE FACTORS

One-child policy

During the middle of the twentieth century, Chinese families were encouraged to have many children.

B

Realising that this was causing an unsustainable increase in population, the Chinese government decided in 1979 to enforce a **one-child per family policy** (photo **B**) and to set a minimum age for marriage. Couples had to apply to be married and again before having a child. Those who failed to conform were deprived of benefits, had to pay a fine and were liable to forced abortions and, in extreme cases, to sterilisation.

In reality, there were exceptions to the one-child policy. Families having a disabled child, belonging to an ethnic minority group or living in more remote rural areas were allowed a second baby. By 2000, the policy had been so successful in reducing the birth rate and population growth that it was relaxed. Women are now offered a wider choice in methods of contraception.

An ageing population

At present, China is more concerned with its ageing population than with its number of children.

China's ageing population results from an increase in **life expectancy**. Life expectancy increased from 40 in 1950 to 70 in 2000 – in other words, a person born in 2000 could expect to live 30 years longer than someone born 50 years earlier (photos **C**).

Predictions suggest that the proportion of Chinese people aged 60 and over will increase from the 10 per cent of the total population in 1980 to 22 per cent by 2030. This change will have a huge impact on Chinese society. It means, for example, that there must be an urgent reform of the provision of:

- pensions – there are none at present for the majority of the population
- health care – the need for more doctors, nurses and accommodation for the elderly.

Selling noodles

Traditional dress

C

Activities

1 Map **D** shows five regions.
   a) For **each** of regions A , B and C:
      - name one large city
      - give three reasons why it has an above average density of population.
   b) For each of regions D and E, give three reasons why it has a below average density of population.

2 In 1979, China introduced the so-called 'one-child per family' policy.
   a) What was the 'one-child' policy?
   b) Why was this policy introduced?
   c) Give one reason why you think it was a good policy.
   d) Give one reason why you think it was a bad policy.

3 China now has an ageing population.
   a) Why is China's population ageing?
   b) What problems result from an ageing population?

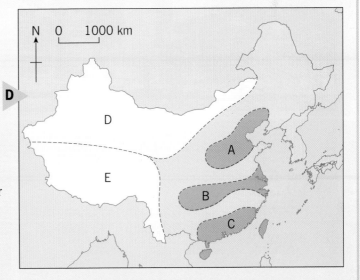

Summary

China's population is very unevenly distributed. It has a low birth rate and an ageing population.

143

China highlights

Before 1980 it was very difficult for the Chinese to travel freely around their own country and for foreign tourists to gain access to it. Since then tourism has developed rapidly. In 2000, China received 27 million overseas tourists, placing it fifth in the world rankings.

Some tourists make visits to remote places like the ancient Silk Road in the north-west or to the snow-covered Himalayas in Tibet. Most, however, take a package tour similar to the one described below (map **A**).

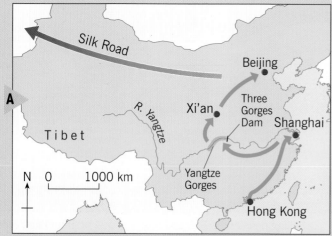

A

DAYS 1 to 3

Hong Kong

Arrive at Hong Kong's new International Airport. Take the funicular railway to The Peak to see Victoria Harbour and Kowloon. Visit the city's numerous modern shopping malls and traditional street markets, some of the many local restaurants, see the world's largest outdoor bronze Buddha and view the city from the harbour at night (photo **B**).

DAYS 4 and 5

Shanghai

Visit the remnants of 'China town'. Take tea in a China tea-house, walk along the Bund to see early nineteenth-century European commercial buildings and gaze with awe at the new (only begun in 1990) city of Pudong across the Huangpu River (photo **C**). Shop in Nanjing Lu and watch a performance of China's top acrobats.

DAYS 6, 7 and 8

The Yangtze

Fly to Chongqing for a three-day cruise down the fabulous Yangtze River. Sail through the scenic Three Gorges (photo **D**), passing towns and temples being flooded as the lake behind the Three Gorges Dam fills up, and visit the Dam itself.

B

C

D

E

F

G

DAYS 9 and 10 — Xi'an

Morning flight to Xi'an. See the Bell and Drum Towers, the two Goose Pagodas, various temples and the Great Mosque. Highlight is the visit to see the Terracotta Army, only discovered in 1974 (photo **E**).

DAYS 11, 12 and 13 — Beijing

Fly to Beijing, China's capital and host to the 2008 Olympic Games. Visit the Temple of Heaven (photo **F**), Tiananmen Square, the Imperial Palace in the Forbidden City, the Summer Palace and the renowned Chinese opera. The tour ends with a visit to the Great Wall of China (photo **G**) and the Ming Tombs. Return overnight from Beijing.

Activities

1 Which six features described in the package tour would you most like to see if you could visit China? List them in order with your 'most like to see' first.

2 Draw three star diagrams like diagram **H** to show four attractions of each of:
   • Hong Kong   • Shanghai   • Beijing.

H

3 Design a poster advertising China as a holiday destination. Try to include:
   • a map to show the places that you mention
   • labelled photos, or a collage of several photos, and a short written description
   • scenic places as well as historic, religious and modern buildings.
You could find more information in travel brochures and on the internet.

Summary

China is a land of contrasts. It has attractive and varied scenery, a long history and differing cultures.

What is life like in Sichuan Province?

Most Chinese people – 70 per cent – live in rural areas, many in villages like Hua Long in the province of Sichuan (map **A** on page 138). Like most rural settlements, Hua Long dates back to the sixteenth century and until the 1990s it underwent little change. Most families are farmers who work long hours and live at a **subsistence** level. They live in farmhouses that are grouped together, in typical Chinese fashion, around a central courtyard (photo **A**). Many families have lived there for several generations.

A

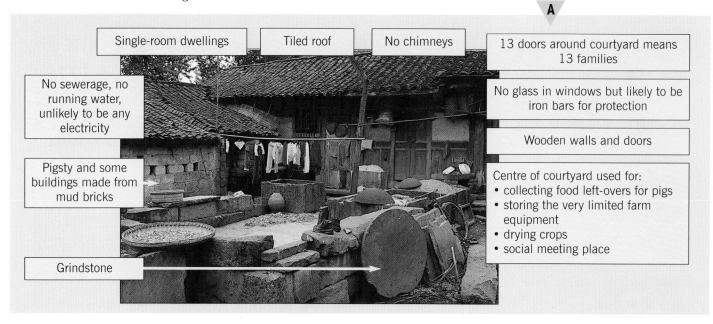

Single-room dwellings

Tiled roof

No chimneys

13 doors around courtyard means 13 families

No sewerage, no running water, unlikely to be any electricity

No glass in windows but likely to be iron bars for protection

Wooden walls and doors

Pigsty and some buildings made from mud bricks

Centre of courtyard used for:
• collecting food left-overs for pigs
• storing the very limited farm equipment
• drying crops
• social meeting place

Grindstone

This farmhouse has recently been pulled down and the families re-housed. The Yang family moved to their new, detached house in 1998. It is located on the outskirts of the village. Mr Yang has two jobs – working on his small farm with his wife, and providing a trishaw taxi service in the nearby town. This enabled the family to save enough money to move from their old wooden single-roomed farmhouse to a double-storeyed, seven-roomed brick-built house (photo **B**). The house includes a kitchen (photo **C**), a living area, two bedrooms and three rooms used for storing crops. Although the house includes a pipe that provides running water and a rather unsafe-looking electricity supply, it lacks sewerage.

B A new farmhouse

C Kitchen inside the new farmhouse showing exposed electricity wire

D The main road in Hua Long

E Recent improvements in Hua Long

Most inhabitants of the village of Hua Long live in buildings that are strung out on either side of the main road (photo **D**). The road is usually dusty during dry weather and muddy after heavy rain. Recent changes to the village include new shops and houses (photo **E**) and

improvements to public buildings (diagram **F**). The new houses indicate an increase in wealth of some of the villagers. Although still very poor, local people claim that their quality of life has improved in the last 20 years.

F

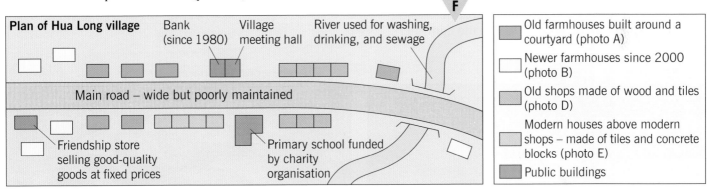

Plan of Hua Long village

Bank (since 1980) Village meeting hall River used for washing, drinking, and sewage

Main road – wide but poorly maintained

Friendship store selling good-quality goods at fixed prices

Primary school funded by charity organisation

Old farmhouses built around a courtyard (photo A)

Newer farmhouses since 2000 (photo B)

Old shops made of wood and tiles (photo D)

Modern houses above modern shops – made of tiles and concrete blocks (photo E)

Public buildings

Activities

1 Make a larger copy of table **G**. Complete it to show differences between old and new farmhouses in Sichuan.

G

	Old farm	New farm
Building materials		
Number of rooms		
Number of storeys		
Central courtyard		
Windows		
Running water		
Electricity		
Sewerage		

2 With the help of diagram **H**, describe the appearance of, and recent changes in, Hua Long.

H

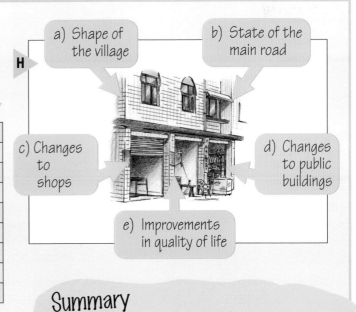

a) Shape of the village

b) State of the main road

c) Changes to shops

d) Changes to public buildings

e) Improvements in quality of life

Summary

Most Chinese people still live in villages. Although they usually have a very low standard of living, there have been improvements in their quality of life.

What is farming like in Sichuan?

As we saw on the last page, most people living in Sichuan are farmers. Like most people living in southern China, and half of the world's population, they rely upon rice for their staple diet. (In the north of China, where it is too cold and dry for rice to grow, wheat provides the staple food.) Diagram **A** explains why Sichuan is ideal for the growing of rice.

Rice is usually grown in **padis**. In Sichuan there are two types of padi:

1 Small fields on the flat fertile flood plains of rivers (photo **B**). The padis are separated by small retaining walls, known as **bunds**. These are built to trap water from the river when it floods following the summer rains.
2 Terraces on steeper hillsides (photo **C**). These also have retaining walls, this time to trap the rainwater itself.

A

Why is Sichuan ideal for growing rice?

- Summers are very warm and the monsoon winds bring plenty of rain.
- Winters are usually mild enough for a second rice crop to be grown.
- Irrigation is needed in the drier winter season.
- The growing season allows crops to grow throughout the year.
- The soil is deep and fertile.
- Most of Sichuan is a low-lying basin surrounded by mountains that give protection against cold winter winds.

B Rice grown on a flood plain

C Rice grown on terraces

Activities

1 Make a larger copy of diagram **E**. Complete it using the headings shown.

2 Imagine that you live in Sichuan and are writing to a friend in the UK.
   a) Explain why rice is so important to your family.
   b) Describe the appearance of the two types of padi.

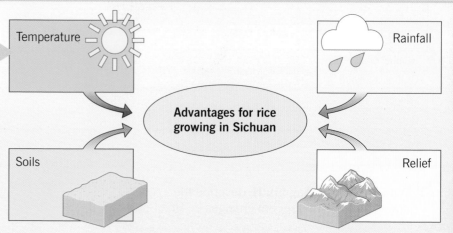

E Temperature — Rainfall — Soils — Relief — Advantages for rice growing in Sichuan

D

1 As soon as the monsoon rains arrive in May, the farmer **ploughs** his land with a wooden plough drawn by a water buffalo.

2 When the fields have been ploughed (into what seems to us a sea of mud), **fertiliser** is spread by hand.

3 Rice seedlings are grown in a **nursery**. When they are strong enough they are collected by the farmer's wife and tied into bundles ready for transplanting.

4 Until recently rice was **transplanted** into padis by women working in a long line. Now it is done by an individual farmer's wife. (This is Mrs Yang whose new farmhouse you saw on page 146.)

5 **Harvesting** is done by hand, usually in September. During the mild winter, a second crop is grown. This is rice if water is available for irrigation, and wheat if it is too dry. Also during winter, farmers grow vegetables such as peas and beans, and repair the bunds.

3 Copy diagram **F**. Complete it by writing the following labels into the correct boxes.

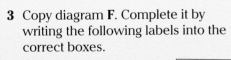

fertiliser added by hand

rice plants tied into bundles

rice planted in a nursery

rice crop is harvested

bunds are repaired

rice is transplanted

padis ploughed by water buffalo

F Rice planted in a nursery

Rice growing in Sichuan

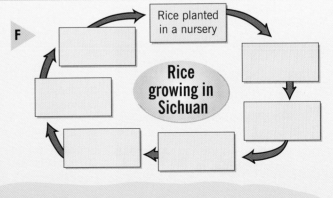

Summary
Most farmers in Sichuan grow rice which is their staple diet.

149

Beijing — Olympic City 2008

Beijing, with an estimated population of 12 million, is the capital of China. It is also the country's centre for culture and education and has been chosen to host the Olympic Games in 2008. This means that before and during this event you are likely to see many images of the city on TV, on the internet and in other forms of the media. These pages show you some of the sights that you are likely to see (map **A**).

Summer Palace Located 17 km north-west of the Forbidden City, the grounds of the emperor's summer palace include a huge lake, a Buddhist pagoda and ornamental gardens.

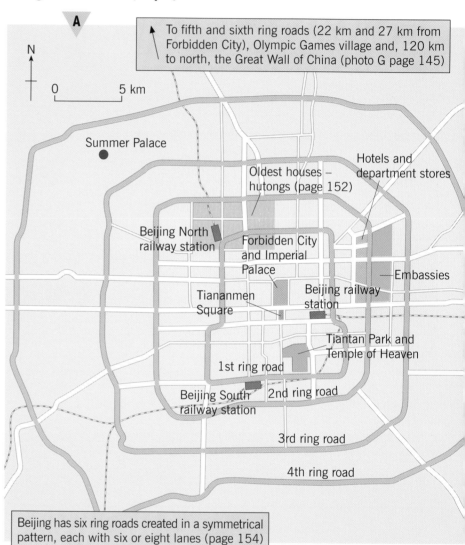

A

To fifth and sixth ring roads (22 km and 27 km from Forbidden City), Olympic Games village and, 120 km to north, the Great Wall of China (photo G page 145)

N

0   5 km

Summer Palace

Oldest houses – hutongs (page 152)

Hotels and department stores

Beijing North railway station

Forbidden City and Imperial Palace

Embassies

Tiananmen Square

Beijing railway station

Tiantan Park and Temple of Heaven

1st ring road

Beijing South railway station

2nd ring road

3rd ring road

4th ring road

Beijing has six ring roads created in a symmetrical pattern, each with six or eight lanes (page 154)

The Forbidden City This is regarded by many to be the centre of the city (although not the CBD). It was the home of emperors from its creation in 1420 until 1924. The entrance is through the Tiananmen Gate (photo **D**). Inside is the Imperial Palace, three large halls, and several pavilions, smaller palaces, courtyards and ornamental gardens (photo **C**).

D

Tiananmen Square This, the largest square in the world, was built to hold over 1 million people. It is surrounded by a huge conference centre, two museums and Chairman Mao's Mausoleum.

Tiantan Park Known to us as the **Temple of Heaven**, this is where the emperor made sacrifices to keep harmony on earth (see photo **F** on page 145). Now a public park, it gives fine views of Beijing's CBD.

Hotels and department stores This area includes more than 25 first-class international hotels and many of Beijing's 70 major department stores.

Activities

1 Copy and complete quizword **H** using the following clues:
   a) Beijing's oldest houses
   b) The city that was home to the emperors
   c) A palace in the centre of the city
   d) A park with fine views of Beijing
   e) Located 120 km north of Beijing
   f) A temple where sacrifices were made
   g) A palace 17 km north-west of the centre
   h) Places to stay east of the centre
   i) The mausoleum of this man is in a large square

Make up a clue for the down-word j.

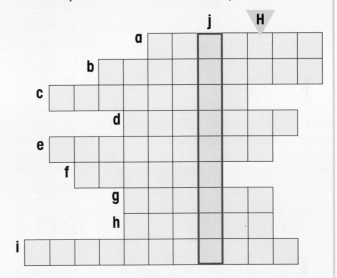

2 Diagram **I** is part of a TV storyboard to advertise Beijing as Olympic City 2008.
   a) Name features 1 and 2.
   b) Name two other features in Beijing.
   c) Write a brief description for each of the four features.

Summary

Beijing, the capital of China, is a huge city with many famous historic and cultural buildings.

What is it like living in Beijing?

Hutongs

Until the 1980s, most of Beijing's inhabitants lived in the 'hutongs'. Hutongs are lanes, or alleys (photo **A**), from which stone gateways give access to courtyards. Many hutongs date back several centuries with some of the courtyard houses up to 200 years old. At the courtyard entrance are letter boxes, a receiver for cable TV and two stone drums – their height indicating the wealth or rank of the inhabitants (photo **B**).

The courtyard in diagram **C** has belonged to Madame Li's family for several generations. Madam Li (photo **D**) is now in her seventies and is one of China's ageing population (page 143). In earlier times the courtyard would have contained a fountain – now it is a place to dry washing and store bicycles. Diagram **C** shows that, today, Madam Li only owns one side of the courtyard. Her home consists of a kitchen (photo **D**), a bedroom, a dining area and a utility room (photo **E**). She considers that with electricity, central heating and a more reliable supply of food, her quality of life is far better than when she was young.

Each courtyard was originally for one family but as Beijing's population grew, they were divided into four or five dwellings. Although the present-day homes are much smaller, so too is the average size of a Chinese family (page 142).

D Madam Li

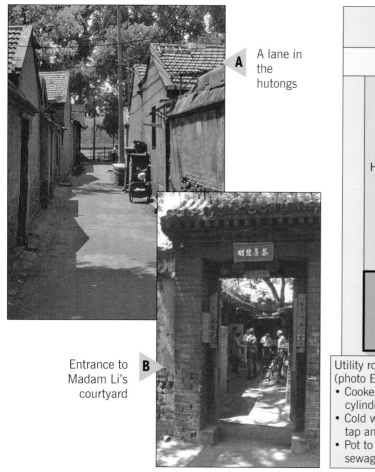
A A lane in the hutongs

Entrance to Madam Li's courtyard **B**

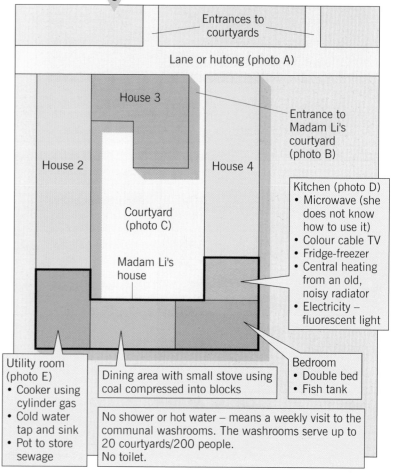
C

Entrances to courtyards

Lane or hutong (photo A)

House 3

House 2

House 4

Entrance to Madam Li's courtyard (photo B)

Courtyard (photo C)

Madam Li's house

Kitchen (photo D)
• Microwave (she does not know how to use it)
• Colour cable TV
• Fridge-freezer
• Central heating from an old, noisy radiator
• Electricity – fluorescent light

Utility room (photo E)
• Cooker using cylinder gas
• Cold water tap and sink
• Pot to store sewage

Dining area with small stove using coal compressed into blocks

Bedroom
• Double bed
• Fish tank

No shower or hot water – means a weekly visit to the communal washrooms. The washrooms serve up to 20 courtyards/200 people. No toilet.

E Utility room in Madam Li's house

F High-rise flats by the third ring road

High-rise flats

Madam Li needed less space because her husband had died and her two children now live in modern high-rise flats (photo **F**). The flats have been built:

- to replace the more run-down hutongs and those pulled down for new ring roads
- to house the rapid increase in Beijing's population.

Many developments are alongside the ring roads.

Madam Li says that her children like living in these flats because they have:

- reliable central heating during the cold winters
- air conditioning for the hot, often humid summers
- hot water, showers and sewerage.

However, she herself does not want to live in them because:

- she knows everyone in her part of the hutongs whereas her children have never spoken to their neighbours in the two years they have lived in the flats
- they are small in size
- they are a long way from shops and places of work.

Activities

1. a) What is a hutong?
   b) When were most hutongs developed?
   c) Answer the questions in sketch **G** to describe the main features of Madam Li's courtyard and home.

2. Copy and complete table **H** to show:
   a) the advantages and
   b) the disadvantages of living in
   • a hutong • a modern high-rise flat.

G

a) What is found at the entrance to a courtyard?

b) What is the courtyard now used for?

f) Why can families now live in smaller houses?

c) How many rooms does Madame Li's home have?

e) How many families now share the courtyard?

d) What has helped to improve Madam Li's quality of life?

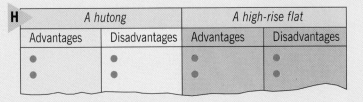

H

A hutong		A high-rise flat	
Advantages	Disadvantages	Advantages	Disadvantages
•	•	•	•
•	•	•	•

Summary

Hutongs are places where most of the people living in Beijing have lived until very recent times.

Two regions compared

As we have seen, there are considerable differences between living in Sichuan and Beijing. Sichuan is mainly a rural area where most people are farmers and live in small towns or villages. However, because it is such an important farming region it has a surprisingly high population density (diagram **E**). The Beijing region is much smaller in size and is dominated by the huge and rapidly growing urban area with its many jobs in secondary and service industries.

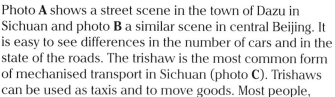

Photo **A** shows a street scene in the town of Dazu in Sichuan and photo **B** a similar scene in central Beijing. It is easy to see differences in the number of cars and in the state of the roads. The trishaw is the most common form of mechanised transport in Sichuan (photo **C**). Trishaws can be used as taxis and to move goods. Most people, however, can only afford to walk. In contrast, Beijing has over 1 million cars and 7 million bicycles (photo **D** was taken outside the city's main railway station). It also has an international airport, two main railway stations and a metro with two lines (the metro is to be extended for the 2008 Olympics).

Diagram **E** shows other differences between the two regions.

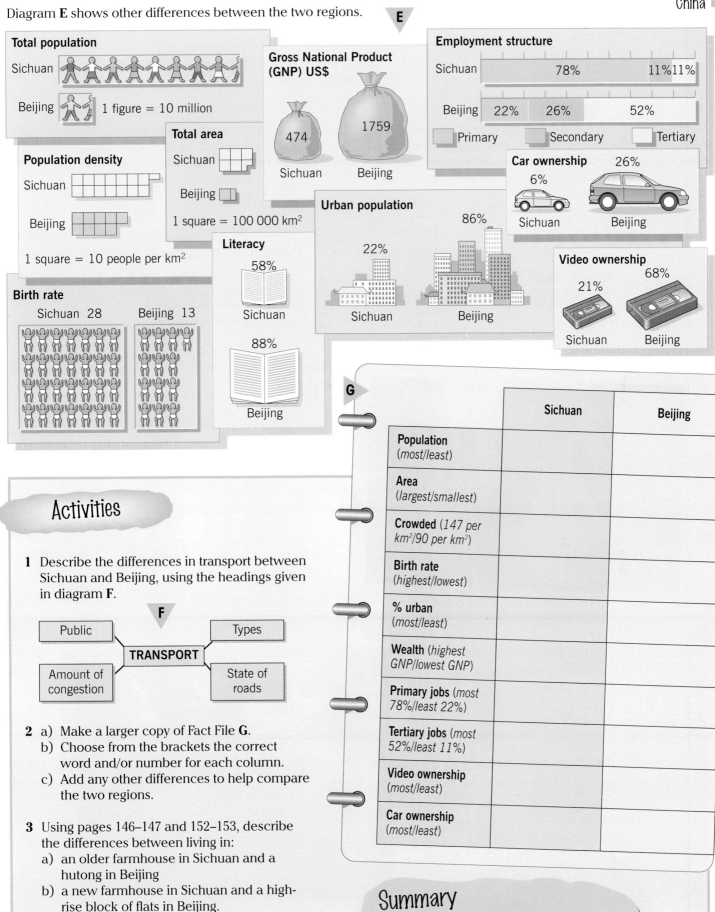

E

Total population

Sichuan
Beijing   1 figure = 10 million

Population density

Sichuan
Beijing
1 square = 10 people per km²

Birth rate

Sichuan 28   Beijing 13

Total area

Sichuan
Beijing
1 square = 100 000 km²

Gross National Product (GNP) US$

474   1759
Sichuan   Beijing

Literacy

58%
Sichuan
88%
Beijing

Urban population

22%   86%
Sichuan   Beijing

Employment structure

Sichuan   78%   11% 11%
Beijing   22%   26%   52%

☐ Primary   ☐ Secondary   ☐ Tertiary

Car ownership

6%   26%
Sichuan   Beijing

Video ownership

21%   68%
Sichuan   Beijing

Activities

1 Describe the differences in transport between Sichuan and Beijing, using the headings given in diagram **F**.

F

Public   Types
TRANSPORT
Amount of congestion   State of roads

2 a) Make a larger copy of Fact File **G**.
  b) Choose from the brackets the correct word and/or number for each column.
  c) Add any other differences to help compare the two regions.

3 Using pages 146–147 and 152–153, describe the differences between living in:
  a) an older farmhouse in Sichuan and a hutong in Beijing
  b) a new farmhouse in Sichuan and a high-rise block of flats in Beijing.

G

	Sichuan	Beijing
Population (*most/least*)		
Area (*largest/smallest*)		
Crowded (*147 per km²/90 per km²*)		
Birth rate (*highest/lowest*)		
% urban (*most/least*)		
Wealth (*highest GNP/lowest GNP*)		
Primary jobs (*most 78%/least 22%*)		
Tertiary jobs (*most 52%/least 11%*)		
Video ownership (*most/least*)		
Car ownership (*most/least*)		

Summary

Living and working in Sichuan is very different from living and working in Beijing.

Sustainable development in China

Sustainable development (page 16) does not waste resources or damage the environment while, at the same time, it helps to improve the living conditions of local people. In Sichuan the natural environment is being threatened as the region begins to develop. Many people fear that this development could lead to the extinction of the giant panda if its natural habitat is destroyed.

The giant panda

What does it look like?

WWF, the World Wide Fund for Nature, uses the giant panda as its logo. A fully grown giant panda is one metre tall at its shoulder and weighs about 100 kg. It has distinctive markings with a white head and black ears, nose and areas around the eyes.

A

What does it eat?

B

Although the giant panda is said to be a carnivore in that it can eat meat, its main diet is that of a herbivore. In fact it relies almost entirely upon one plant – bamboo. The giant panda has flat molar teeth and has developed strong jaw and cheek muscles. Together these help it crunch the fibrous bamboo plant. The giant panda has a very poor digestive system. To overcome this an adult consumes 20 kg of bamboo a day which in spring can increase to 45 kg (imagine eating almost half your body weight each day!). The giant panda can spend up to eight hours a day eating – and most of the rest sleeping while the food is digested.

Where is it found?

C

The giant panda is an **endangered species**. It is believed that, at present, there are probably fewer than 1000 still living. Of these:

- Nearly a half live in the forested, mountainous areas in the Chinese province of Sichuan (map **A** page 138). The animals do not live here by choice, but have been forced upwards to between 2000 and 3000 m by the activity of rice farmers (pages 148 and 149).
- Nearly another half live in a semi-wild habitat in two reserves, also in Sichuan.
- The few remaining animals live in several zoos spread across the world.

Why is it endangered?

- The giant panda tends to live a solitary life which reduces its opportunities of mating.
- The mating season is very brief as females are on heat for only 12–15 days a year, with a peak fertility period of only 2 to 7 days.
- Food supply is extremely limited as the bamboo forest has been cleared by farmers and logging companies.
- Every 60 or so years, for some unknown reason, every bamboo plant dies down. Although new plants soon grow, this may be too long for such a hungry animal.
- Animals may be caught by poaching – although the giant panda tends to be caught in traps set for other animals rather than for the panda itself.

How can it be protected?

1 By captive breeding in zoos. However:
   - only three zoos outside China have successfully bred giant pandas
   - of 51 born in captivity in China, only 20 reached adulthood
   - animals born and bred in captivity are unlikely to survive if released into the wild
   - most of their natural habitats have been destroyed.
2 By conserving what is left of the giant panda's natural forest home. The photos on these two pages were taken in China's Research Centre for Giant Panda Breeding at Chengdu in Sichuan. This, and a nearby nature reserve, are the only two protected areas in the world.

Sustainable development is essential in this part of China if people are to improve their low standard of living (diagram **E** page 155), the environment is not destroyed and the giant panda is to survive.

Activities

1 a) What is meant by the term 'endangered species'?
   b) Why is the survival of endangered species an example of sustainable development?

2 a) Where do most giant pandas live?
   b) Describe the diet of the giant panda.
   c) Why is it increasingly difficult for giant pandas to find sufficient food?
   d) Give two reasons, other than diet, that threaten the giant pandas' survival.

3 Design a poster aimed at protecting the giant panda. Remember that it will have to:
   - be eye-catching
   - convince people of the need to help protect the animal.

Summary

Careful management of the environment is essential if the giant panda is to survive.

How interdependent is China?

Countries need to work together if they are to progress and improve their standards of living. Countries that work together or rely on others are said to be **interdependent**.

One way by which countries become interdependent is by selling and buying from each other. No country has everything that its people want or need. To provide these things a country has to exchange goods ands materials with other countries. This exchange is called **trade**.

A country will buy (**import**) things which it lacks. These may either be:

● **primary goods**, such as foodstuffs and minerals, which are often low in value, or
● **secondary goods**, such as machinery and electronics, which are high in value.

In order to pay for these a country has to sell (**export**) goods of which it has a surplus. Ideally a country aims for a **trade surplus**. This means that it earns more money from its exports than it spends on its imports. Until 1978, China was a closed country. This meant that not only did it not trade with other countries, it was also very difficult for foreigners to gain entry to China or for Chinese people to leave.

In 1978, China introduced its 'open door policy'. Since then, it has been catching up with other developing countries and 'integrating with the global economy'. In other words, China is rapidly becoming more interdependent. Most of its trade is with the more developed countries, e.g. the USA, in eastern Asia and in Europe (map **A**). China's trade has doubled in each of the last five years and it now has a small trade surplus (graphs **B**). This increase in trade is partly due to China's changing types of export (diagram **C**).

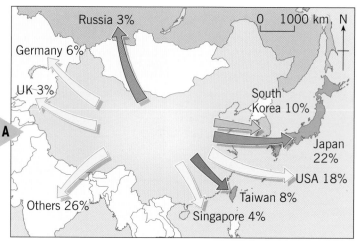

A

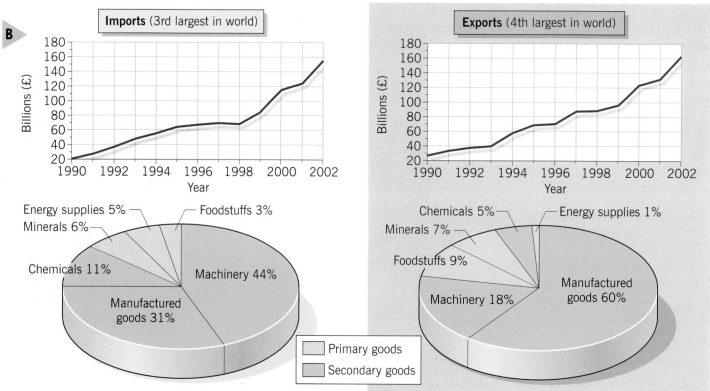

B

Imports (3rd largest in world)

Energy supplies 5% — Foodstuffs 3%
Minerals 6%
Chemicals 11%
Machinery 44%
Manufactured goods 31%

Exports (4th largest in world)

Chemicals 5% — Energy supplies 1%
Minerals 7%
Foodstuffs 9%
Machinery 18%
Manufactured goods 60%

☐ Primary goods
■ Secondary goods

C China's exports

At first, China exported simple manufactured goods such as cane baskets and garden furniture or processed raw materials such as green tea.

Later it began to export trainers and sportswear produced by large overseas companies such as Adidas, Nike and Reebok.

Now it is concentrating on high-quality technical goods such as computers, digital cameras and mobile phones. These are also produced for large overseas companies.

In many cases, large overseas companies locate in China. This is:

● partly because China has the necessary raw materials with which to make the goods, but

● mainly to take advantage of China's plentiful supply of cheap labour. In some sportswear and textile factories, people can only earn £3 a day even if they work for over 12 hours.

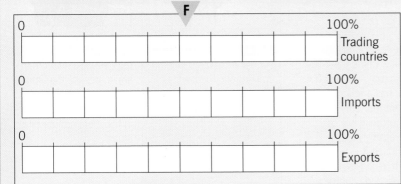

D

Activities

1 a) What is meant when a country is said to be interdependent?
  b) How can being interdependent help a country?

2 Complete the definitions in table **E** by matching the terms on the left with the correct ending from the list on the right.

3 a) Draw three bar graphs like those shown in diagram **F**.
  b) Complete the first to show the countries with which China has most trade.
  c) Complete the second to show China's major imports.
  d) Complete the third to show China's major exports.
  e) On the last two graphs, colour primary goods in green and manufactured goods in red. How does this help to explain China's trade surplus?

E

Trade	Things that are made from primary goods
Imports	Buying goods or materials from another country
Exports	Raw materials such as foodstuffs and energy resources
Trade surplus	Cost of imports is greater than money obtained from exports
Trade deficit	The exchange of goods and materials between countries
Primary goods	Money from exports is more than money paid for imports
Manufactured goods	Selling goods made in or obtained from a country

F

```
0                                        100%
┌──┬──┬──┬──┬──┬──┬──┬──┬──┬──┐ Trading
│  │  │  │  │  │  │  │  │  │  │ countries
└──┴──┴──┴──┴──┴──┴──┴──┴──┴──┘

0                                        100%
┌──┬──┬──┬──┬──┬──┬──┬──┬──┬──┐
│  │  │  │  │  │  │  │  │  │  │ Imports
└──┴──┴──┴──┴──┴──┴──┴──┴──┴──┘

0                                        100%
┌──┬──┬──┬──┬──┬──┬──┬──┬──┬──┐
│  │  │  │  │  │  │  │  │  │  │ Exports
└──┴──┴──┴──┴──┴──┴──┴──┴──┴──┘
```

Summary

China has only recently begun to trade with other countries and to become interdependent.

How developed is China?

You should now be aware that there are many differences between living in China and in other countries such as the United Kingdom. These differences may include ethnic background, housing, jobs, religion, language and wealth. You will also be aware that different countries are at different levels of **development**.

We have already seen in unit 1 that development is not easy to define. To many people development means how rich a country is and how high a standard of living it has. The easiest way to measure wealth and to make comparisons between countries is to use the **gross national product (GNP)**. Remember that GNP, described on page 8, is the amount of money earned by a country divided by its total population. Diagram **A** shows that almost three-quarters of the countries in the world have a higher GNP than China. This suggests that China is not, as yet, one of the world's more developed countries.

Wealth is not the only way to measure, or to describe, development. Diagram **B** shows that it can also be measured by differences in population (page 10) as well as in health, education, jobs and trade (page 12). Yet each of these measures can in turn be linked with wealth. Poorer countries are unlikely to be able to provide enough money to spend on things such as schools, health care and birth control. It is also harder for them to develop new industries or to improve transport and housing.

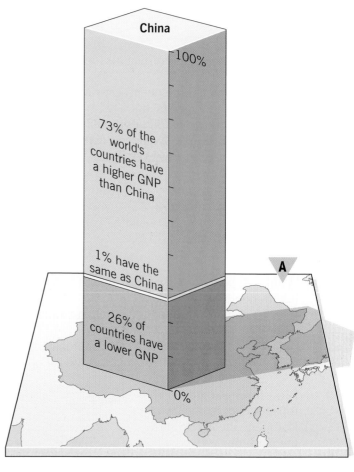

China

100%

73% of the world's countries have a higher GNP than China

1% have the same as China

26% of countries have a lower GNP

0%

A

Jobs	**Trade**	**Population**	**Health**	**Education**
Although many Chinese people still have primary jobs (such as farming and mining), a rapidly increasing number are being employed in secondary (especially high-tech) and service industries.	Until recently, China had very little world trade. It now tends to import machinery and to use this to make high-tech goods such as computers, digital cameras and mobile phones.	Due to its 'one-child' policy, China has a low birth rate – although it still has a relatively high infant mortality rate. Life expectancy is also increasing rapidly, although it is not yet as high as in the more developed countries.	China has relatively little money to spend on training the thousands of doctors and nurses it needs, and on providing hospitals and medical care for its huge population.	China has a high literacy rate, especially in urban areas, despite the limited resources available. Education is harder to find in the more remote rural areas.

B

C Shops and traffic on Nanjing Lu, Shanghai

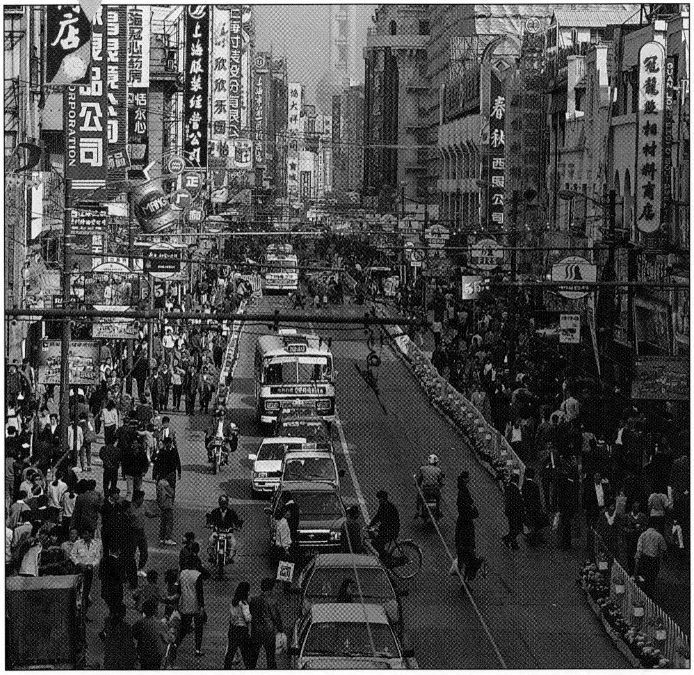

What diagrams **A** and **B** do not show, however, are the differences in wealth within China itself. A small but increasing number of Chinese are now wealthy and have a high standard of living. Most of these live in large cities near to the east coast (photo **C**). In contrast, the majority of Chinese are still very poor and have a low, even if slowly improving, standard of living (photo **D**). Most of these live in rural areas away from the coast (map **E**).

The gap between the rich and the poor is a major problem in China as it is in other developing countries.

E

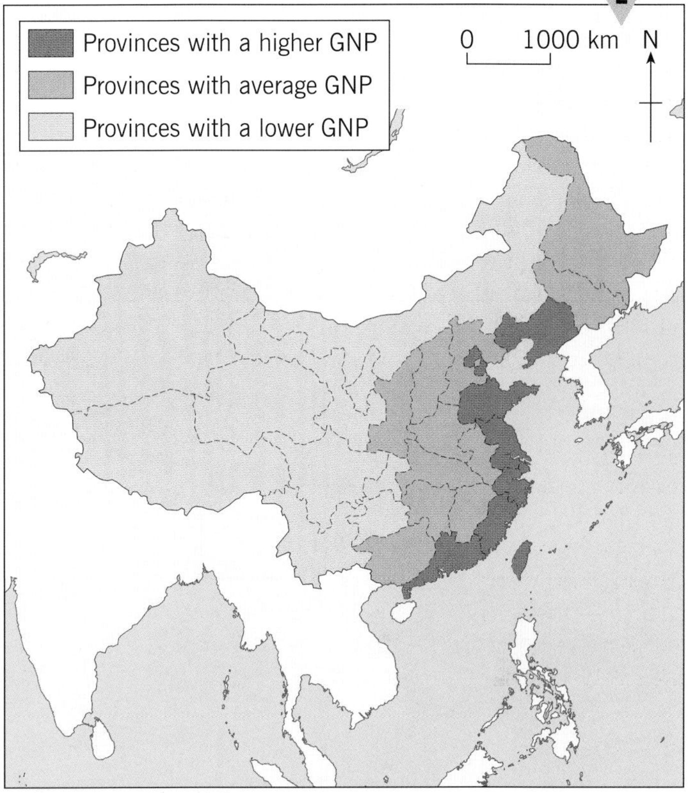
Provinces with a higher GNP
Provinces with average GNP
Provinces with a lower GNP
0
1000 km
N

D Farming families in Sichuan

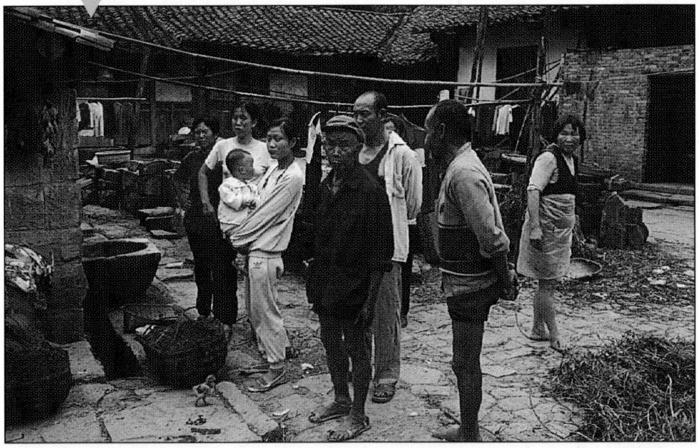

Activities

1 a) Name the seven measures shown in diagram **F** which can be used to describe a country's level of development.
b) Explain how each one can be used to measure development.
c) Which ones suggest that China is still a developing country?
d) Which, if any, suggest that China is beginning to develop more rapidly?

2 a) Why is GNP not always a good measure of a country's development?
b) What does map **E** show about levels of development in China?

F

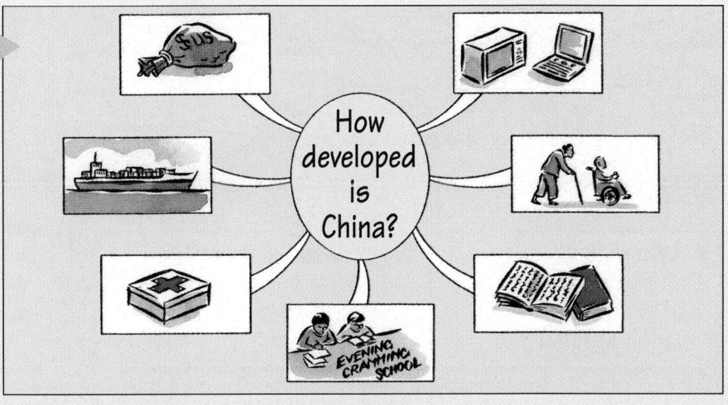
How developed is China?
$US
EVENING CRAMMING SCHOOL

Summary

Although China is still a developing country it has the potential to develop rapidly in this century.

8 Comparing places

How can we learn about places?

What do you do when you want to know something? You ask questions. Geographers do the same thing. They ask questions about people and places and how they affect each other. Asking questions can help us learn about countries, about regions and about our own local area.

Some questions that can help us learn about places are shown below. These same questions can be used when we are looking at large areas as well as small areas like the shanty town shown in the drawing. You may think of many other questions that you would like to ask.

The questions that geographers ask include words like **who**, **what**, **where**, **how**, **why** and **when**.

A

1 Where is it?
Can you name the place and say where it is in relation to other places?

2 What is it like?
What are the physical and human features?

3 Why is it like this?
What has happened to make it like this?

4 How is it changing?
Are there changes in the landscape, buildings or economy?

5 What have been the effects of these changes?
In what way have they affected places and people?

6 What links are there?
Is there good transport? Is there trade, aid or other links between places?

7 How developed is it?
What is the standard of living and quality of life? Is there any improvement?

8 What do you think and feel about the place?
What are your views? What are the good points and bad points?

162

Another way of learning about places is to compare one with another. No two places in the world are exactly the same. Comparing places helps us to identify differences but also to recognise similarities. That can help us learn about and understand our world.

Sometimes we may simply want to compare places in terms of relief, vegetation and climate. At other times we may be interested in human factors like population, settlement and jobs. Comparing places can also help us understand differences in quality of life and levels of development

B The Dolomites, northern Italy

C Guilin, China

Activities

1 a) Match each of the statements below with a question from drawing **A**.
   - Improved housing being built
   - Low level of development with poor quality of life
   - Favela in Rio de Janeiro, Brazil
   - Aid given by other countries
   - Crowded shanty settlement on a steep slope
   - Improved living conditions
   - Lack of money for housing

   b) Write your own answer to question 8.

2 Look at the lettered features on photos **B** and **C**. Match the letters to each of the features in box **D** below. Some may be used more than once.

D
- Flooded fields • Bare rock • Grassy slopes
- Small village • Vegetated mountain
- Flat land • Steep mountains • Wide river
- Dense forest • Farmland

3 a) Make a larger copy of diagram **E**. It is called a Venn diagram.
   b) Add the features from box **D** as shown.
   c) Write a comparison of the two places.

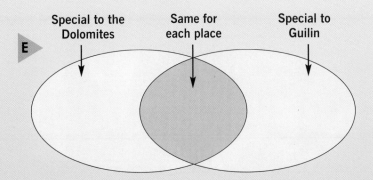

Special to the Dolomites   Same for each place   Special to Guilin

E

Summary

Asking questions and comparing places can help us learn about and understand our world.

How does development affect quality of life?

All countries are different. Some are rich, have high standards of living and are said to be developed. Others are poor, have lower standards of living and are said to be developing.

It is true to say that **most** people in developed countries have a better quality of life than those in developing countries. However, it would be wrong to think that this is always the case. Not everyone in rich countries is wealthy and has an enjoyable life. Similarly, not everyone in a poor country is without money and lives a miserable life. The link between standard of living and quality of life is just not as simple as that.

Drawings **A**, **B**, **D** and **E** look at the lifestyles of different groups of people in different parts of the world.

Standard of living is a measure of how well-off a country or a person is. It is mainly about economic factors such as wealth and earnings and how these can affect people's lifestyle.

Quality of life is a measure of a person's well-being. It is about how happy and content they are with their lifestyle and surroundings.

A   Xinos and his family

B   John and Joanne

We live in a clearing in the Amazon rainforest. Our homes are wooden buildings with thatched roofs. Two or three families live in each hut.

We live mainly by hunting, fishing and collecting food from the forest. We all work together and everyone helps each other. The elders in the tribe teach us the skills we need in our lives. There are plenty of children here so we play together and have good fun. We are never bored as there is always something to do.

We live in a new house in a suburb of Manchester. Dad has a small business and mum is a part-time teacher.

We go to the local school which is just a few minutes away. After school we both plan to go to university. Most of our friends live nearby and there is always plenty to do. At weekends the family often go to the Lake District where we have a caravan. In summer we usually rent a villa in Spain where we stay with friends.

Activities

1 Make a larger copy of the table below. Put the statements from drawing **C** into the correct columns.

Standard of living	Quality of life

2 Look at drawings **A**, **B**, **D** and **E**.
a) Who has the lowest standard of living?
b) Who has the highest standard of living?
c) Who has a good quality of life?
d) Who has a poor quality of life?
e) Who lives in developed countries?
f) Who lives in developing countries?
g) Who has most opportunities in the future?
h) Who is most contented with their lives?
Suggest a reason for each of your answers.

C

MEASURES OF DEVELOPMENT

School attendance House prices
Food supply Taxes
Yearly earnings Car ownership
Television use Holidays taken
Take home pay Life expectancy
GNP per capita People per doctor
Cost of living Crime rates
Income from trade

Summary

Most people in developed countries have a better quality of life than those in developing countries. Sometimes, however, the opposite can be true.

D Jarwin

I live with my parents and four brothers in a shanty town slum on the outskirts of Nairobi. Our house is made of mud and corrugated iron. There are only two small rooms so it is very crowded.

I go to school three days a week but only in the mornings. There are very few books and over 40 of us in the class. After school and at weekends I go to the city centre to work in the market. Life is very difficult here. Our family is poor and despite working hard, we don't seem able to improve our lifestyle.

E Nahito and Kiko

We live in a large house on the outskirts of Tokyo. Our parents both have well-paid jobs in the city. They leave home at 7 in the morning and don't get back till 7 at night. They work very hard and always seem to be tired. They are always complaining about crowded trains and congestion on the roads.

We have a nanny to look after us so do not see much of mum and dad. Making friends is difficult here so we spend most of our time doing homework or watching TV. Sometimes we find life quite boring.

How can we compare regions?

Use the information on these pages to compare two of the UK's regions, the South West and the South East.

Total population (millions)

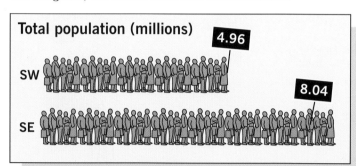

SW — 4.96

SE — 8.04

Population density (per km²)

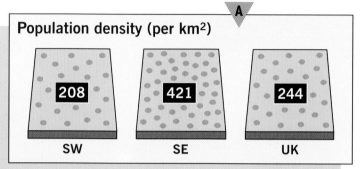

SW	SE	UK
208	421	244

Average weekly earnings

SW	SE	UK
£463	£555	£514

Employment structure

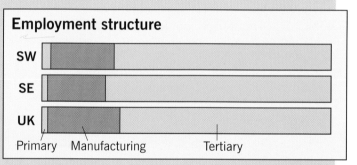

SW

SE

UK

Primary   Manufacturing   Tertiary

Average house prices

SW	SE	UK
£157,000	£193,000	£148,000

Households with car

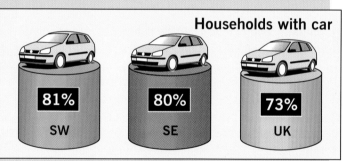

SW	SE	UK
81%	80%	73%

Climate

	Plymouth	Brighton
Jan temp	7°C	6°C
July temp	17°C	17°C
Rainfall	960mm	782mm

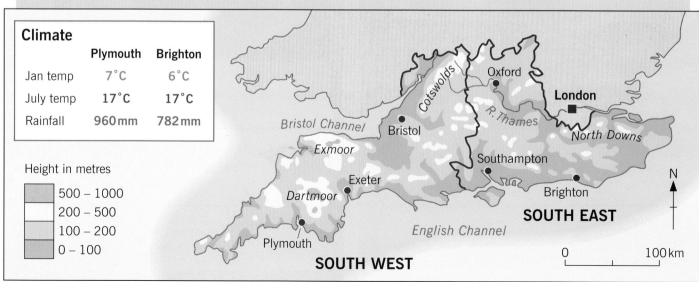

Height in metres
- 500 – 1000
- 200 – 500
- 100 – 200
- 0 – 100

Cotswolds, Oxford, London, R. Thames, North Downs, Bristol Channel, Bristol, Exmoor, Southampton, Exeter, Dartmoor, Brighton, SOUTH EAST, English Channel, Plymouth, SOUTH WEST

0   100 km

N

B Fowey, in the South West

C Folkestone, in the South East

D Other comparisons

	SW	SE	UK
Traffic congestion (vehicles per mile per day)	2500	4900	3800
Travel to work time (% more than one hour)	2.9	7.5	4.4
Unemployment rate (%)	3.8	3.8	5.0
Crime rate (recorded crimes per 1000 people)	85	80	104
Mobile phone ownership (%)	51	57	52

Activities

1 a) Make a larger copy of table **E**.
   b) Tick the correct column for each statement.
       More than one column may be ticked.

E

	SW	SE
Has most high land		
Has most rainfall		
Has warm summers		
Has sheltered harbours		
Has attractive countryside		
Has most people		
Is most crowded		
Has highest earnings		
Is an expensive place to live		
Has few people in primary jobs		
Has above average car ownership		
Has worst traffic congestion		
Has low unemployment rates		
Has low crime rates		

2 Look at photos **B** and **C**. List three main features
   that are:
   a) similar in both places
   b) only in the South West
   c) only in the South East.

3 Choose the region that interests you most. Write a
   brief description of that region using these headings:
   a) Physical features
   b) Wealth
   c) Quality of life.

4 Compare two other UK regions.
   You will find information at
   www.statistics.gov.uk/neighbourhoods
   and www.statistics.gov.uk/statbase

Summary

Regions may be compared using a variety of maps,
graphs, photos and facts and figures.

How can we compare countries?

Use the information on these pages to compare the UK with Japan.

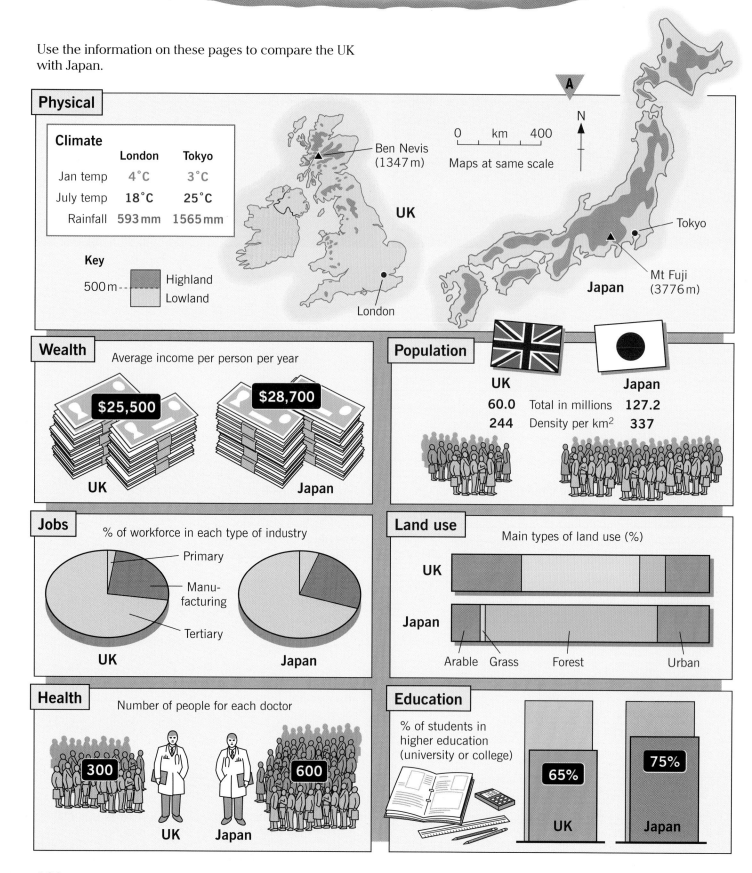

Physical

Climate

	London	Tokyo
Jan temp	4°C	3°C
July temp	18°C	25°C
Rainfall	593 mm	1565 mm

Key

500 m - - - Highland / Lowland

Ben Nevis (1347 m)

UK

0 km 400

Maps at same scale

N

London

Tokyo

Mt Fuji (3776 m)

Japan

Wealth

Average income per person per year

$25,500 — UK

$28,700 — Japan

Population

UK		Japan
60.0	Total in millions	127.2
244	Density per km²	337

Jobs

% of workforce in each type of industry

Primary

Manu-facturing

Tertiary

UK   Japan

Land use

Main types of land use (%)

UK

Japan

Arable   Grass   Forest   Urban

Health

Number of people for each doctor

300 — UK

600 — Japan

Education

% of students in higher education (university or college)

65% UK

75% Japan

B Ullswater in the Lake District, England

C Mount Fuji, Japan

	UK	Japan
Urban dwellers (% living in towns)	92	78
Food consumption (as % of needs)	130	110
Unemployment (%)	5.0	5.4
Car ownership (number per 1000 people)	476	554
TV ownership (number per 1000 people)	521	686

D Other comparisons

Activities

1 a) Make a larger copy of table **E**.
  b) Tick the correct column for each statement. More than one column may be ticked.

E

	UK	Japan
Has most high ground		
Has most rainfall		
Has cold winters		
Has warmest summers		
Has most people		
Is most crowded		
Has highest earnings		
Has few people in primary jobs		
Is mainly forested		
Has most people living in towns		
School attendance is high		
Getting a doctor may be difficult		
Most people have plenty to eat		
Has low unemployment rates		

2 Look at photos **B** and **C**. Describe two features that are similar in both places and two features that are different.

3 Write a brief description of Japan using these headings:
  a) Physical features
  b) Wealth
  c) Quality of life.

4 Compare the UK and China. You will find further information on the back cover and at
www.un.org/pubs/CyberSchoolBus
www.worldbank.org/data and
www.odci.gov/cia/publications/factbook

Summary

Countries may be compared using a variety of maps, graphs, photos and facts and figures.

Where in the world? ... Physical

Look at the map showing some of the world's physical features. It is based on millions of satellite images carefully put together to give a picture of the world. The colours and relief have been enhanced to make the features clearer and easier to identify.

Activities

1 Find four rivers, four mountain ranges and two deserts on the map. Name them and give the continent that each one is in.

2 Answer the following questions. You will find all of the answers on the map.
   1 Covers a third of the earth's surface
   2 Mauna Loa is on this island
   3 A river in Asia
   4 Desert in Africa
   5 Ocean east of Africa
   6 Great Barrier Reef is made of this
   7 Vostok is on this continent
   8 Country with highest temperature
   9 Large area of coral
   10 World's highest mountain
   11 The Arctic is the most northern one
   12 Shallow water teeming with fish
   13 This one is 6680 km long
   14 Has had no rain for 400 years
   15 Volcano in Central America
   16 Al'Aziziyah is this
   17 River flows into Pacific Ocean

3 Take the first letter of each of your answers to spell out a suitable heading for the map.

4 Use the map to make up your own clues for the word below:

PLACES

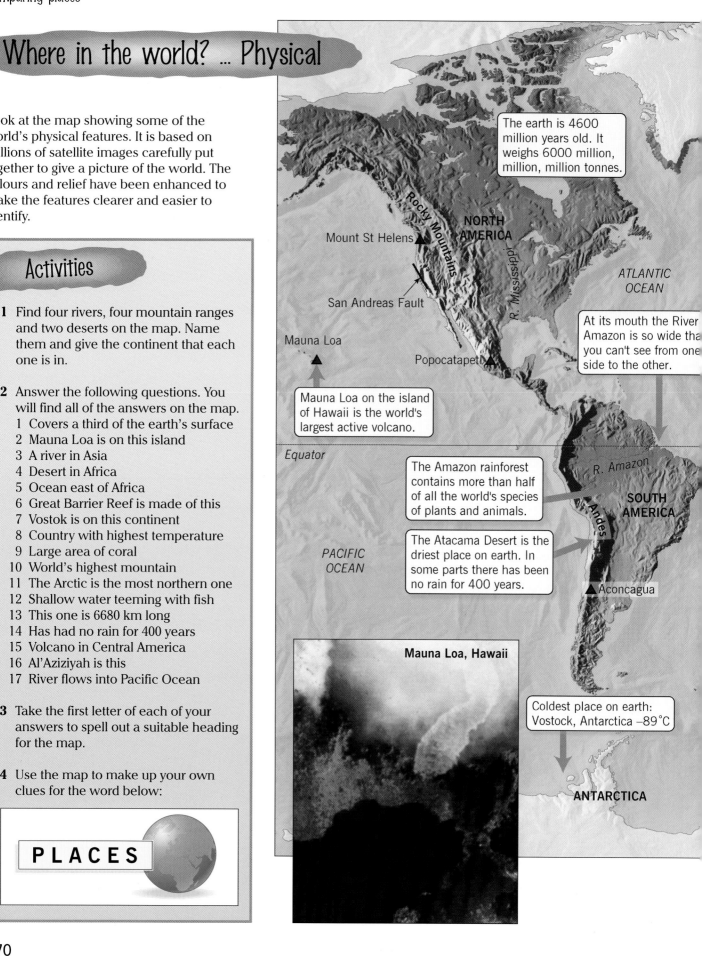

The earth is 4600 million years old. It weighs 6000 million, million, million tonnes.

Rocky Mountains

NORTH AMERICA

Mount St Helens ▲

San Andreas Fault

R. Mississippi

ATLANTIC OCEAN

Mauna Loa ▲

Popocatapetl ▲

At its mouth the River Amazon is so wide that you can't see from one side to the other.

Mauna Loa on the island of Hawaii is the world's largest active volcano.

Equator

The Amazon rainforest contains more than half of all the world's species of plants and animals.

R. Amazon

Andes

SOUTH AMERICA

The Atacama Desert is the driest place on earth. In some parts there has been no rain for 400 years.

PACIFIC OCEAN

▲ Aconcagua

Mauna Loa, Hawaii

Coldest place on earth: Vostock, Antarctica −89°C

ANTARCTICA

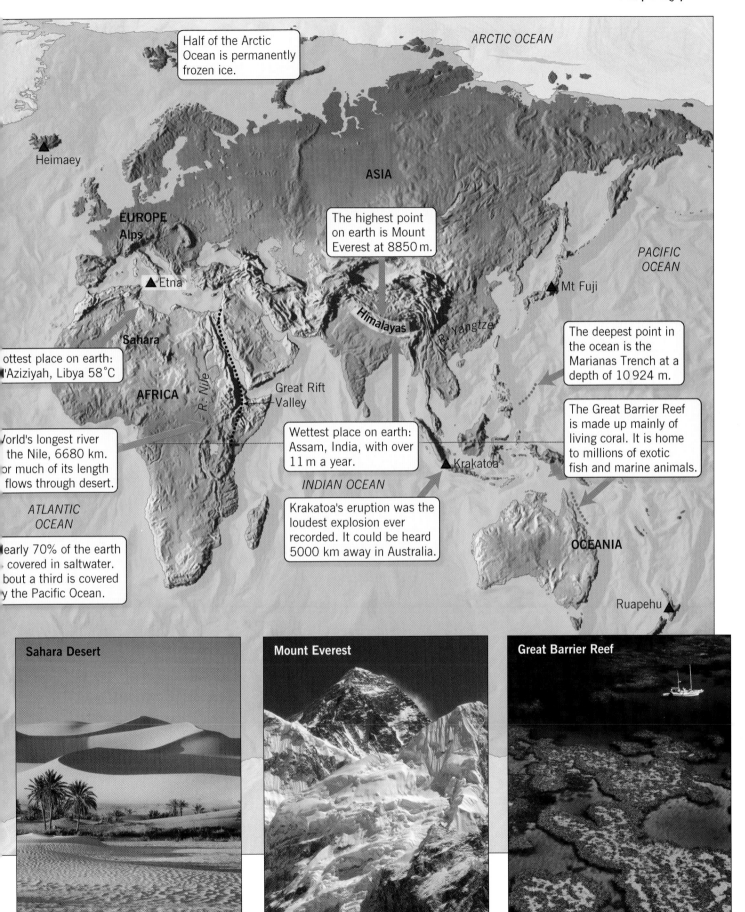

Half of the Arctic Ocean is permanently frozen ice.

ARCTIC OCEAN

Heimaey

ASIA

EUROPE
Alps

The highest point on earth is Mount Everest at 8850 m.

PACIFIC OCEAN

▲ Etna

▲ Mt Fuji

Himalayas

R. Yangtze

Sahara

The deepest point in the ocean is the Marianas Trench at a depth of 10 924 m.

ottest place on earth: 'Aziziyah, Libya 58°C

AFRICA

R. Nile

Great Rift Valley

The Great Barrier Reef is made up mainly of living coral. It is home to millions of exotic fish and marine animals.

Vorld's longest river the Nile, 6680 km. or much of its length flows through desert.

Wettest place on earth: Assam, India, with over 11 m a year.

Krakatoa

INDIAN OCEAN

ATLANTIC OCEAN

Krakatoa's eruption was the loudest explosion ever recorded. It could be heard 5000 km away in Australia.

early 70% of the earth covered in saltwater. bout a third is covered y the Pacific Ocean.

OCEANIA

Ruapehu ▲

Sahara Desert

Mount Everest

Great Barrier Reef

171

Where in the world? ... Human

Activities

1 Answer the following questions. You will find all of the answers on the map.
1 Capital city of Japan
2 Proportion of people living in cities
3 France is in this continent
4 May reach 8.5 billion by 2020
5 Australia is part of this continent
6 World's largest country
7 City on west coast of USA
8 Least crowded country (last letter)
9 Time for population to increase by 9000
10 Country with highest GNP/capita
11 Most spoken language
12 Where 60% of world's people live
13 City on east coast of USA
14 Nearest country south of the UK
15 Line around the middle of the Earth
16 Sydney is in this country
17 Second part of the name of an African city
18 Country in North America
19 Largest country in Asia
20 Goes through Kenya
21 Coastal city of China

2 Take the first letter of each of your answers to spell out a suitable heading for the map.

3 Make a larger copy of the table below.
a) Write in the names of the 12 countries that are named and located on the map.
b) Complete the table using the statistics at the back of the book.
c) List the 12 countries in order of wealth. Give the richest first.

Country	Area	Population	GNP/capita

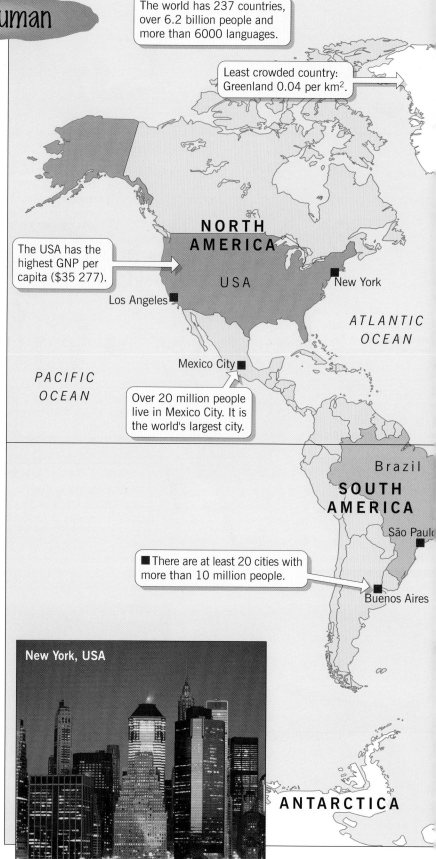

The world has 237 countries, over 6.2 billion people and more than 6000 languages.

Least crowded country: Greenland 0.04 per km².

NORTH AMERICA

The USA has the highest GNP per capita ($35 277).

USA

New York

Los Angeles

ATLANTIC OCEAN

PACIFIC OCEAN

Mexico City

Over 20 million people live in Mexico City. It is the world's largest city.

Brazil

SOUTH AMERICA

São Paulo

There are at least 20 cities with more than 10 million people.

Buenos Aires

New York, USA

ANTARCTICA

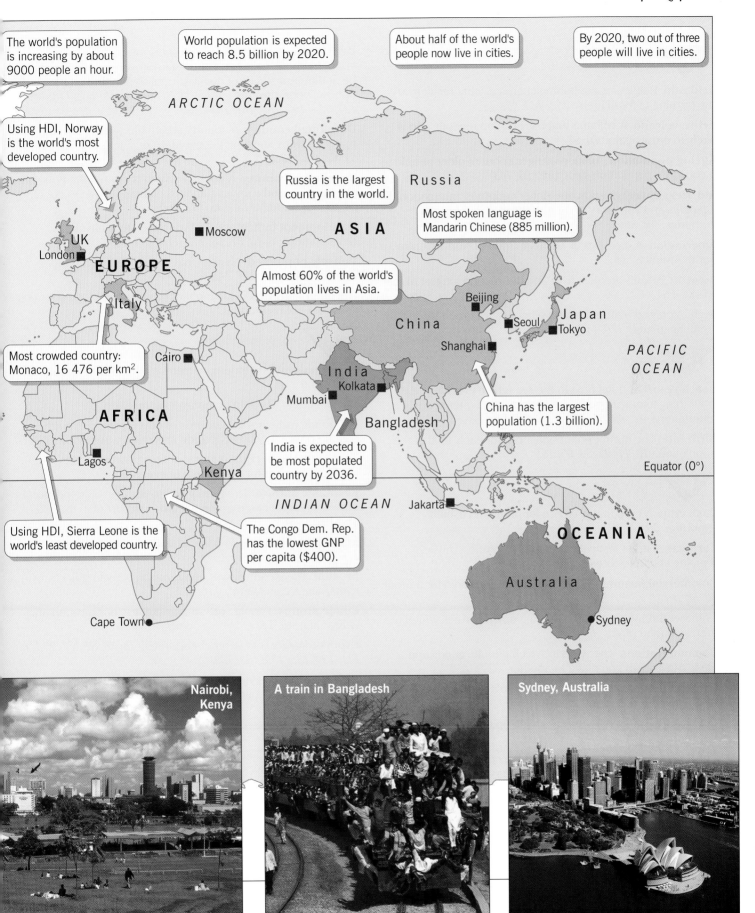

The world's population is increasing by about 9000 people an hour.

World population is expected to reach 8.5 billion by 2020.

About half of the world's people now live in cities.

By 2020, two out of three people will live in cities.

ARCTIC OCEAN

Using HDI, Norway is the world's most developed country.

Russia is the largest country in the world.

Russia

Moscow

ASIA

Most spoken language is Mandarin Chinese (885 million).

UK
London

EUROPE

Italy

Almost 60% of the world's population lives in Asia.

Beijing

China

Japan
Seoul
Tokyo

Shanghai

Most crowded country: Monaco, 16 476 per km².

Cairo

PACIFIC OCEAN

India
Kolkata

AFRICA

Mumbai

Bangladesh

China has the largest population (1.3 billion).

Lagos

Kenya

Equator (0°)

India is expected to be most populated country by 2036.

INDIAN OCEAN

Jakarta

OCEANIA

Using HDI, Sierra Leone is the world's least developed country.

The Congo Dem. Rep. has the lowest GNP per capita ($400).

Australia

Sydney

Cape Town

Nairobi, Kenya

A train in Bangladesh

Sydney, Australia

Glossary

Acid rain Rainwater containing chemicals that result from the burning of fossil fuels. *132, 133*

Active volcano A volcano that has erupted recently and is likely to erupt again. *70, 92*

Ageing population An increasing number of older people in a country's population structure. *95, 143*

Aid Help usually given by the richer countries, international agencies and voluntary organisations mainly to poorer countries. *14, 38*

Amerindian A member of an indian tribe of North, Central or South America. *18*

Amazon Brazil's greatest river and the second longest in the world. *20*

Arch A coastal feature formed when waves erode through a small headland. *116, 117*

Beach resort A hotel next to the sea which provides everything a tourist needs, e.g. restaurants, water sports, entertainments. *49, 51*

Birth rate The number of people born for each 1000 of the population. *10, 11, 47, 56, 95, 155*

Cash crop A crop that is grown for profit and usually exported. *58*

Carnival A street festival with parades, parties, music, dancing and fancy dress. *24*

Commercial farming When farm produce is sold for a profit. *26, 58*

Commercial logging The chopping down of trees which are then sold for a profit. *40*

Communications The ways in which people, goods and ideas move from one place to another. *82*

Commuter A person who lives in one place and travels some distance to work in another. *101*

Coral A type of limestone rock made up of the skeletons of tiny marine creatures. *44, 45, 49, 51*

Coral reef A band of coral lying off the coast which forms a fragile environment and protects the coast. *44, 45, 49, 51*

Conservation The protection of the environment. *40*

Death rate The number of people who die per 1000 of the population. *10, 11, 47, 95*

Deposition The laying down of material carried by rivers, sea, ice or wind. *116, 117*

Development Development means growth. It involves changes and usually brings about improvement. Countries can be at different stages of development depending on how 'rich' or how 'poor' they are. *4–17, 36, 37, 64, 88, 89, 112, 113, 136, 137, 154, 155, 160, 161, 163–165.*

Developed country A country which has a lot of money, many services and a higher standard of living. *6–17, 36, 37, 52, 54, 62, 64, 112, 113, 136, 137*

Developing country A country which is often quite poor, has few services and a lower standard of living. *6–17, 36, 37, 52, 54, 62, 63, 64, 112, 113, 136, 137, 160*

Development indicators Methods used to measure development. *8–13, 37, 88, 112, 113, 155, 160*

Densely populated An area that is crowded with people. *23, 46, 68, 82, 94, 124, 125, 142*

Dormant volcano A volcano that has erupted in the last 2000 years but not recently. *92*

Earthquake A movement, or tremor, of the earth's crust. *70, 92, 93, 100*

Earth's crust The thin outer layer of the earth. *70*

Economic indicators Measures of development that are based on wealth, e.g. GNP, trade and energy use. *9, 12, 37, 164*

Economic Union (EU) A group of European countries working together for the benefit of everyone. *86, 87*

Economic miracle The term given to Brazil's rapid industrial growth and great increase in wealth. It occurred in the 1960s and 1970s. *40*

Endangered species Wildlife in danger of becoming extinct. *156, 157*

Erosion The wearing away and removal of rock, soil, etc. by rivers, sea, ice and wind. *116, 117*

Ethnic groups People with similar culture, background and way of life. *46, 142*

Exports Goods sold to other countries. *14, 38, 62, 63, 86, 110, 111, 134, 135, 139, 158, 159*

Extinct volcano A volcano that has not erupted in historic times and is not expected to erupt again. *92*

Favela The Brazillian name for a shanty settlement – a collection of shacks and poor quality housing which often lack electricity, a water supply and sewage disposal. *29*

Fazendas Coffee plantations in Brazil. *24*

Fold mountains Layers of rock that have changed shape because of pressure on them and formed mountains. *71*

Forest garden Small clearings in the forest where people of the Kayapo tribe grow food. *30, 50*

Fragile environment Parts of the natural world that can easily be damaged. *50*

Golden triangle The name given to the industrial area in south-east Brazil. *26, 27*

Gross National Product (GNP) The wealth of a country. The total amount of money earned by a country divided by its total population. It is used as an economic measure of development. *8, 9, 13, 64, 112, 155, 160*

Heavy industry Large scale secondary industries such as shipbuilding, steel and chemicals. *26*

Human Development Index (HDI) A social measure of development. *13*

Humus The remains of plants and animals left in the soil. *56*

Hutongs Traditional housing in Beijing. *152, 153*

Immigrant A person who arrives in a country with the intention of living there. *120*

Imports Goods brought into a country. *38, 62, 63, 86, 110, 111, 134, 135, 158*

Infant mortality The number of children out of every 1000 born alive who die before they reach the age of one year. *10, 11, 37, 47, 89, 95*

Intensive farming Farms which cover small areas but which use either many people or a lot of capital. No land is wasted. *103*

Interdependent When countries work together and rely on each other for help. *14, 15, 38, 62, 63, 86, 110, 134, 135, 158, 159*

Isolated Difficult to reach. Far from other places. *82*

Land values The cost of land. Land in the middle of a town or city usually has the highest value. *100*

Landscapes The scenery. What the land looks like. *116, 117*

Life expectancy The average number of years a person can expect to live. *10, 11, 91, 143*

Literacy rate The proportion of people who can read and write. *65, 155*

Magma Molten rock below the earth's surface. *92*

Manufactured goods These are the things that are made from raw materials, e.g. cars, machinery and electrical goods. They are usually of high value. *14, 15, 38, 63, 110, 158, 159*

Mediterranean climate Places which have hot, dry summers and mild, wet winters. *72*

Migration The movement of people from one place to another to live or to work. *120*

Multicultural A society where people with different beliefs and traditions live and work together. *121*

Multi-nationals Large companies with offices and factories throughout the world. *38, 159*

National debt The total amount of money owed by a country. *38*

National Park An area of countryside where spectacular scenery and wildlife are protected by law. *48, 50, 54, 82*

Natural hazards A great force of nature, such as an earthquake or volcano, which is a threat or danger to people and their way of life. *70*

Natural increase The difference between birth and death rates. *10, 11, 140, 141*

Natural resources Raw materials which are obtained from the environment, e.g. water, coal, soil. *16, 17*

Negative factors Things that discourage people from living in an area. *22, 68, 142*

Non-renewable resources Resources that can only be used once. *16, 17*

Pacific Rim Countries around the edge of the Pacific Ocean. *110*

Padis Small fields where rice is grown. They are flooded for part of the year. *148, 149*

Pastorals Farmers who look after herds of animals. *54*

Physical features Landforms that are a result of natural processes. *16, 17, 40, 41, 64, 65, 88, 89, 116, 117, 140, 141*

Plate boundary Where plates meet on the earth's surface. *70, 71, 92, 93*

Plates Large sections of the earth's crust. *44, 45, 70, 71, 92, 93*

Pollution Noise, dust and other harmful substances produced by people and machines, which spoil an area. *16*

Population density A measure of how crowded a place is. *22, 23, 68, 94, 142*

Population distribution How people are spread out over an area. *22, 23, 46, 68, 94, 142*

Population pyramid A type of graph that shows the population structure of a country. *10, 11*

Positive factors Things that encourage people to live in an area. *22, 68, 142*

Primary goods Raw materials such as minerals, timber and foodstuffs. They are usually of low value. *14, 38, 63, 110, 111, 158*

Quality of life A measure of a person's well-being – how happy and content they are with their lifestyle and physical surroundings. *7, 17, 60, 84, 134, 137, 147, 152, 163–165*

Rainforest Tall, dense forest found in hot, wet climates such as the Amazon region of Brazil. *20, 30–35*

Recession A decrease in wealth in a country. Usually associated with a decline in industry, fewer jobs available and less money to go round. *104*

Redeveloped To knock everything down and start all over again. *124*

Resources Things which can be useful to people. They may be natural like coal and trees, or of other value like money and skilled workers. *16, 17*

Renewable resources Resources that can be used over and over again. *17, 40, 108*

Richter scale A measure of the strength of an earthquake. *93*

Rift valley A steep-sided valley formed by the sinking of land between two faults or cracks caused by plate movement. *44, 45*

Safari The name given to a type of holiday where wild animals are viewed in their natural habitat. *42, 50*

Sand dune A mound or ridge of sand shaped by the wind. *117*

Shamba A small plot of cultivated land around houses in rural Kenya. *56*

Shanty settlement A collection of shacks and poor quality housing which often lack electricity, a water supply and sewage disposal. *29, 53*

Shifting cultivation A type of farming where land is cultivated for a few years before the people move on, clear another patch and allow the old plots to recover and the natural vegetation to return. *30*

Site The actual place where a settlement first grew up. *98*

Social indicators Development indicators that help measure standards of living, e.g. school attendance and literacy rates. *9, 11, 37*

Sparsely populated An area that has few people living in it. *22, 23, 46, 67, 82, 94, 142*

Spit A long narrow tongue of sand and shingle which grows out from the shoreline. *117*

Stack A pillar of rock on a sea coast separated from the mainland by erosion. *117*

Standard of living How well-off a person or country is. *7–9, 13, 17, 60, 88, 89, 108, 136, 137, 164, 165*

Subsistence farming Growing just enough food for your own needs with nothing left to sell. *30, 56, 146, 148, 149*

Sustainable development A method of progress that does not waste resources and looks after the needs of today without damaging resources for the future. *16, 17, 40, 53, 60, 85, 88, 108, 132, 133, 156, 157*

Tourism When people travel to places for recreation and pleasure. *24, 25, 44–47, 72, 73, 124, 125, 144, 145*

Traffic grid lock A serious traffic jam. *81*

Trade The movement of goods and services between countries. *9, 14, 38, 62, 63, 86, 110, 111, 134, 135, 139, 158, 159*

Trade deficit When the cost of imports is greater than the money made from exports. *36, 62*

Trade surplus When the money made from exports is greater than the cost of imports. *38, 110*

Trading partners Countries which trade with each other. *40, 63, 86, 87, 110, 111, 158*

Transportation The movement of eroded material by rivers, sea, ice and wind. *117*

Urban dwellers The proportion of people in a country who live in towns and cities. *12, 13*

Urban life Living conditions in towns and cities. *28, 29, 52, 53, 80, 81, 98–101, 126, 127, 152, 153*

Village life Living conditions in small rural settlements. *30, 31, 54, 55, 102, 146, 147*

Volcano A cone-shaped mountain or hill, often made up from lava and ash. *56, 70, 71*